THE HIDDEN HISTORY OF THE SECRET BALLOT

Hidden History of the Secret Ballot

List price $24.95
Discount price $19.95

Purchased by _Bahram Rajee_

ROMAIN BERTRAND
JEAN-LOUIS BRIQUET
PETER PELS
editors

The Hidden History of the Secret Ballot

INDIANA UNIVERSITY PRESS
BLOOMINGTON AND INDIANAPOLIS

This book is a publication of

Indiana University Press
601 North Morton Street
Bloomington, Indiana 47404-3797 USA

http://iupress.indiana.edu

Telephone orders   800-842-6796
Fax orders   812-855-7931
Orders by e-mail   iuporder@indiana.edu

First published in the United Kingdom by
C. Hurst & Co. (Publishers) Ltd.
41 Great Russell Street, London WC1B 3PL
www.hurstpub.co.uk

The paper used in this publication meets the minimum requirements of
American National Standard for Information Sciences—Permanence of Paper
for Printed Library Materials, ANSI Z39.48-1984.

Printed in India

Cataloging information is available from the Library of Congress.

ISBN 978-0-253-21942-8 (pbk.)

ISBN 978-0-253-34963-7 (cl.)

1 2 3 4 5 12 11 10 09 08 07

CONTENTS

CONTRIBUTORS

MAHMOUD ALINEJAD: social anthropologist, post-graduate student, Amsterdam School of Social Science Research.

RICHARD BANÉGAS: political scientist, Assistant Professor, University of Paris I-La Sorbonne.

ROMAIN BERTRAND: political scientist, Research Fellow, Centre d'Etudes et de Recherches Internationales (CERI), Fondation Nationale des Sciences Politiques, Paris.

JEAN-LOUIS BRIQUET: political scientist, Research Fellow, Centre d'Etudes et de Recherches Internationales (CERI), Centre National de la Recherche Scientifique, Paris.

JOHN CROWLEY: political scientist, Chief Editor, International Social Science Journal, UNESCO, Paris.

CHRISTOPHE JAFFRELOT: political scientist, Director, Centre d'Etudes et de Recherches Internationales (CERI), Centre National de la Recherche Scientifique, Paris.

DENIS LACORNE: political scientist, Research Director, Centre d'Etudes et de Recherches Internationales (CERI), Fondation Nationale des Sciences Politiques, Paris.

FRANK O'GORMAN: historian, Professor, Manchester University.

PETER PELS: social anthropologist, Professor, Leiden University, Research Associate, Amsterdam School of Social Science Research.

JOHN PEMBERTON: social anthropologist, Associate Professor, Columbia University.

DAVID RECONDO: political scientist, Research Fellow, Centre d'Etudes et de Recherches Internationales (CERI), Fondation Nationale des Sciences Politiques, Paris.

INTRODUCTION

TOWARDS A HISTORICAL ETHNOGRAPHY OF VOTING

Romain Bertrand, Jean-Louis Briquet and Peter Pels

Today the technology of the secret ballot is regarded as the self-evident tool of representative democracy. It underpins the globally dominant conception of voting as a universal and individual political act. At the core of this conception stands the idea—laid down in Article 21 of the Universal Declaration of Human Rights—that secrecy is the *sine qua non* condition of free expression of the voters' will. Vigorously promoted by United Nations bureaucrats and in World Bank and IMF reports stressing 'good governance' and 'transparency', as well as by other governmental or non-governmental institutions and experts devoted to electoral engineering, this idea has become the current *doxa* of democracy-builders worldwide.[1] It is an assumption with deep historical references: it may seem as old as the imaginary nexus that first equated *demos* and *kratos*. Indeed, we find that in Ancient Greece the decision to ostracise someone (*ostraka*) was taken through a secret voting process, while in second-century Rome 'tabular laws' involving the use of 'ballot boxes' and small wax plates were passed in an effort to downplay the political influence of the aristocracy and allow plebeian social groupings to free themselves from the former's unchallenged domination of the *res publica*. Such historical references feed the impression that there exists an indissoluble and common-sense link between some form of voting secrecy and individual political freedom, and that modern Western representative democracy has finally managed to institutionalise this universal link to the benefit of humanity as a whole. However, this volume calls into question the supposed universality of this link, by means of historical ethnographic studies of a number of different 'cultures of voting' produced by institutionalisation of the secret ballot in modern societies.

A ballot bearing the names of all the candidates of all parties, so arranged as to ensure absolute secrecy and liberty in voting first became compulsory in Australia in 1837 (hence the name 'Australian ballot').

---

1 See, for example, the special issue of *Critique internationale* (2004) on promoting democracy.

Only after much wrangling was a similar technology legally adopted in Britain in 1872; in 1896 a secret ballot was accepted by four-fifths of the United States (Fredman, 1969); Germany instituted it in 1903; France in 1913 (Garrigou, 2002). Each of these historical trajectories leading up to the legal act of instituting the secret ballot displays different emphases on different reasons for adopting the technology and a different balance of interests. In England, for example, the discussion about the Australian ballot rarely referred to the political ideologies that divided élite from plebeian or proletarian interests: instead of a debate about political freedoms, the secret ballot raised worries about the extent to which secrecy allowed for fraud by both canvassers and voters (O'Gorman, 1992 and this volume). In the southern states of the United States the secret ballot provided a form of literate discipline that in practice disenfranchised a large segment of the lower-class black vote and thus restricted rather than expanded individual political freedom (Crowley, this volume). In France the emphasis on individual choice and freedom emerged from the mutual interest of the state and political entrepreneurs in standardising the ballot, rather than the other way around (Garrigou, 1993). Such historical studies not only raise doubts about the universality of the link between secret ballot technology and the achievement of free individual political choice, they also question the assumption that there is a single technology that can be referred to as 'the' secret ballot as such.

These suspicions grow stronger when cultural differences are introduced into the analysis. After the Second World War most ideologies of modernisation and building of democratic nation-states were based on the implicit assumption that representative democracy by the secret ballot came with a purely Western copyright stamp—that it could be transferred to non-Western societies but not reinvented by them, since reinvention would automatically result in the 'failure' of such ready-made democracy. In places where the technology of the secret ballot was introduced by a colonising state matters were often much more complicated: at the local government level in Mexico, for example, although the secret ballot had been established at the national level, it stood in a complex, hybrid relation to forms and patterns of voting by public acclamation (Recondo, this volume). In late-colonial Tanganyika the embedding of the secret ballot in anti-colonial political routines seems to have led to a corporate rather than individualised culture of voting (Pels, this volume). In Benin an increasingly individualised culture of voting did indeed result from the introduction of multiparty politics, but by means of clientelistic buying and selling of votes rather than through the secret liberation of the individual voice from such patronage (Banégas, this volume). The complex assumptions about the link between individual choice and the technology of the secret ballot that usually remain unquestioned in the West—assumptions about literacy, the isolation of the individual voter and the reliability of state and media apparatuses in quantifying and processing votes for public consumption—are reshuffled, recombined and reinvented as soon as that technology travels to another set of social, political and economic circumstances.

Thus the essays in this volume, written by anthropologists, historians and political scientists, all examine the socio-cultural specificity of the historical trajectories in which the secret ballot was adopted in their particular areas of study. They do not deny that the technology of the secret ballot is a potent socio-political force—on the contrary, they all wonder how it so successfully attained the status of prime mediator of popular sovereignty. All the essays bring their own perspectives to bear on this question, and not all of them agree on the answers. Nevertheless, this introduction intends to sketch out the approach they all have in common, if to different degrees, starting with an outline of the ideology that identifies the secret ballot with freedom. Subsequently, we hope to make clear why one needs to study 'cultures of voting': not because of relativism that identifies the different 'political cultures' in which the secret ballot is implemented, but because the secret ballot itself is a specific emanation of a culture of modernity that consists of several different, sometimes separable and even contradictory traits that have to be disaggregated in order to understand how they can be reassembled in variable socio-historical circumstances. This requires a perspective on the secret ballot that stresses first its character as a *technology* (something that makes it, like all material culture, a relatively autonomous agent in specific social circumstances, but able to be modified to fit new forms of use) and second, its character as a *performance*, by highlighting the fact that its production can be observed from both a front-stage and a back-stage point of view, making 'secrecy' contingent on a tenuous relationship with the publicity given to it in specific socio-historical circumstances.

THE SECRET BALLOT AS FETISH

The 'secret ballot is freedom' ideology conveys the idea that there is only one form of legitimate opinion: a personal opinion produced when numerous social constraints in which citizens are routinely and universally enmeshed—community or religious allegiances, the patronage of big men, employers or notables, parties, 'political machines'—are kept at bay. Once established at the heart of the political institutions of a number of globally dominant modern nation-states, the technology was assumed to help free the individual citizen from such everyday forms of political alienation, to identify him or her with the nation and to neutralise non-institutionalised—lower-class, potentially disruptive—forms of protest. In a number of cases this did indeed happen: in the United States the partial dismantling of political machines went together with the intentional or unintentional exclusion of threatening—often black—electoral constituencies; in Britain the secret ballot helped to break the influence of trade union networks on the electorate; and in France it consolidated the power of the centralising state against so-called 'clientelistic' networks of mutual recognition and support, in the name of freeing 'sincere' political choices. The promoters of the democratic ideal wanted to disembed and abstract the modern, individual citizen from such sociopolitical relationships in order to free him/her for the unfettered exercise of individual reason.

These assumptions, whether practically realised or not, henceforth became unchallenged criteria of democratic virtue that in turn defined roles which had to be learned by voters and which defined their proper performance in public settings (Garrigou, 1993: 15). In France under the Third Republic (1875–1940) a democratic worldview came to the fore that morally devalued and legally prohibited 'communitarian forms of voting': Republicans kept denouncing the influence exercised by notables, the underground 'pressures of the Church' and practices of political clientelism (for similar developments in Britain, see O'Gorman, this volume). The electoral arena was meant to become a place where the newly defined civic virtues of individual rationality and independent choice would play out, sanctioned by the majesty of state power: an Enlightenment dream come true. The rules of the electoral game—whatever their actual historical provenance—came to be conceived as practical realisations of this civic ideal. In French this is poignantly summarised in the very term used to designate the polling booth (*l'isoloir*), a material means of 'isolating' the voter from the outside social world, allowing the free expression of one's political choice. As Alain Garrigou aptly puts it:

The *isoloir* seemed to make compulsory a requirement of maximum sincerity by intending to prevent any loss of legitimacy [i.e. cheating] and annihilating those barely perceptible constraints whose very existence it pointed out. ... By giving a specific technological shape to a peculiar mode of political relationships, the *isoloir* thus takes on the active characteristics of a fetish, as if the tool had the intrinsic ability to transform both the voter's person and the content of the vote. (Garrigou, 1988: 29, 42)

In other words, the new ideology of the citizen-turned-individual-voter was seen as taking concrete form in a set of novel and peculiar technologies: a material culture characterised by literacy, individual isolation and the neutralisation of a public voting space that ensured control by public authorities and political parties in a docile performance of political commitment. At the same time, those material mechanisms also defined electoral deviance and enforced sanctions against it: they disallowed improper practices of influencing voters (such as public festivities) and promoted a new, 'normal' form of political action. The more voting came to mean the free expression of one's inner judgment, the more the ideology of the enlightened voter redefined political legitimacy:

In order to gain legitimacy in political struggles, elected leaders came to interpret the votes they had gathered as signs of approval of their ideas. Thus they gave the act of voting the status of a political opinion *per se*. This conception of a voter freed from social bindings was an ideal representation. (Garrigou, 1988: 30)

Not only did this ideology transform a specific *quantitative* practice of abstraction and tallying into a new legitimation of a *qualitative* political standpoint, it also translated this ideal representation into 'normal' behavioural patterns, a specific material culture and sets of procedures validated by the state's legal establishment. Despite efforts to restore alternative forms of voting—such as John Stuart Mill's critique of secret voting in the name of a public 'moral of the assertion of opinions' (Manin, 1997)—the secret ballot eventually emerged as the winner. A core assumption of such voting ideology and the instruments that materialise it is that this set of technical devices possesses an intrinsic persuasive force, such that its implementation is a necessary and almost sufficient condition to create an inexorable movement towards the democracy of the citizen-individual. This assumption amounts to a form of technological determinism in which the medium—the secret ballot—is often taken to produce the message—free individual political choice. At worst it devolves into a 'fetishism of the electoral moment' that is strongly advocated by democracy-building agencies (see Bertrand, this volume).

The result of this combination of an ideology of unfettered political choice and its materialisation in a set of techniques, both fetishised as powerful agents in processes of political reform, is that we are left with a large hiatus in the qualitative research into global politics. The fetishisation of the secret ballot obscures the complicated genealogy of this electoral technology, which, even in relatively long-standing electoral democracies such as the British and French, can be shown to consist of numerous conflicts of interests and ideals and a slow and incremental assembling of separate technical devices that we now tend to regard as inextricably bound together. This volume builds on and brings together research into the contrasting effects of the genealogy and implementation of the secret ballot in different times and places—research that, with a number of important exceptions, has barely begun, and requires input from a variety of disciplines: socio-cultural anthropology, history and political science (to name just those disciplines from which scholars have taken part in this particular project).

This calls for a sceptical attitude towards the specific cultural features of political modernity—the ideology outlined above. It also implies adopting an explicitly historical and comparative perspective towards the secret ballot, not just in 'the West' but, more important, by studying its implementation and development in non-European democracies. Lastly, it forces us to recognise that *all* political technologies are forms of subjectivisation in a double sense (Foucault, 1978): they subject the people targeted by their disciplinary regimes, but also allow these people to position themselves as subjects in sometimes subversive appropriations of these technologies 'from below' (Bayart, 1993). To do so we need to discuss further what is meant by 'cultures of voting', by the idea of the secret ballot as a 'technology' and by the idea of a public 'performance' and what the secrecy of the secret ballot is taken to mean. The result may well be even greater scepticism, if not towards the principle of 'one man, one vote', then certainly towards the ideology that intends to draw on it. But if that enables us to understand better how democracy is actually achieved in different socio-political circumstances, this may be a small price to pay.

CULTURES OF VOTING

In a world where the word 'culture' is increasingly 'on the streets' and anthropologists are uncomfortable about a term over which they once thought to wield a scientific near-monopoly, a clarification of the title for this volume is required.[2] Our use of the term 'cultures of voting' is intended to counter the idea that there is such a thing as a universal or a-cultural way of voting realised in the institutions of representative democracy in general and in voting by secret ballot in particular. Thus we do not use the word 'culture' in terms of the common American political science notion of 'political culture'—if that is taken to mean the culturally predetermined evaluative or affective attitude of an individual towards the political system (which is itself made up of universal institutions or functions of politics).

Indeed, one of the main intentions of this volume is to show that the secret ballot can be made to fit widely different situations. Like any other technology, it boasts a kind of relative autonomy that allows it to be transported from one situation to another without radically changing shape. This perspective, even when not implying total cultural relativism, stresses a certain moral relativism, saying it is impossible to equate the secret ballot with stable normative content, and acknowledging that the values the secret ballot carries in one situation will probably change when it is transported to another—to such an extent that, as we have seen, the goal of 'freeing' individual voters from external pressures in one context can actually be replaced by the exclusion of voters from electoral

---

2 For two influential critiques of the notion of culture, see Abu-Lughod (1991) and Stolcke (1995).

practice in another. One of the main aims of this volume is to free the study of the institution of voting by secret ballot from such normative presumptions, and make room for a genealogy of the cultural features characterising the use of the secret ballot in different circumstances. The globalisation of the secret ballot as a desirable democratic ideal is itself the strongest argument against both ideal-typical absolutism and cultural relativism: apparently this political technology is both sufficiently autonomous from specific socio-cultural and historical circumstances to travel widely without seeming to change shape radically, and yet flexible enough to adapt successfully to many different circumstances.

In order to grasp this particular aspect of the secret ballot as a relatively autonomous political technology that can nevertheless be transposed to very different circumstances, it is necessary to interpret 'cultures of voting' as different 'cultures of modernity'—that is, as different disaggregations and recombinations of what can be called specifically 'modern' cultural features.[3] These cultural features of modernity are limited in number—in the case at hand we are specifically referring to certain beliefs and practices that define and constitute a regime of values consisting of the individual choice of the political actor, the neutrality of the state in setting the political stage, the essentiality of the act of secretly marking a ballot to achieve political freedom, and the necessity and desirability of a quantitative translation of political choice. These cultural features are thus found in each and every situation where some form of voting by secret ballot is practised—but there is no guarantee that all these cultural features are adopted with the same force and in the same relation to each other in each case. The value of individual choice may be challenged by more corporate relationships, the neutrality of the state may be in doubt, the dominance of oral tradition or audio-visual media may diminish reliance on the written word and undercut trust in secrecy, the need for or possibility of reliable quantitative representation may be questioned.

Thus we must speak of 'cultures of voting' in the plural. This plurality does not refer to radically incommensurable instances, but to a multitude of historical trajectories within a genealogy that nevertheless retains the recognisable features of political modernity—even if only at the level of the native point of view of the moderns themselves. At the very least this perspective points up the intention of the authors herein to question the ideology of achieving freedom through the principle of 'one man, one vote', and to reposition this ideology in relation to its different concrete manifestations. But it also raises two questions. First, where does this ideology, the 'fetishism of the electoral moment' that denies such cultural and historical differences, come from? We argue below that the

---

3 We therefore explicitly adopt Charles Taylor's critique of the 'a-cultural' theories of modernity (2001) that often still dominate part of political science.

answer must be sought in our understanding of 'technology'. Second, how have the specifically modern features of this political technology become so diversified? To answer this we need to scrutinise the inherently *performative* character of the secret ballot as a political ritual.

TECHNOLOGY

A 'ballot' is something that wavers between a material substance, an organised system of secret voting and a quantified measure of votes cast. The secret ballot therefore partakes of the 'awkward' oscillation between *technique*—'matters of practical construction'—and *technology*—'a system of such means and methods' (Williams, 1983: 315). It is, in other words, material culture as well as an organisation of social relationships: it is a causal factor in social change, a 'tool' to be manipulated, as well as a social construction, an effect with often unintended consequences. Seen as a technology, the secret ballot is the material objectification of a certain rationalising drive, but also a tool to control 'the people' politically (as an electorate) and a means for the people to appropriate, and possibly subvert, political control.[4] This simultaneously material and social nature of technology explains why technology 'subjectivates' in a double sense. On the one hand it subjects people to its system of constraints as an object—especially where a state apparatus invests it with power to produce docile 'citizen-individuals'—which explains the fetishism of the electoral moment and the tremendous investment of the engineers of democracy in the material culture of the ballot. On the other hand the existence of such a tool also provides subjects with a capacity to act against those wielding political power. It is therefore vital, for the historical ethnography of the secret ballot, to acknowledge the *material mediation* of such forms of subjectivation in different cultures of voting by the secret ballot as a technology.

The chapters in this volume provide ample illustration of such a double-edged process. Rather than endorsing the liberal 'one man, one vote' requirement that portrays the secret ballot as enabling the freedom of the individual voter, many chapters (O'Gorman, Crowley, Pels) illustrate how the secret ballot was frequently devised to keep the electorate under control and politically marginalise 'dangerous' groups of voters. The material culture of literacy, taxation and registration that usually

---

4 We do not have the room to elaborate further on our understanding of 'technology' here, except to fall back on an earlier definition inspired by, among others, Bijker *et al.* (1987), Foucault (1988) and Gell (1992): '"[T]echnology" refers to a regulation of human practice that comes in a certain objectified form, as a set of objects (tools, machines, buildings), as a set of more or less explicit rules of their use, as a ritual or an exemplar of conduct, or as a disciplinary apparatus (of course, a technology usually combines two or more of these)' (Pels, 2000: 137).

underpins the working of voting by secret ballot provides its own mediations of the act of voting and determines people's access to the so-called 'free' election. Electoral technologies are therefore by no means neutral. Indeed a forceful reminder of the material impact of voting technology was presented when in 2000 George W. Bush won the presidential race in the United States even though he gathered fewer votes than his challenger—a result that was strongly influenced by the paradox that all the material mechanisms set up in Florida to keep out corruption and enable the expression of the 'crystal-clear will of the people' in fact made the electorate's choice all the more obscure, and greatly diminished the effective participation of black Democrats in particular (see Lacorne, this volume). At a more general level, the fetishism of the electoral moment—the obsession with engineering the material culture of 'free and fair polls'—can be seen to conceal larger political processes of institutional deadlock and the rise of criminalised political militias. As Bertrand argues in his chapter, in Indonesia the quest for a perfect voting technology—i.e. for a technocratic management of political change—led to a proliferation of electoral regulations that helped to prevent cheating but also made the election issues all the more obscure (and hence suspect) in the eyes of the voters. He thus reinforces the insight that the material mediation of the secret ballot is, in itself, by no means transparent, and that it would be wrong to assume *a priori* that electoral technologies are neutral (see also Pels, this volume).

Christophe Jaffrelot shows in his chapter that in India's 500-million-voter-strong democracy such techniques of preventing fraudulent behaviour are mobilised on an enormous social scale without, in fact, resulting in the 'freeing' of the act of voting from solid networks of social dependencies. But he also indicates that such electoral procedures were put to strategic use by more subordinate networks: low-caste groups could indeed successfully pursue their anti-high-caste politics by electoral means—if not in the classical liberal sense of 'disembedding' the individual voter from such networks of ethnic and patrimonial alliance. The relative autonomy of voting technologies, which resides to a large extent in their materialisation as objects, places and written and legally sanctioned sets of regulations, implies that these technologies can also be appropriated by voters and imbued with possibly subversive social meanings. Thus the introduction of the secret ballot to the Uluguru district in colonial Tanganyika in the 1950s may first have been perceived by the inhabitants of the district as bringing in an alien form that was not suited to their more or less 'traditional' political routines, a position that could reinforce the British colonial officials' view that they were not yet 'mature enough' for the secret ballot—i.e. that they were not yet citizens, but still subjects (cf. Mamdani, 1996). But they quickly appropriated this technology six years later, when a corporate understanding of membership of the main opposition party, TANU, had redefined citizenship in the terms of anti-colonial racialism. Again 'politics from below' produced an outcome unexpected by the engineers of democracy, and distinct from their desired production of the citizen as individual. As in other fields of the study of material culture, the tool was 'diverted' by ordinary practitioners and consumers from its officially endorsed aims and officially prescribed uses, and inserted into a different political performance from the one anticipated (cf. Appadurai, 1986: 26–7).

Hence, Alain Garrigou's (1993) thesis that the voter is 'disciplined' through electoral procedures, while important, requires qualification. On the one hand one can indeed speak of a process of 'domestication' of political passions when the literate material culture of registration and voting by written and later printed ballot increasingly displaced and outlawed the festive and public oral mobilisation of voters that characterised earlier electoral cultures. On the other hand these new forms were also appropriated at once by voters according to local political routines, and even rejected or regarded with suspicion or contempt. Jean-Louis Briquet shows in his chapter such a discrepancy between the meanings and functions attributed to voting tools by public authorities and those assigned to the secret ballot by Corsican voters: here universal franchise and the secret ballot did not provide freedom from clientelistic networks but instead articulated the alienness of state-endorsed forms of political authority to these networks and thereby further adapted the latter to the former—by making the lack of secrecy about the vote a public secret among voters. David Recondo's chapter similarly shows that 'modern' voting by secret ballot does not make 'traditional' means of public voting disappear in a present-day Mexican village, but instead leads to forms of mutual accommodation between the two systems in a hybrid and culturally specific compromise.

Lastly we should note that these double-edged effects that can be identified in the implementation of the secret ballot often occur simultaneously. As Richard Banégas argues in his chapter, the first multi-party elections in Benin were characterised by at least two different effects: one was that an authoritarian and autocratic regime presented a newly 'democratic' face to foreign donors and thus secured, under a different guise, the continuation of a political economy of predation initiated during the era of single-party democracy; the other was that the electoral process was embedded in the monetary culture of clientelism and patronage in such a way that a measure of individualised voting behaviour emerged. This partly shows that, at least in a globalised world, understanding how the secret ballot is performed before different audiences is crucial for our qualitative analyses—we turn to that below. But Banégas' attention to the broader material culture of monetarised exchange and its impact on electoral procedure also reinforces the point that a historical ethnography of the secret ballot requires us to pay close attention to the material culture not just of voting technology, but also of the broader social relationships in which it is caught up.

Such an analysis is necessary, in the first place, because of the technology of the secret ballot itself—as noted earlier, the polling booth is an object imbued with modern presuppositions and electoral engineers pay the utmost attention to its construction and the surroundings in which it is placed as well as the rules and procedures governing its use. It has a direct political impact, especially when we consider what effect the *literate* technology of voting had on excluding certain electoral groups or disciplining both voters and candidates for election and their parties. But, in the second place, as social scientists we cannot espouse fetishism of these electoral technologies that those same engineers often take for granted, and instead must study carefully the material practices in which these technologies are caught up—whether this implies 'make-believe' elections, 'hybridising' elections or the straightforward rejection of the technology. In the third and last place, this relative autonomy of the material technology of the secret ballot explains why it lends itself to modes of subjectivisation that are sometimes radically opposed, disciplining voters as much as allowing them room for subversive action, and generating a mix of strategic and tactical action that, in historical ethnography, is best understood in terms of performance.

PERFORMANCE

As suggested by Michel de Certeau, the tactical appropriation of a technological device is always a creative performance, leading to unpredictable but long-lasting changes in its functioning (Certeau *et al.*, 1980). For a historical ethnography of the secret ballot, the concept of *performance* is vital for understanding this unpredictability: it locates the technology's material manifestations in concrete relationships between producers of the act of voting and its audiences. Thinking of the secret ballot as performance allows us to ask whether we should see an election as ritual, as drama, as (stage-)fight, as riot or as revolution. The answer may differ depending on the audience: while, for example, the colonial officials who organised the first territorial election in Tanganyika in 1958 preferred it to be a quiet ritual of political participation (often described by them in terms of theatrical metaphors), a majority of the African voters looked upon it as a revolution (Pels, this volume); while the Golkar party may have hoped that the 1982 elections in Solo on Java would turn out to be a political ritual as well (without, in any case, changing the composition of parliament in any radical way), the actual event was the occasion for riot and rebellion (Pemberton, this volume); while the electoral system devised by the Iranian revolutionary regime was intended to reduce revolutionary fervour to domesticated participation, it actually turned out to become a performance of the Khatami regime's reforms (Alinejad, this volume); and while the elections in Benin were partly meant to perform to the audience of external donors as a theatre of political choice, they turned into an electoral fight over patronage relationships with the voters (Banégas, this volume). Even when state bureaucrats generally want an election to occur without major upheavals, either before, during or after the act of voting, the material culture of the secret ballot mediates relationships between its producers and its audience, and it derives much of its ambivalence and unpredictability from the variability of these relationships.

The notion of performance is also vital in understanding the specific nature of the *secrecy* of the secret ballot. We have already referred to the ideological conception that holds the secrecy of the secret ballot to be the key to the voter's freedom to express his or her political choice. But seen within the larger context of the performance of voting as a whole, it becomes immediately obvious that the secrecy of the secret ballot is restricted, at least for the audience of the voters, to the moment of marking a ballot paper in the individual isolation of the polling booth. In other words, the voter is cast in a specific role within a larger performance, the staging of which largely escapes the perception of the majority of voters. How are voters' registration lists composed before they are used to check the right to vote? What happens to the ballot box once it is off-stage, out of sight of the voters? As Peter Pels puts it in his chapter: 'the secret ballot is *always* doctored behind the stage by state officials', even when the preparations for or the results of the election have *not* been tampered with in fraudulent ways (our emphasis). The example of the 2000 Presidential Elections in Florida, scrutinised in Lacorne's chapter, is enough to remind us that the material culture of the secret ballot leads to speculation about its 'off-stage' performance, with the results of this speculation depending on the audience concerned. The public performance of the secrecy of individual choice is only a small part of what remains concealed in an election—the processes of drawing up the lists of registered voters, canvassing votes and tallying them all have their public and hidden dimensions. And as the chapters by O'Gorman and Briquet remind us, the performance of secrecy itself can be suspect as well.

Such suspicion of the performance of secrecy was partly fuelled by the fact that it takes place in a larger landscape of political performance, a landscape that it also influences. One reason why the fetishism of the secret ballot has been so successful is that it can contribute to the marginalisation, delegitimation or dismissal of alternative political performances: collective forms of the shaping and voicing of opinion and criticism such as street protests and collective demonstrations like petitionary processions, subversive happenings or carnivalesque rituals—in fact, the performance of the secret ballot has a tendency to discredit *all* forms of collective political action in favour of the individual expression of political preference.[5] At the same time, the context of voting by secret ballot is characterised by its own collective performances: campaigning and canvassing for votes have turned into a veritable theatrical and media industry, and, as John Pemberton reminds us, these occasions can turn into riotous performances themselves.

Campaigning and canvassing remind us that collective performances not only accompany but are in fact generated by voting by secret ballot: current campaigns are impossible without a new figure of technocratic politics, whose role is directly dependent on the culture of tallying that characterises the secret ballot—the survey-man or pollster, who interprets polling results as a soothsayer used to interpret entrails, and thus monopolises production of the meaning of the vote. Since voting has been turned into a secret voice, enclosed in the individual's political heart and sometimes not even disclosed to one's intimate friends, it cannot express itself directly. Its divination calls for specialists, be they professional politicians (who always speak 'in the name of the voter') or spin-doctors (who read political destinies in poll figures) (see Geschiere, 2003). Their performances enclose the act of voting in a vast machinery of theatrical action and *trompe l'oeil*, and this may be the reason why Jean-Paul Sartre once said in the early 1970s that elections were 'booby-traps' (*'Elections, piège à cons'*).

Again we should emphasise that these performances engender their own appropriations and interpretations among different audiences: today, there are few European journalists who, when questioned about the declining rates of participation in local and national polls, will not talk at great length about the 'crisis of representative democracy'—again, as if participation in voting by secret ballot was the special symptom from which to diagnose politics in general. Indeed the procedural perfection for which electoral engineers strive does not prevent increases in abstention, political indifference or 'anti-system' votes—it may even foster these phenomena, as is shown by the rising criticism, in most Western democracies, of the secret ballot technology and the attempts to invent new modes of political expression (in the name of a still elusive 'participative democracy' in which voting would become a minor form of political assertion). But whatever the case may be, our understanding of these developments will necessarily have to build on the kind of historical ethnographies of voting by secret ballot and its ideologies, material culture and performances that this volume aims to provide.

---

5 Irene Gendzier, for example, has remarked on this conservative function of elections as proscribing organised dissent, in her critique of modernisation theory (1985: 4, 104).

This volume is one outcome of a series of research seminars jointly organised by the Centre d'Etudes et de Recherches Internationales (CERI, Paris) and the Amsterdam School of Social Science Research (ASSSR) from 2000 onwards.

Abu-Lughod, L., 1991, 'Writing Against Culture' in R.G. Fox (ed.), *Recapturing Anthropology: Working in the Present*, Santa Fe, NM: School of American Research Press, pp. 137–62.

Appadurai, A., 1986, 'Introduction: Commodities and the Politics of Value' in A. Appadurai (ed.), *The Social Life of Things*, Cambridge University Press, pp. 3–63.

Bayart, J.-F., 1993, *The State in Africa: The Politics of the Belly*, London: Longman.

Bijker, W. *et al.*, 1987, *The Social Construction of Technological Systems*, Cambridge University Press.

Certeau, M. de *et al.*, 1980, *L'invention du quotidien*, Paris: Union générale d'éditions.

Critique internationale, no. 24 (July), 2004, 'Promouvoir la démocratie?', C. Perron (ed.).

Foucault, M., 1978, *Histoire de la sexualité*, vol. I: *La volonté de savoir*, Paris: Gallimard.

——, 1988, 'Technologies of the Self' in L.H. Martin, H. Gutman and P.H. Hutton (eds), *Technologies of the Self: A Seminar with Michel Foucault*, Amherst, MA: University of Massachusetts Press.

Fredman, L.E., 1969, *The Australian Ballot: The Story of an American Reform*, East Lansing, MI: University of Michigan Press.

Garrigou, A., 1988, 'Le secret de l'isoloir', *Actes de la recherche en sciences sociales*, nos 71–2, pp. 22–45.

——, 1993, 'La construction sociale du vote. Fétichisme et raison instrumentale', *Politix*, no. 22, pp. 5–42.

——, 2002, *Histoire sociale du suffrage universel en France (1848–2000)*, Paris: Seuil.

Gell, A., 1992, 'The Technology of Enchantment and the Enchantment of Technology' in J. Coote and A. Shelton (eds), *Anthropology, Art and Aesthetics*, Oxford: Clarendon Press, pp. 40–63.

Gendzier, I.L., 1985, *Managing Political Change: Social Scientists and the Third World*, Boulder, CO and London: Westview Press.

Geschiere, P., 2003, 'On Witch Doctors and Spin Doctors: The Role of "Experts" in African and American Politics' in B. Meyer and P. Pels (eds), *Magic and Modernity*, Stanford University Press, pp. 159–82.

Mamdani M., 1996, *Citizen and Subject: Contemporary Africa and the Legacy of Late Colonialism*, Princeton University Press.

Manin, B., 1997, *The Principles of Representative Government*, Cambridge University Press.

O'Gorman, F., 1992, 'Campaign Rituals and Ceremonies: The Social Meaning of Elections in England, 1780–1860', *Past and Present*, no. 135, pp. 79–115.

Pels, P., 2000, 'The Trickster's Dilemma: Ethics and the Technologies of the Anthropological Self' in M. Strathern (ed.), *Audit Cultures: Anthropological Studies in Accountability, Ethics and the Academy*, London and New York: Routledge, pp. 135–72.

Stolcke, V., 1995, 'Talking Culture: New Boundaries, New Rhetorics of Exclusion in Europe', *Current Anthropology*, vol. 36, no. 1, pp. 1–24.

Taylor, C., 2001, 'Two Theories of Modernity' in D.P. Gaonkar (ed.), *Alternative Modernities*, Durham, NC and London: Duke University Press, pp. 172–96.

Williams, R., 1983, *Keywords: A Vocabulary of Culture and Society*, New York: Oxford University Press (revised edition).

THE SECRET BALLOT
IN NINETEENTH-CENTURY BRITAIN

Frank O'Gorman

I

In 1872 the British Parliament passed 'An Act to Amend the Law relating to Procedure at Parliamentary and Municipal Elections', usually known as the Ballot Act. The Act replaced a traditional system of public voting with a set of procedures which allowed electors to vote in secret. It has conventionally been regarded as an essential part of a wider process of democratisation which dominates British political history in the nineteenth century and is usually linked to the Reform Acts of 1832, 1867 and 1884–5, which massively increased the size of the electorate from less than half a million to over five and a half million. The Ballot Act of 1872 thus appears as an integral element in an enlightened programme of electoral reform. Taken together, these reforms became the foundations of the democratic body politic completed in the twentieth century.[1]

However, as recent historians have recognised, democratisation in nineteenth-century Britain was an intermittent and haphazard process. The twenty-first-century observer may see in the Reform Acts of 1832, 1867 and 1884–5 a consistent, linear process. They were, in fact, a series of almost entirely unrelated responses to a sequence of very different political crises. Few contemporaries interpreted either the Reform Acts or the Ballot Act of 1872 within a democratic context. Both of the major political parties, the Whigs (Liberals) and the Tories (Conservatives), were normally against extending the right to vote. They only passed Reform Acts when it was politically expedient for them to do so, especially when popular demand for reform threatened their political supremacy. Furthermore they were usually careful to concede as little as possible to the reformers and, where possible, to control the process of political change. The great Reform Acts, then, were meant just as much to check the speed and to dilute the force of democratisation as to encourage it.[2]

---

[1] The enfranchisement of all adult males and of women over the age of thirty came in 1918. Women between the ages of twenty-one and thirty were enfranchised in 1928.

[2] Indeed the Reform Act of 1832, which extended the vote to the £10 householder in the boroughs, was for over a decade regarded as a final settlement of the electoral system by

While successive measures sought to transform the old electoral system, the political élite ensured that as much of it as possible would be salvaged.[3] Calculated concessions could take the sting out of future popular agitation. This is why, for example, down to the legislation of 1884–5 every effort was made to keep urban and rural interests as separate as possible.[4] This process of incremental adaptation ensured that reforming legislation was rendered as acceptable as possible to defenders of the old system. Consequently, the nineteenth-century political élite in Britain was strikingly successful in moulding the shape and influencing the pace of democratisation in a manner which enabled it to cling to power both in parliamentary and in local politics.

What this meant in practice, both in 1832 and in 1867, was the slow and gradual abandonment of unacceptable and illegitimate features of the old electoral regime. The 1832 Act, for example, removed the worst of the rotten boroughs, in which the electorate was notoriously small and thus susceptible to social and political pressure. At the same time, the 1832 Act accelerated the inclusion of newer social and economic groups within the electorate. In a similar fashion, the Reform Act of 1867 permitted the enfranchisement of sections of the working classes. Such was the price that both Whigs and Tories were prepared to pay for the preservation of their social and political order.

The persistence of the old electoral order was not only a question of political calculation. After all, the old system was operationally efficient and until the closing decades of the century continued to conform to social and economic realities. Although historians have very naturally concentrated on the progressive changes which ultimately transformed the political system in the nineteenth century, they have until recently tended to neglect those elements of the electoral system which were much slower to change. Indeed electoral culture was intensely traditional, preoccupied as it was with historic forms and rights of election, with ancestral recollections of past struggles, with customary party vendettas and established habits of thought. For the first half of the nineteenth century, and in some cases for much longer, contemporaries were content to regard the vote as a piece of freehold property on which it was legitimate for the elector to make a profit either by selling it or by seeking to secure other concrete material gains for disposing of it in a certain manner. During this period it was regarded as perfectly normal for electors to seek

much of the political nation.
3 Or, indeed, even re-strengthened. The 1832 Act gave the vote for the first time to tenants-at-will in the counties who were among the most vulnerable of rural voters.
4 The county constituencies, which down to the end of the nineteenth century were the preserve of the landed élite, were in effect 'sealed off' from the rapidly expanding boroughs so that urban voters were prevented from voting in the counties. For this issue see Moore (1976: 256–89).

the advice of their landlord, employer or minister in disposing of their vote. In the counties, for example, a landlord who provided work for his dependents and housing for their families, and who sponsored a variety of local institutions which provided a civilised framework in which they could live their lives, might well expect to be rewarded with the political support of his tenants. As Lord John Russell said during the Reform Act debates in 1831:

'Wherever the aristocracy reside, receiving large incomes, performing important duties, relieving the poor by charity, and evincing private worth and public virtue, it is not in human nature that they should not possess a great influence upon public opinion.'[5]

Even in the boroughs, social influence was legitimately exercised by factory owners, bankers and others with rich resources. As John William Croker remarked, 'feelings of gratitude for the benefits which have been conferred upon them' were a perfectly normal consequence of philanthropy, charity and paternalism.[6]

Most contemporaries recognised that electoral influence of this type was not simply a right of property but a public trust which involved distinct and well-recognised paternal obligations to the community as a whole. This may have been an idealised view of social relationships in the constituencies and there are many examples of departures from this norm, but this was nevertheless the standard by which such relationships were judged. For example, to provide a small favour, a feast or a small job to an elector and his family might be nothing more than natural paternalism. At what point such harmless generosity might be deemed to have drifted over the borderline into corruption is difficult to say. Certainly to provide food, lodging and a small sum to cover expenses for an elector would be nothing more than a natural courtesy. But for an electoral patron to attempt to threaten, intimidate and browbeat an elector against his conscience would be regarded as illegitimate and unjustifiable.[7] More specifically, before 1885 most constituencies were double-member constituencies and electors, consequently, had two votes. Electors might thus choose to allocate both of their votes to the candidates approved by his patron or, if they disapproved of one of them, they might deliver only one vote. The range of choices thus available to an elector was complex and the room for negotiation considerable. The delivery of a vote, therefore, was a complicated matter and involved reciprocal duties and responsibilities. Most important of all, these duties were performed and these responsibilities carried out in the public eye, in which the activi-

5 Hansard, 3rd series, II, 1086 (19 February 1831).
6 Hansard, 3rd series, III, 102 (4 March 1831).
7 For this interpretation of a reciprocal relationship between voters and electors, see O'Gorman (1989: 225–85).

ties of those with the vote were scrutinised to an extraordinary degree. Down to the middle of the nineteenth century this public scrutiny of electors was staunchly defended by many contemporaries who argued that if there were a secret ballot the vote would become the voter's property and would thus be exercised for his own, not the public's interest. Consequently, secrecy, hypocrisy and even dishonesty would ensue. As many contemporaries continued to argue down to the passage of the 1872 Act, legitimate political action was the consequence not of secrecy and concealment but of manly honesty and public debate.[8]

II

The pre-1872 system of voting was characterised by tumultuous popular participation which was in turn generated by local political rivalries. The poll began with the nomination ceremony which was conducted from the hustings, a temporary, raised wooden structure from which speeches were delivered during the nomination process and during the poll. The candidates would reach the hustings at the head of rival processions, accompanied by large and noisy bands of their own supporters, resplendent in their respective colours. The nomination consisted of speeches nominating the candidates followed by the acceptance speeches of the candidates themselves. Even if the election was not contested, a formal nomination would still be held in which the candidates went through the public processes described. If the election was to be contested, the nomination would be followed by a show of hands, usually inconclusive or confused by the participation of non-electors, after which any of the candidates could demand a poll.

The nomination was a raucous, public occasion, much enjoyed by onlookers, and included considerable audience participation, such as heckling, booing and cheering. Occasionally members of the public made their own speeches for or against particular candidates. Whether much of the audience could actually hear the speeches is doubtful but is nevertheless beside the point. The nomination was an opportunity for the non-electors to make their opinions or, at least, their presence felt. They were there to remind the local élite, impressively turned out and displayed on the hustings, elevated above the audience, of their presence and of the well-understood convention that elections were conducted on their behalf. The nomination was followed, usually the next day, by the taking of the poll, which before 1832 was a prolonged and tortuous affair. The poll was usually open from about 8.00 a.m. to around 4.00 or 5.00 p.m. and might last for several days. Until 1785 there was no limitation on the length of a poll, but the inordinate length of the poll at the Westminster

8 See, for example, the speeches against the Ballot Act on 22 June, 6 July and 8 July 1871 in Hansard, 3rd series, CCVII, 432–43 and 1231; CCVIII, 1113.

constituency in 1784 led to an act the following year restricting polling to fifteen days. Very few polls lasted as long as that, but before 1832 for one to last over a week seems not to have been uncommon. The 1832 Reform Act restricted the poll to two days, a change which seriously diminished the prospects for lengthy, 'carnivalesque' entertainment, and in 1835 borough polls were restricted to one day. In 1853 county polls were also limited to a single day.

Votes were tendered by individual voters not at the hustings but at specially erected polling booths. Voters were brought to the poll in tallies or groups of ten, sometimes more. They would proceed by shuffling through a succession of bars, each guarded by a constable. The polling booths were enclosed structures but they were not secret. On his arrival there the voter would encounter a representative of the returning officer, a polling clerk who would note the voter's spoken preference, and agents and messengers of both sides in the election. The voter would approach the bar or table and would be asked by the returning officer, or his representative, for proof of his entitlement to the franchise. In a county election he would have to give his name, address and occupation and evidence of his freehold. In the various types of boroughs evidence of the entitlement would have to be similarly provided. At this point the poll agents for either side might question the validity of the credentials thus claimed. The voter might then have to endure some minutes of examination and scrutiny. Indeed poll agents were free to administer loyalty oaths to voters whose loyalty to the state or, more usually, the church might have been suspected, such as Jacobites, radicals or dissenters. Alternatively they might administer the oath against bribery. The returning officer would have to reach a decision on each case. Once his credentials had been verified, the voter would orally inform the poll clerk how he wished to dispose of his two votes. These choices would then be entered in the official poll book. The voter would then exit through the rear door of the booth.

Polling could be a slow and arduous business. Its pace could be determined by a number of factors including the number of voters, the number of polling booths to accommodate them and the firmness and efficiency of the returning officer. Indeed it was by no means unknown for one side to slow down the pace of polling, perhaps by querying the credentials of their opponents' voters. Their purpose in so doing might vary. If they were in the lead they would wish to make it difficult for their opponents to catch up. On the other hand they may simply have wished to cause their opponents more trouble and expense. Voting could thus be a complex, time-consuming and even daunting process. It was characterised by intense organisation and elaborate, bureaucratic legality against a backcloth of partisanship and excitement. Although the voters declared their voting choices quietly and in an enclosed booth, the event was by no means private. The disposal of each elector's vote could be known in minutes and the entire election proceeding was, and was expected to be, publicly known. In most places poll books and the lists of electors together with the distribution of their votes were published after the contest. Most of all the process of polling was characterised by public competition. For example, for each side to publish the state of the poll at hourly intervals was normal—galvanising their own and their opponents' supporters. Furthermore, at the end of each day the returning officer would announce the state of the poll. Such public encouragement of public competition might even then be followed by speeches of optimistic gratitude from the candidates, together with further processions, treating and other forms of entertainment of the voters. This aspect of elections was marvellously and mercilessly satirised by many artists and cartoonists, not least William Hogarth, whose *Four Prints of an Election* (1755–8) amounted to nothing less than a systematic critique and condemnation of the popular excesses of contemporary electoral culture.

This system of polling did not go unchanged. As we have seen, the length of the poll was severely curtailed after 1785. However, the above description relates exclusively to parliamentary elections. In the arena of local elections the status of the public poll was being seriously undermined long before 1872. The Poor Law Amendment Act of 1834 allowed for a form of secret voting in vestry elections. In this system ballot papers were delivered to the homes of electors, completed and collected two days later. In such a manner electors could cast their suffrages without the noise of the mob or the pressure of election agents. Nevertheless, in parliamentary elections the principle and practice of public polling continued down to 1872.

III

The political culture in which the ballot was embedded was boisterous, competitive and, above all, public. Many contemporaries were disposed to adopt a permissive attitude to at least three features of the ballot which later generations were to find intolerable. First, there were the pressures, social, financial and even occupational, placed upon electors to vote in a certain manner; second, contemporaries revelled in the publicity given both to the disposal of the vote during polling and to the record of the voting in so-called poll books published after the election; third, the enormous length of time which the election leading to the ballot required debilitated the normal routines of life for weeks and sometimes months. Taken together, these three features of the electoral system were condemned as corrupt by reformers and radicals.

Yet the existing electoral system was cherished by the landowning and other propertied classes because it allowed them, in their role as electoral

patrons with interests in parliamentary constituencies, considerable control of the electoral system and its output: members of parliament and the
opinions they professed. Consequently leadership of the parliamentary
parties, the control of parliament, the power of government and thus of
the political system more widely were enormously facilitated. However,
by the early nineteenth century an increasingly sensitive public opinion
was beginning to demand the reform of some of the more questionable
aspects of electoral life in Britain and a small radical group in parliament
began to question some of the less defensible features of the existing
electoral system. In this they were keenly supported by middle-class
radicals throughout the country, especially in the rising mercantile and
manufacturing towns.

In 1806 a leading Whig, George Tierney, moved a Treating bill which
would have ensured that electors voted at their own expense. Although
his intention was to restrict the financial inducements offered to voters, it
proved impossible to differentiate legitimate election expenses from illegal financial inducements. Furthermore it was argued that such a measure
might disenfranchise poor voters. The bill was defeated, as was a similar
measure in 1814. Furthermore a bill to prevent agents from interfering
with voters after the start of the poll failed to pass in 1818. The failure
of these attempted reforms was one element in the continued search for
a more comprehensive cure for electoral corruption and intimidation. By
the second decade of the nineteenth century systematic arguments for
the secret ballot were being put forward.[9] Only through the ballot, it was
argued, could voters exercise the franchise free of intimidation. In 1817
Jeremy Bentham published a *Plan of Parliamentary Reform* which included demands for annual elections, equal electoral districts and the secret ballot (Cannon, 1972: 175–6)—demands which were to be repeated
later by the radicals of the late 1820s and early 1830s, the Chartists and
radical elements within the Gladstonian Liberal party. The most famous
early propagandist for the ballot, however, was James Mill who in 1830
published his anonymous *On the Ballot*, in which he characterised the
existing situation of the elector:

The unfortunate voter is in the power of some opulent man; the opulent man
informs him how he must vote. Conscience, virtue, moral obligation, religion, all
cry to him that he ought to consult his own judgement, and faithfully follow its
dictates. The consequences of pleasing, or offending, the opulent man, stare him
in the face; the oath is violated, the moral obligation is disregarded, a faithless, a
prostitute, a pernicious vote is given.[10]

---

9 Demand for the secret ballot goes back at least to the Levellers and other radical groups
of the mid-seventeenth century. It was revived in the later eighteenth century by Major
Cartwright and other reform leaders (Cannon, 1972: 22, 26, 54–5, 61, 82, 102).
10 Quoted in Park (1931: 52).

These ideas informed the debate over the passing of the Reform Act of 1832, when demand for the ballot was quite widely voiced. The first major debate on a demand for ballot came on 28 May 1830 when the great Irish radical Daniel O'Connell moved resolutions in favour of universal suffrage, triennial parliaments and vote by ballot.[11] Although O'Connell's motion was roundly defeated, support for the ballot out of doors was building. In January 1831 a periodical, the *Ballot*, was launched, devoted to the passing of a Ballot Act, and by March 1831 no fewer than 280 petitions demanding the ballot had been presented to the House of Commons.[12] Perhaps surprisingly, the Whig government of Lord Grey, which was a government of landowners, seriously considered including the ballot in the first plan of reform.[13] However, even if the government had been in favour of the measure, it would have stood no chance either of passing the House of Lords or of being accepted by King William IV. Indeed there was considerable doubt that it would have even passed the House of Commons. In any case, Lord John Russell, one of the most enthusiastic Whig reformers, thought there was no need for it:

Our object should be rather to place the power of choice in men of property and intelligence, who will exercise it with honesty and discrimination. (Quoted in Cannon, 1972: 208)

Between 1832 and 1867 further attempts were made to purify electoral practices without going as far as the ballot, but little headway was made. In fact the 1832 Reform Act had been accompanied by a Bribery Act, which, having passed the Commons, failed to pass the Lords because of lack of time. Its sponsor, Lord John Russell, tried again in 1841 and 1842 after the General Election of that year had witnessed electoral bribery on an unprecedented scale. Russell proposed to outlaw payments and other gifts to voters, but no progress was made. One line of approach was to extend the boundaries of corrupt boroughs in an attempt to include large numbers of respectable voters with which to swamp established interests. Scarcely more effective were attempts to disenfranchise certain classes of voters in notoriously corrupt constituencies. It was in fact easier to disenfranchise them completely. Thus Sudbury and St Albans were disenfranchised in 1844 and 1852 respectively. But to attack individual constituencies was an exhausting and time-consuming process. The wider problem of electoral corruption still remained. In truth, the

11 The motion was overwhelmingly defeated by 31 to 13 (Kinzer, 1982: 9–10).

12 Hansard, 3rd series, III, 787, quoted in Seymour (1915: 207).

13 It must be admitted that there were tactical reasons for this. The cabinet committee entrusted with drafting the first plan of reform proposed a £20 householder franchise. The ballot was included as an inducement to reformers to accept this high entry level to the franchise. The government later lowered the entry level to £10 and the ballot was no longer needed (Brock, 1973: 138–42; Seymour, 1915: 208).

issue of electoral corruption and intimidation was not rated as an urgent political priority in these years. There was always resistance from the electoral patrons in the House of Lords, who could be relied upon to block or to delay any measure that threatened to weaken the control of constituencies in which they had an interest. Even those party leaders who entertained some enthusiasm for the project, such as Russell, were not prepared to whip their followers in either House through the division lobbies. Finally, it was commonly believed that further reforms of electoral processes might precipitate yet greater demands for more radical reforms of the franchise.

Consequently, in the years after 1832 the demand for the ballot declined, albeit only very slowly. Pro-ballot candidates in some of the larger boroughs had in fact performed quite respectably in the first election after the Reform Act (Kinzer, 1982: 16–17). Meanwhile, on the liberal wing of the Whig party and in radical circles the demand for the ballot continued unabated, not least because there was a widespread conviction that the Reform Act of 1832, with its hundreds of thousands of additional voters, many of whom were vulnerable to influence and intimidation, had worsened the problem of electoral corruption. This was the theme of George Grote's magnificent hour-long speech to the Commons on 25 April 1833, in which he argued that only the secret ballot would enable the fruits of the Reform Act to be harvested. In spite of Grote's oratory, the motion for the ballot was lost by a significant majority, 211 to 106. The radical impetus which had done so much to ensure the passing of the 1832 Reform Act was steadily weakening. However, these years are not devoid of significance. Between 1835 and 1839 George Grote launched an impressive campaign characterised by petitions, pamphlets, meetings and annual motions in Parliament.[14] In the parliamentary session of 1837–8 no fewer than 365 petitions for the ballot were received, signed by over 181,000 signatories.[15] However, during the 1840s, even though it was enthusiastically championed by the Chartists, support for the ballot eventually declined in popularity. Grote retired from Parliament in 1841. The Chartists demanded the ballot but only as part of a comprehensive reform of the electoral system, thus alienating many moderate Whig and liberal reformers who might otherwise have persevered in their support for the measure. Nevertheless, the ballot refused to go away. Indeed, in 1853 a Ballot Society was formed of which Cobden and Bright were members. Its leader was Henry Berkeley, who had led the parliamentary campaign for the ballot since 1847. He proceeded to move annual motions for the ballot in the Commons between 1848 and 1866. In 1848 and 1851 such motions actually passed thin Houses by small majorities. In

14 For a summary of these pamphlets and their contents, see Park (1931: 59–63).
15 These figures are given in *The British Almanac*.

other years he obtained a promising number of votes, most dramatically 172 (against 232 in 1853), 189 (against 257) in 1857 and 197 (against 294) a year later (Seymour, 1915: 226). Yet these were little more than ritual gestures. So long as the leaders of the major political parties, the House of Lords and the monarchy remained opposed there was no prospect of achieving vote by ballot.

The years of the Crimean War (1854–6) and of Palmerston's supremacy (1859–65) left most of the public uninterested in the issue of the ballot. In 1859 John Stuart Mill announced his opposition to the ballot and, in lending his enormous authority to the retention of open voting, argued that the ballot, far from cleansing electoral politics, would only encourage deceit and hypocrisy.[16] Berkeley's motions were attracting fewer supporters. In 1862 and 1865 he could not even muster 100 votes. A mass of contemporary evidence suggests that many observers were irritated by the old demand for the ballot (Park, 1931: 71–3). Even the Ballot Society, now almost moribund, recognised in the middle of the 1860s that it could not compete with other issues of the day. Worst of all, the Whig and Liberal leaders remained indifferent if not hostile. In 1866 Gladstone confessed that neither in the present nor in the future would a Liberal government bring in a ballot bill (Seymour, 1915: 428).

Yet even in these dismal days enthusiasm for the ballot never quite disappeared. Many of the larger and more open constituencies supported it, as did their MPs, in Berkeley's annual motions. Much of the Northern liberal press, such as the *Leeds Mercury*, continued to canvass the issue in their columns. There are at least four reasons for this continuing bedrock of support. First, many contemporaries remained convinced that the amount of electoral corruption, far from diminishing after 1832, was actually increasing, in line with the increased number of voters. Second, the Ballot Society had done much useful and enduring work. It had acted as an umbrella group for local ballot societies, issued tracts and sent out public speakers. Not least, it maintained pressure on MPs (Park, 1931: 74). Third, the public demand for the ballot remained respectable. Even in the very quiet year of 1860 no fewer than sixty-five petitions containing over 7,000 signatures were raised. Four, the granting of the secret ballot to Victoria and three other Australian colonies seriously weakened intellectual opposition to it.

IV

Towards the end of the 1860s the popularity of the ballot began to revive. Many contemporaries took objection to the fact that many elements of electoral corruption had survived the Reform Act of 1832 and continued

16 *Edinburgh Review*, July 1860.

to attract attention. The blatant influence of individuals, families and institutions over voters in some small constituencies had not disappeared and cases of electoral malpractice and intimidation were now more widely and more sensationally reported than ever. In the 1860s political parties were beginning to cultivate a popular middle-class membership in an attempt to establish bureaucratic national and constituency party structures. This professionalisation represented a direct challenge to the old personal and informal politics of influence and treating. At the same time, the Industrial Revolution in Britain saw the emergence of a huge industrial proletariat which was effectively barred from the franchise by the property qualifications imposed by the 1832 Reform Act. As mid-Victorian prosperity began to wane in the 1860s, a new generation of working-class leaders began to demand political reform while trades unions agitated for improved wages and conditions. A popular reform agitation in 1866–7 demanded not merely the extension of the franchise but in many places the ballot as well. It was back on the political agenda. In 1867 the Conservative party, which had been in opposition for most of the years since 1832, saw an opportunity to make a political comeback by passing a further measure of reform which would enfranchise sections of the new industrial working class to its own electoral advantage.

The Reform Act of 1867 changed the situation in important respects. The appearance of one million new voters, many of them working men, unprotected by the ballot caused considerable discussion. How free would they be to vote as they wished? In fact many of these class-conscious voters bitterly resented the interference of their social superiors with their newly acquired franchise. After all, the Act enfranchised many constituencies where industrial employers turned out to have an influence over the voters comparable to that of landlords in rural areas. Places like Blackburn, Bury, Darlington, Jarrow, Mansfield and Northwich allowed new electoral patrons to emerge with powers that almost equalled many of their rural counterparts.[17] Elsewhere, where both the local economy and the pattern of employment were more mixed, voting behaviour was much more individualistic and voters enjoyed considerably more freedom of choice.

During the reform agitation of 1866–7 the ballot attracted less extra-parliamentary support than it had done in 1831–2. Within parliament, however, it was a different story. On 12 July 1867 Berkeley moved to include the ballot in the Reform Bill and his motion was only defeated by 161 to 112. Many Liberal MPs supported the measure, but others were suspicious of its likely consequences.[18] In some ways, however, the

---

17 See the interesting discussion in Pugh (1982: 12–13).
18 At the General Election of 1868 the ballot was to appear in the election addresses of 151 Liberal MPs (O'Leary, 1962: 46).

Reform Act had a positive effect on the fortunes of the ballot. Insofar as it highlighted the problems of so many dependent voters it provided a powerful further impetus for Liberal MPs and their supporters to champion the cause. After all, the ideological purpose of Gladstonian Liberalism was to attack the power of the landed ruling class at all levels. The ballot could be portrayed as a perfect example of Gladstonian Liberalism in action. As Disraeli, at least, noted, Liberal MPs would in future be 'compelled by the double pressure of the ministry and their constituents to vote in its favour'.[19] Indeed they began to exert such pressure on Gladstone that he started to reconsider his earlier opposition to the ballot.

The General Election of 1868 was vigorously contested on the new franchises as both parties sought to appeal to the new voters. Following the lacklustre campaigns of the previous three general elections, 1857, 1859 and 1865, this was a lengthy and fiercely contested election and reports of rioting, bribery and intimidation were common. No fewer than thirty-four petitions for corruption were heard following the election, although the extent of corruption was very much greater than even this number might suggest. Gladstone was appalled at the scale of these electoral abuses and was not inclined to resist too strongly when, in bringing Bright into the cabinet at the end of the year, he was forced to concede an inquiry into the issue of the ballot. Nor could he have been unaware that at least half of his supporters in the House of Commons were supporters of the ballot. Consequently, the new Liberal government recommended the establishment of a Select Committee to inquire into the whole subject of electioneering at both parliamentary and municipal levels. In moving its appointment, Henry Bruce commented on the disfavour into which the exercise of influence had fallen in recent years (Moore, 1976: 412). The establishment of the Committee and its early meetings aroused immense anticipation in the press and among the liberal public to which Gladstone aspired to appeal. Between December 1868 and August 1869 no fewer than ninety-nine petitions signed by over 25,000 signatories were organised. This degree of support could not be maintained during the next few years. The number of petitions in 1870, 1871 and 1872 was 9,228, 9,339 and 2,214 respectively, impressive but by no means decisive. Nevertheless, it was to prove sufficient to soothe the anxieties of a government indecisive on the issue of the ballot.

This all-party committee took evidence from a variety of sources until July 1869. The committee concluded that in English counties undue influence was often exercised. In English boroughs 'undue influence in a modified form' was common. Although intimidation was not so widespread in Scotland, especially in the new constituencies, in Ireland the

19 8 July 1871, *Diaries of the 5th Earl of Derby* (1994, ed. J. Vincent, Camden 5th series, IV, 83–4).

influence of the clergy often rivalled that of landlords. The committee concluded that there were four possible remedies: the abolition of public nomination, the abolition of paid canvassers and agents, an increase in the number of polling places and, not least, the introduction of the secret ballot. Its report was laid before the Commons on 15 March 1870.[20] In May the cabinet approved a comprehensive bill which included both the ballot and the abolition of public nomination. Moreover, the bill forbade the use of public houses as committee rooms, lengthened polling hours and charged election expenses to the ratepayers, this latter clause opening the door to working-class candidates. Most disappointing to radicals, however, the bill included a provision for scrutiny by which ballot papers could be checked against the names of the electors in cases of alleged corruption. Such a measure, they argued, seriously compromised the secrecy of the ballot. However, the bill had not even reached its second reading before the session ended and with it the bill's prospects. Nevertheless, the session was not devoid of significance. During July Gladstone announced a change of mind on the ballot, withdrawing his earlier opposition. Almost as significant, a clause was inserted into Forster's Education Bill, then making its way through Parliament, providing for the ballot in School Board elections in London, a vital, symbolic measure.

A second ballot bill was introduced into the Commons by Forster on 20 February 1871. It was considerably more radical than the first, extending not only the ballot but the abolition of public nomination to municipal elections. After much heart-searching the government decided to abandon the scrutiny. However, this bill too failed to complete its parliamentary stages. The main business of the session was the contentious Army Regulation Bill, which abolished the practice of buying army commissions. The bill monopolised both the time and the attention of parliament to such an extent that over thirty measures, not least the ballot bill, were seriously delayed. The bill's second reading could not be scheduled until 3 April. It passed easily but serious opposition came with the committee stage, which opened as late as 22 June. The committee wearily worked its way through the amendments—over 200 of them—which had been tabled, no fewer than half of them by Liberal MPs. By the time the bill reached its third reading on 8 August the committee members had endured twenty-seven sittings and had divided no fewer than seventy-three times. However, on second reading in the Lords on 10 August the bill was overwhelmingly defeated by 97 to 48. There was no prospect of the bill passing in what little remained of the session and it had to be deferred until the following year (O'Leary, 1962: 74–81).

---

[20] The best summary of the activities of the Committee is contained in O'Leary (1962: 57–67).

Believing that the radical extent of the measure had partially contributed to the failure in 1871, the government now divided the bill into two to facilitate its passage in the session of 1872. The main bill concentrated on election procedure, in both municipal and parliamentary elections. The other confined itself to the elimination of corrupt practices. The passage of these bills through Parliament was without incident. The bills passed their second reading in the Commons on 15 February and in a thin House the bills were committed on 29 February. Gladstone faced down wrecking resistance in the Lords, which demanded the restoration of a scrutiny. The Conservative opposition had no stomach for the threat of a general election on the issue if the ballot proposal were defeated, and the bills received the royal assent on 18 July 1872.

Why was a Ballot Act passed in 1872? By the 1870s public opinion was much more susceptible to evidence of electoral corruption than had been the case in the 1830s, and after the General Election of 1868 there can be no doubt that public opinion was largely, if in many places unenthusiastically, in favour of the measure. This, however, was not the decisive factor: as Disraeli argued, less than one quarter of MPs were pledged to the measure.[21] Yet *The Times* was full of reports of pro-ballot meetings and opinion.[22] There were also warnings and murmurings against the obstructive attitude of the House of Lords, which may have persuaded some MPs and peers not to oppose the measure.[23] Nevertheless, as Bruce Kinzer argues, middle-class radicalism had largely faded by the early 1870s: witness Bright's acceptance of office in Gladstone's cabinet (Kinzer, 1982: 99–103). The early 1870s saw the gradual erosion of resistance until in the end even some Conservatives accepted the ballot.

A principal reason for this development was the weakening of some of the traditional arguments against the ballot. The harsh light of publicity and decades of press reporting of cases of electoral corruption had steadily eroded the legitimacy of public voting. One of the most powerful ideological props of the old electoral order had been the conviction that the vote was a public trust exercised on behalf of the non-voters by the voters. Such a public trust, it followed, had to be exercised in public. Supporters of the ballot argued that if the vote *was* a public trust then voters, especially in their immense numbers after 1867, ought to be able to exercise that trust without intimidation or corruption, and thus privately. If the laws made the voter theoretically responsible to the public, then why was he so frequently under the thumb of some private person rather than being able to exercise his political choices

21 On 8 August 1871, see Hansard, 3rd series, CCVIII, 1098–100.
22 See the issues of 24 December 1868, 16 January 1869, 6 April, 19 May 1870 and 1st June 1872. See also *Saturday Review*, 5 February, 27 May 1870, 3 March, 21 June and 7 July 1871 (Park, 1931: 71–2).
23 *The Times*, 11 July and 23 August 1871.

freely?[24] Similarly the old scare stories that the ballot would usher in an age of chaos and democracy seemed rash and extravagant after its widespread adoption in other countries and in school board and vestry elections.[25] Finally, the old argument that open voting bred a sturdy independence of mind and character that was quintessentially English could be difficult to sustain. As one contemporary observed, 'what takes place in every contested election under the "English" system ought to make the ears of every Englishman tingle with shame' (quoted in Dennis and Skilton, 1987: 34–5).

Nevertheless, the political initiative for the ballot in 1869–72 came not from outside parliament but from within, and, in particular, from the Liberal party. Quite simply, the ballot was a central feature of Gladstonian Liberalism. Many Liberal MPs were in favour of the ballot. They had recognised that after 1867 the pressure for it was irresistible. Within the context of Gladstone's administration of 1868–74 the Ballot Act may be judged as part of the Liberals' sustained campaign to reduce landed and ecclesiastical power. Already the Victorian middling orders, encouraged by the Municipal Corporations Act of 1835 and the Northcote-Trevelyan Report (1853), were making inroads into the structures of aristocratic power. During his administration Gladstone directly attacked aristocratic privilege through reforms in the army and civil service, through the abolition of the purchase of army commissions, through the ending of privileged access to the civil service and through the abolition of religious tests at the universities. By 1871 the administration appeared to be running out of steam, a consideration that may have persuaded Gladstone to throw the weight of his ministry behind the cause of the secret ballot.

In any case, the purpose of the Ballot Act was to reform and re-legitimate electoral influence, not to destroy it. Democracy was as far from the ambitions of the men responsible for the Ballot Act of 1872 as it had been from those responsible for the Reform Acts of 1832 and 1867. Although some of its most enthusiastic proponents might occasionally make a gesture in favour of 'the full representation of the people', they were in truth anxious to ensure that 'the voter should give his vote according to the dictates of his conscience and for the benefit of his country.' The main objective of the bill was to keep the voter 'free from illegitimate influences' while securing for him 'the full force of all those legitimate influences arising from the education, the character and the tone of those with whom he lived'.[26] Far from exposing the voter to democratic influences,

---

24 See Mr Baker's speech in the Commons on 22 June 1871, Hansard, 3rd series, CCVII, 472–3. See also O'Leary (1962: 26) and Moore (1976: 406).
25 See Mr Walter's speech in the Commons on second reading on 15 February 1872, Hansard, 3rd series, CCIX, 491–2.
26 See Assheton Cross's speech in the Commons on 22 June 1871, Hansard, 3rd series, CCVII, 410–11.

the object of the bill was to protect voters from agitators and mob orators just as much as from electoral patrons. The ideal of the Act, therefore, was the independent voter freed from influence from below as well as from above.[27] The objective of the government was even less exciting. As W.E. Forster put it, the government wished 'to make elections as orderly as possible, and to induce the peaceful portion of the voters to take as large a part as possible'.[28] Others simply wished to 'promote the tranquillity, the freedom and the purity of elections'.[29] The context of the measure, then, was to preserve a reformed electoral influence at a time of rapid population increase, local and regional economic change and new social relationships which collectively threatened to undermine the traditional sources of social and electoral influence. To some extent Moore is right to argue that because canvassers could no longer, after their experiences of the 1868 election, predict the outcome of contests with any precision, the system of open voting had become redundant to the retention of patronal control (Moore, 1976: 406–7 and 412). Consequently, it was safe to pass a Ballot Act in 1872 because its passage did not represent a threat to aristocratic or upper-class power.

V

In the end the Ballot Act provided for a nomination in writing to be proposed and seconded by two registered electors and signed by eight others. Voters would vote by entering a private booth within a polling station, marking a ballot paper and placing it in a ballot box. The box would be sealed at the end of polling and entrusted to a returning officer. The boxes would be sent to the returning officer, accompanied by an account of the number of ballot papers issued, a copy of the register and the counterfoils. The ballots would be counted in a central place in the constituency, witnessed by party agents and the candidates. A declaration of the result of the poll would then be publicly made. The new polling system was drastically different from the old one. The cultural context was now significantly different. It was not just that the actual act of voting was now a private as opposed to a public act. As we shall see later, the traditional nomination and its attendant public rituals were abolished. Furthermore electors no longer voted in tallies. They could walk quietly into one of the (more numerous) polling stations free of outward intimidation and their votes were no longer publicly recorded. There were no

27 See Baillie Cochrane's speech to the Commons, 22 June 1871, Hansard, 3rd series, CCVII, 446.
28 See Forster's speech on 6 July 1871, Hansard, 3rd series, CCVII, 1268. See also his speech on 18 April 1872, Hansard, 3rd series, CCX, 1482–3.
29 See Assheton Cross's speech in the Commons on 24 July 1871, Hansard, 3rd series, CCVIII, 668–9.

announcements of the state of the poll, no speeches and, for the most part, little or nothing by way of entertainment during the period of the poll itself.

There was no question, then, that the Ballot Act largely succeeded in its objectives. Most of its deficiencies were the result of inexperience, such as the sponsors' neglect of some of the more practical aspects of organising a ballot. For example, only three days were allowed for the preparation of the ballot papers and boxes and in the large urban constituencies this was inadequate. However, on the whole the secret ballot worked well (O'Leary, 1962: 90–2). Secrecy was observed and no systematic attempts were made to breach it. Since all the ballot boxes for a constituency were counted together no certain conclusions could be reached about an individual's vote. Consequently, poll books could no longer be published. As contemporaries recognised, this was crucial because the poll books revealed how individuals had disposed of their votes.[30] Moreover, any fears that the new secret system of voting might disenfranchise ignorant or illiterate voters who might need advice and direction did not amount to much. Only a very small proportion of ballot papers were spoiled (Seymour, 1915: 432–3). It is significant that no attempt was ever made to return to the *status quo ante* 1872. A House of Lords amendment had restricted the operation of the Act to eight years only, but there was never the slightest chance that it would not be renewed. After 1880 the Act was renewed annually and it became permanent with the passage of the Representation of the People Act in 1918 (Kinzer, 1982: 247–8).

The effects of the Ballot Act must be measured by its objectives and not by the hysterical fears of its opponents, who gloomily predicted the end of all influence, the onset of universal suffrage and, worst of all, votes for women.[31] We should not, for example, be surprised that the Act did not see an immediate end of electoral influence. For the ordinary voter to fully realise there were no overt pressures on him to vote in a particular manner would take time. After all, the Marquis of Hartington in his famous report of 1870 had not come out against the principle of influencing electors but only against 'the improper means to influence them' (Seymour, 1915: 433–4). Again and again supporters of the Ballot

---

[30] See Bereford-Hope's speech in the Commons on 28 February 1872, Hansard, 3rd series, CCIX, 501–2.

[31] See Newdegate's speech in the Commons on 6 July 1871, Hansard, 3rd series, CCVII, 1231. Sir Stafford Northcote asserted that the Ballot Act would put an end to 'that kind of influence which a candidate, and those interested in an election, had to know how such and such a man voted, because how a man voted was an important fact in the eyes of the constituency' (14 July 1871, Hansard, 3rd series, CCVII, 1758). On 15 February 1872 Stephen Cave declared that the Ballot Act would 'annihilate that neighbourly influence of education and station' (Hansard, 3rd series, CCIX, 488).

Act argued that the purpose of the legislation was to stop the intimidation of voters, not to destroy legitimate influence.[32] As we have already seen, the Ballot Act of 1872, like the Reform Acts of 1832 and 1867, was designed less to abolish electoral influence than to preserve it in an acceptable and legitimate form. Consequently, even after 1872 landlords and patrons in both counties and boroughs continued to issue requests to voters to support the candidates of their choice. Treating and gifts, election breakfasts and the 'employment' of voters all continued. Such activities were simply not regarded as bribes. If anything, one of the unexpected consequences of the Ballot Act was to promote collective forms of treating, such as picnics and parties. Moreover, it is likely that although direct instructions to individual voters declined after the Ballot Act, the expectations that agents could generate among voters could be enough to secure their support just as strongly as in the days of open voting (Seymour, 1915: 433–4).

In the counties social pressures still maintained their subtle yet powerful hold on the dispositions of the voters. There was certainly no sudden weakening of electoral influence in the counties at the General Election of 1874.[33] There were few contests and most tenants seem obediently to have done what was asked of them by their patrons. In Lincolnshire, one of the counties most closely studied, the ballot made little difference either to patterns of voting or to patterns of representation (Olney, 1973: 179). This was also the case in many boroughs. 'The medium-sized company town was almost as secure a stronghold for influence as the landed estates of the agricultural counties' (Pugh, 1982: 12–13). In the larger boroughs the combination of more numerous voters and the more fragmented nature of influence may have produced a greater freedom in the disposal of votes. On the whole, however, the patronal classes were able to rest easily with the Ballot Act since they did not believe it posed an immediate threat to either their electoral influence or their social pre-eminence. Consequently it is not difficult to see why the Act passed Parliament relatively easily.

After the Ballot Act of 1872, then, influence persisted but the influence of individual electoral patrons was gradually integrated into the increasingly bureaucratic structures of the great political parties. This occurred because the Act made it absolutely essential for parties to organise themselves much more comprehensively than had been necessary in the past, when influence and instructions together with a hearty dose of treating would have been enough to deliver votes. Here was work for

[32] Leatham denounced intimidation and even viewed influence as 'a system of organised pressure' which was all the more insidious for being so subtly applied (see his speech in the Commons on 22 June 1871, Hansard, 3rd series, CCVII, 452–3).

[33] As late as 1874 'the dominant mode of county politics remained influence' (Nossiter, 1975: 104).

parties to do. Candidates were now to be less dependent upon traditional patterns of influence for their return and almost entirely dependent upon the efficient operation of party workers and institutions together with that of other, less political, groups such as churches and trades unions. In many ways, of course, the influence of the parties, with their 'elaborate paraphernalia of agents, canvassers and committee rooms', was not unlike the older politics of patronage (Pugh, 1982: 137). Indeed, as Seymour remarks, canvassing of electors became more important after 1872 than it had been before. In fact the functions and powers of political parties gained rather than lost as a result of the Ballot Act (Seymour, 1915: 433). In that sense the Ballot Act is an important date in the development of party institutions in Britain.

The effect of the Ballot Act upon corruption is more difficult to estimate since it was overtaken by the Corrupt Practices Act of 1883. In the eleven years of its independent operation there was certainly no immediate and dramatic curtailment of corruption. Supporters of the bill argued that the ballot would limit bribery because those exerting pressure could never be certain how electors had voted. It was surely impossible for the large number of voters enfranchised in 1867 to be individually bribed.[34] Opponents of the bill predicted that both impersonation and bribery would inevitably increase if open voting were abandoned. In their opinion a secret ballot would increase the opportunities for bribery because it would in practice be impossible to prove that bribery had occurred.[35] Their fears should not be dismissed out of hand. The General Election of 1874 was no less corrupt than that of 1868 (Ostrogorski, 1902: 469). Everything depended on the constituency. Where patterns of corruption were well entrenched there was probably little immediate change. In traditionally corrupt boroughs corruption may even have increased if electors took money from both sides. To judge from the General Election of 1874 little had changed: 'Voters were canvassed, intimidated, and almost certainly bribed with the difference this time that the principal agents were not the masters but the men' (Nossiter, 1975: 99). Indeed Hanham (1972: 266) has declared that within a few years 'the old ways ... were resumed with a new zest.' By 1880, according to Cornelius O'Leary (1962: 157), there was 'an unparalleled orgy of extravagance'. After that election no fewer than eight constituencies were disenfranchised for corruption (Hanham, 1972: 266–73). Moreover there was little to suggest that the Ballot Act reduced election expenses, despite the optimistic forecasts of its support-

34 See, for example, the speeches of Mr James and Mr Platt in the House of Commons on 26 June 1871, Hansard, 3rd series, CCVII, 560–2, 584 and 628; see also that of the Marquis of Ripon in the Lords on 10 August 1871, Hansard, 3rd series, CCVIII, 1256–60.
35 See the speech of Bentinck to the Commons on 29 June 1871, Hansard, 3rd series, CCVII, 746–50; see also Russell's speech on 8 July 1872, reported in Hanham (1969: 275–6).

ers. Forster admitted that the provision of more polling stations would cost money but thought that the Act would reduce the number of paid canvassers, lessen the need to convey voters and abolish the costs of the hustings and nomination.[36] However, Ostrogorski (1902: 159) estimated the election of 1880 was the worst in this period for illicit expenditure by the candidates. There was to be no limit on expenses before the Corrupt Practices Act of 1883, which at last restricted the amount of money that each side could spend on elections.

The Ballot Act could not reduce electoral malpractice to any extent so long as the conditions for it persisted. As Fielden told the Commons, such corruption would continue while society was founded upon such massive social inequalities.[37] More specifically, the persistence of small and therefore vulnerable electorates, the idea of the vote as a piece of property from which electors were prepared to take a profit, and the continuing tolerance of electoral corruption ensured that further assaults on abuses of electoral campaigning would be required. The Ballot Act had surprisingly little effect on the distribution of seats between the political parties. As the table below shows, the Conservatives certainly gained ground on the Liberals in 1874 by comparison with their performance in 1868 but, as *The Morning Post* commented in December 1872, the Tory party was bound to revive its electoral fortunes after its defeat in 1868 largely because it commanded more property than its rivals.[38]

	1868; votes	1868; seats	1874; votes	1874; seats
Liberal	1,422,677	385	1,388,988	301
Conservative	906,045	273	1,088,532	351

Where the Ballot Act might have been most expected to make a difference, namely in the single-member smallest boroughs, little change was discernible. Analysing the fourteen smallest boroughs, Martin (1874) found that the number of Liberal votes in these seats increased from 5,466 in 1868 only to 5,527 in 1874. The Conservative vote was similarly little changed, dropping by only a hundred between 1868 and 1874. In spite of what may have been expected, the most notable success for the Conservatives in 1874 was actually in the English counties, where the Liberal share of the vote dropped by 2.75 per cent while the Conservatives' share increased by a striking 7.75 per cent.[39] It is possible

36 See Forster's speeches to the Commons on 3 August 1871 and 14 March 1872 (Hansard, 3rd series, CCVIII, 851–7; 1972–6).

37 29 February 1872, Hansard, 3rd series, CCVIII, 499–500.

38 See the detailed calculations in Martin (1874: 193–230).

39 This cuts clean against Kinzer's argument that the Ballot Act had little effect in the

that in the boroughs the elector found greater freedom, but his employer was just as likely to be Conservative as Liberal. In Scotland and Wales the voters had demonstrated their resistance to influence even before the ballot had been enacted. The Act of 1872 simply reinforced their pre-existing independence of mind.

The Ballot Act is supposed to have had the greatest effect in Ireland, where the extent of landlord and clerical influence as late as the General Election of 1868 was very great:

The great majority of the seats were allocated without any reference to the people at all, as fifty-four of the sixty-four county seats and eleven of the thirty-nine borough seats were uncontested. But even where there was a contest the voters were rarely left to decide for themselves. In the towns (even in Dublin) money and mobs were the masters, with the consequence that petitions were presented in eleven of the twenty boroughs contested. In the countryside ..., the landlords or their agents escorted their tenants in batches to the polls. (Hanham, 1972: 180)[40]

Indeed the level of education in the electorate was much more basic than in England. Consequently the Act did not work as well in Ireland as it did in England. In Athlone in 1874 no fewer than one in eight of the ballot papers was incorrectly filled in, owing in part to illiteracy (Hoppen, 1984: 73). Because the Ballot Act weakened the power of landlords, Parnell's task of organising the electoral base of the Home Rule movement was almost certainly made considerably easier than it might otherwise have been. After the election of 1874 there were no fewer than fifty-nine MPs 'returned on Home Rule principles' to Westminster (Hoppen, 1989: 116); in 1868 there had been none. However, it is likely that the Ballot Act, far from injecting novel patterns of behaviour into Irish electoral politics, did little more than quicken certain of its principal features. Indeed, Michael Hurst argued in 1965 that the trail of by-election victories for the Home Rule movement between 1868 and 1872 shows that the Ballot Act merely accelerated existing tendencies (Hurst, 1965: 326–52). Nevertheless, although the effects of the Ballot Act should not be exaggerated, in the case of Ireland, at least, some of the more gloomy prophecies as to the effect of the Act were justified. Ireland did slip further out of electoral control than was already the case, with incalculable effects upon the future relations between the two countries.

VI

The most significant, immediate effect of the Ballot Act was to be found less in its legislative and social consequences than in the considerable

---

country (Kinzer, 1982: 246–7).

40 Some MPs who opposed the Ballot Act in England nevertheless recognised the need for it in Ireland. See the debate of 15 February 1872, Hansard, 3rd series, CCIX, 479.

impact it made in the pattern and structure of electoral culture. Admittedly the economic and social context within which that culture existed was steadily undergoing change in the last three decades of the century. The beginning of the 'great depression' in agriculture may be dated from the middle of the 1870s, when some Conservative peers were already starting to bemoan the decline of their influence in the counties.[41] The timing of the decline of influence was very varied. In Cornwall the gentry and aristocracy had already conceded their electoral pre-eminence before the 1880s (Jaggard, 1999: 283). In Lincolnshire it was still alive and well even after that date (Olney, 1973: 206–22). The landed interest began to feel threatened and isolated in an increasingly urban and industrial society. Its loss of electoral influence did not begin with the Ballot Act, but was certainly marked by it and most likely accelerated by it. The old assumptions about élite influence and the obedience of blocs of electoral support were changing. Indeed, by the later 1880s the aristocracy had yielded the larger towns to middle-class interests. As Pugh remarks, 'by the 1880s even entrenched MPs were vulnerable to political issues' (Pugh, 1982: 13).

However, the Ballot Act did not merely presage the decline of old electoral influence but more fundamentally the passing of a traditional form of electoral culture. This culture, with its rowdy and popular pattern of election rituals, was several centuries old. It provided a narrative structure to the election campaign, beginning with the formal entry rituals of the rival candidates into the constituency; continuing with the elaborate formalities of canvassing the electors, with the public processions and speeches, the treating and entertainment of the electors and, what is often overlooked, of the non-electors too; culminating with the formalities of the nomination of the candidates and, where necessary, the taking of the poll. This pattern of electioneering concluded with the formal chairing of the victorious candidates around the constituency and in many places the formal departure of the candidates from the constituency. This pattern of electioneering, boisterous, popular, rowdy and very expensive, frequently brought the normal life of the constituency to a halt for days and even weeks. With all of its manifest failings and abuses, the old electoral culture had brought on to the streets the mass of the people, participating in a series of political and social ritualistic events which had publicised local issues, asserted local identities, voiced local complaints and combined rich and poor alike in a carnivalesque world of dramas between good and evil, the great and the lowly and the free and the unfree.

The Ballot Act not only accelerated the decline of this old, rowdy and vigorous electoral culture but directly legislated against several of

---

41 *Derby Diary*, 20 May 1870.

its key elements. In particular the Act of 1872 saw the disappearance of a whole series of electoral rituals and ceremonies. Almost immediately the Act was put to the test. At a by-election at Pontefract in August 1872 the first election under the Ballot Act took place. Observers at once noted the difference:

> No bands of music paraded the town. No colours or banners were seen in procession. The church bells were silent .... It hardly seemed like an election.[42]

As *The Spectator* of 17 August 1872 commented, not only was there little bribery and corruption but some people even complained that the election had been too quiet (Park, 1931: 84). One of the next by-elections occurred at Preston, a traditionally lively town, a few weeks later. *The Times'* reporter on 28 September 1872 noted 'the marked absence of drunkenness until late in the day, and my firm conviction of the purity of election' (quoted in O'Leary, 1962: 86). When the next general election came round, in 1874, many observers commented on the change. *The Times* observed, 'mobs, processions, favours, free fights and punch-drinking have become for the most part things of the past, and where rioting did occur during the late Elections it was probably not aggravated by any political duplicity.'[43] In fact there was very little incident worth reporting on the polling day of the General Election of 1874 (O'Leary, 1962: 89). Another source commented, 'since the passing of the Ballot Act we have never had the slightest trouble at any election that has taken place in London, and the places that used to be the worst are now the best' (quoted in O'Leary, 1962: 90).

The Act of 1872 made a number of important changes in the old electoral culture. The introduction of written nominations removed public nomination, which had been such a lively piece of popular theatre. The nomination had been the focal point of electoral campaigning. It had been the first occasion when all voters—and non-voters too—were able to congregate together. Most important of all, it had been a great civic occasion, punctuated with displays of civic festivity such as bell-ringing and elaborate displays of corporate and civic ceremonial. All this was now gone. Many MPs celebrated the passing of these ritualistic displays of popular festivity which had so frequently been marked by riot and disorder.[44] As one MP put it, the nomination had been 'a Saturnalia for all the roughs and rowdies of society', for which crowds could be hired to shout down the speeches of opponents.[45] All of this was now replaced with the quiet and efficient operation of the secret ballot.

---

42 Quoted in Seymour (1915: 432). See also O'Leary (1962: 86).
43 *The Times*, 11 February 1874.
44 See Colonel Edwards' comments to the House of Commons about nominations on 22 June 1871, Hansard, 3rd series, CCVII, 437.
45 See Osborne's comments, 29 June 1871, Hansard, 3rd series, CCVII, 752–3.

James Vernon has argued that the disappearance of public nomination, 'the occasion on which the disfranchised exercised most influence',
was much to be regretted. Together with the provision of an increased
number of polling booths, the ending of public nomination tended to
reduce the number and disperse the force of election crowds. Indeed the
Ballot Act forbade the admission of non-electors to the new indoor polling places. 'In short, many of the electoral events which had previously
afforded the disfranchised their most powerful role were eroded or abolished' (Vernon, 1993: 157–8). This opinion merely reflected the attitude
of the Tory opponents of the measure who glorified public nomination,
'the most free and popular form of election that was possible.' Certainly
the nomination ceremonies had publicised the election and enabled voters and non-voters alike to quiz the candidates.[46] However, this rarely
went beyond the level of booing and hissing. As many supporters of
the measure—and even Disraeli—recognised, it was inconsistent to re-
tain public nomination alongside the introduction of the secret ballot.[47]
The same argument led logically to other features of the Act, not least
the ending of hourly announcements of the state of the poll, which had
historically done so much to maintain election excitement. This was consistent with the desire to ensure the voter's privacy and protect him from
outside interference of any kind.[48] In a similar way, the Act forbade the
use of rooms in public houses for electoral purposes, where voters had
frequently been 'cooped' for hours before the poll, during which time a
heady mixture of ale and entertainment might cloud his judgement.[49]

The decline in the old electoral culture was not initiated by the Ballot
Act of 1872. It had been under way since the middle of the century. For
example, even as early as the 1830s there had been reports that some of
the old ceremonies were being abandoned. The chairing was dispensed
with in Liverpool in 1831 and in Dover in 1852. In the constituencies
newly enfranchised in 1868 chairings were to be rare. The victorious
candidates were simply carried on the shoulders of their supporters
(O'Gorman, 1992). As the decline of the old rituals accelerated in the second half of the century, the traditional pattern of electoral campaigning
was being slowly replaced with a formal, municipal and party-controlled
pattern with its own narratives, symbols and rituals. Both parties saw the
need to establish new national organisations which would be rooted in
the constituencies but centrally directed. In an age of mass electorates,
especially after the Reform Act of 1867, the results of elections could not

---

46 See the debates of 4, 6 and 7 July 1871, Hansard, 3rd series, CCVII, 1101; 1262–3;
1307.
47 See the debates of 7 and 13 July 1871, Hansard, 3rd series, CCVII, 1306; 1671.
48 See the debate of 11 July 1871, Hansard, 3rd series, CCVII, 1424.
49 See the debates on 29 June and 24 July 1871, Hansard, 3rd series, CCVII, 753; CCVIII,
675–7.

be left to the independent vagaries of electoral patrons and the old casual management of elections through ritual deployment.

The Ballot Act, then, was only one contributory element in a long-term decline of the traditional electoral culture. This process may be attributable to certain underlying developments. First, the functions the old electoral rituals had fulfilled could now be carried out by other agencies, by pressure groups and, most important, by political parties. At the end of the nineteenth century crowds could be deployed and controlled, entertainment provided and a sense of excitement generated by the political parties. Second, Victorians were beginning to lose patience with the tumultuous violence associated with electoral campaigning. These elements of greater sensitivity relate back to the stiffening of social respectability, which included questioning of drunkenness and violence and a growing aversion to brutal animal sports, such as bull baiting (Garrard, 2002: 273). Third, the spread of education through Sunday Schools, Ragged Schools, Mechanics Institutes and after 1870 a national system of primary education, and—not to be forgotten—the availability of news and newspapers, all made for a much better educated electorate.[50] Fourth, the rise of local civic cultures, the emergence of a new ritual year centred on the town hall and the mayor's parlour, overwhelmed the relevance of the old electoral activities and thus civilised the old electoral passions (Garrard, 2002: 273–4).

Indeed it is impossible to take the Ballot Act out of context in any attempt to assess its significance. Other legislative enactments were just as relevant. Arguably of greater significance than the Ballot Act of 1872 in the decline of traditional electoral culture was the Corrupt Practices Act of 1883. As O'Leary says of the Act, it was 'by far the most stringent ever passed in Britain against electoral malpractices' (O'Leary, 1962: 175). The Liberal government had been shamed by the reports of further and continued malpractice in the General Election of 1880. Although there was no vociferous public demand for such an act, the party leaders realised that something more needed to be done even after the Ballot Act. The Act of 1883 laid down stringent standards of electoral behaviour and severe penalties for their infringement. For example, parliamentary candidates involved in electoral malpractice were liable to lose their seats and face one to five years' imprisonment. Electoral expenditure in each constituency was to pass through a single agent and accounts were to be paid within four weeks. No candidate could spend more than £100 on personal expenses and very low maxima were set for the employment of agents and canvassers. Such issues would be decided by an independent returning officer. Unlike earlier legislation, the Act of 1883 was stringently applied. Consequently, the General Election of 1885 was the pur-

---

50 See the discussion in Tholfsen (1961: 227–33).

est on record (Hanham, 1972: 281). Electoral corruption steadily and significantly declined thereafter. The number of election petitions trickled into single figures and very few MPs were subsequently unseated. Even this was not the end for the old electoral culture. As we have seen, the reform legislation of 1883–5, which added 2.5 million voters, bringing the total to 5.6 million, was vital in the final decline of electoral influence and the expiry of the old electoral culture. This remodelling of the electoral system, together with the swamping of the old structures with uncontrollable numbers of new voters, was the final straw. Even if the Ballot Act had not been passed, it is hard to see how electoral influence and the old electoral rituals could have survived the legislation of 1883–5. At the General Election of 1885 the Liberals at once began making inroads into counties traditionally Conservative.[51] Although Blewett (1965: 27–8) has remarked that much of the old electoral culture survived even after 1885, in truth most of it was already gone. Some remnants of it continued to survive in some fifteen to twenty seats in market and cathedral cities where family influences remained strong and payments to some voters were still made (Hanham, 1972: 282–3), but these were now widely recognised as anachronistic and atypical. The old electoral world had passed. In its demise the Ballot Act occupied an essential political and symbolic place. But the displacement of one electoral culture by another is always a complex and subtle process which can never be attributed to a single cause or a single act.

Blewett, Neal, 1965, 'The Franchise in the United Kingdom, 1885–1918', *Past and Present*, no. 32, pp. 27–56.

Brock, Michael, 1973, *The Great Reform Act*, London: Hutchinson and Co.

Cannon, John A., 1972, *Parliamentary Reform, 1660–1832*, Cambridge University Press.

Dennis, Barbara and David Skilton (eds), 1987, *Reform and Intellectual Debate in Victorian England*, London: Routledge.

Garrard, John, 2002, *Democratisation in Britain: Elites, Civil Society and Reform since 1800*, Basingstoke: Palgrave.

Hanham, Harold J., 1959, *Elections and Party Management: Politics in the Time of Disraeli and Gladstone*, London: Longmans Green.

——, 1969, *The Nineteenth Century Constitution*, Cambridge University Press.

——, 1972, *Electoral Facts from 1832–1853: Impartially Stated, Constituting a Complete Political Gazeteer. Edited with an Introduction and Bibliographical Guide to Electoral Sources, 1832–1885*, Brighton, Harvester Press.

---

[51] Although Pugh (1982: 69–70) argues that the Liberal victories would not have been so impressive without the Ballot Act.

Hoppen, Theodore, 1984, *Elections and Society in Ireland, 1832–1885*, Oxford: Clarendon Press.

——, 1989, *Ireland Since 1800: Conflict and Conformity*, London: Longmans Green.

Hurst, Michael, 1965, 'Ireland and the Ballot Act of 1872', *Historical Journal*, no. 8, pp. 326–52.

Jaggard, Edwin, 1999, *Cornwall Politics in the Age of Reform*, London: Royal Historical Society.

Kinzer, Bruce L., 1982, *The Ballot Question in Nineteenth Century English Politics*, New York: Garland.

Martin, J.B., 1874, 'The Elections of 1868 and 1874', *Journal of the Statistical Society of London*, June, pp. 193–230.

Moore, David C., 1976, *The Politics of Deference: A Study of the Mid-Nineteenth Century Political System*, Hassocks: Harvester Press.

Nossiter, Thomas J., 1975, *Influence, Opinion and Political Idioms in Reformed England, 1832–1874*, Brighton: Harvester Press.

O'Gorman, Frank, 1989, *Voters, Patrons and Parties: The Unreformed Electoral System of Hanoverian England, 1734–1832*, Oxford University Press.

——, 1992, 'Campaign Rituals and Ceremonies: the Social Meaning of Elections in England, 1780–1860', *Past and Present*, no. 135, pp. 79–115.

O'Leary, Cornelius, 1962, *The Elimination of Corrupt Practices at British Elections, 1868–1911*, Oxford: Clarendon Press.

Olney, R.J., 1973, *Lincolnshire Politics, 1832–1885*, Oxford University Press.

Ostrogorski, Moisej, 1982 [1902], *Democracy and the Organization of Politics*, New Brunswick, NJ: Transaction.

Park, Joseph H., 1931, 'England's Controversy over the Secret Ballot', *Political Science Quarterly*, no. 1.

Pugh, Martin, 1982, *The Making of Modern British Politics*, Oxford: Malden.

Seymour, Charles, 1915, *Electoral Reform in England and Wales*, New Haven, CT: Yale University Press.

Tholfsen, Trygve, 1961, 'The Transition to Democracy in Victorian England', *International Review of Social History*, no. 6, pp. 225–48.

Vernon, James, 1993, *Politics and the People*, Cambridge University Press.

USES AND ABUSES OF THE SECRET BALLOT IN THE AMERICAN AGE OF REFORM[1]

John Crowley

I

Modern democracies—viewed as systems for the distribution of authority, power and influence and for the embodiment of an abstract entity called the 'people'—have a protean character. Of their many faces, two form a particularly stark contrast. On the one hand democracy, at a normative level, is predicated upon some understanding of the general will or the general interest, of which, precisely, the abstract 'people' is the subject. Many very tangible aspects of democratic rule, including in particular the fundamental principle of legal sovereignty, would be either incomprehensible or profoundly misleading in the absence of such a presumption. This normative perspective is not always taken very seriously. Indeed it is so sharply at variance with a whole range of easily observable facts that it is often dismissed as, at best, a myth—or perhaps a rather sick joke. But myths sometimes matter—when they are believed in or when institutions have been designed with reference to them. In fact the institutions tend to matter more than the beliefs, because they are at least partly autonomous. They have a degree of social 'thickness' that enables them to rely on habit, tacit coercion or systematic incentives, even where self-conscious belief is lacking. Among the interesting institutions that bring into play some idea of the general will or interest is the secret ballot.

Now 'bring into play' is a very vague phrase—and designedly so. A whole family of political techniques goes under the name 'secret ballot'. The US case considered here will offer some idea of the sheer range of possible implementations of one apparently simple idea: that citizens should cast their vote with reference only to their own judgement. Some of the observable variation, which the US case by no means exhausts, is itself technical in origin. To say that the voter should, at the moment of

---

1 This chapter is an extensively revised version of a paper first published in French as 'Le vote secret contre la démocratie américaine (1880–1910)', *Politix*, 22 (1993), 69–83.

voting, be 'isolated' or 'insulated'—the two words are etymologically identical; indeed, in French, both senses are covered by *isoler*, whence comes *isoloir* for polling booth—from external influence is not to say exactly how this is to be achieved. No doubt some kind of booth is required, and either some kind of envelope in which the ballot paper is placed before re-emergence into the public gaze or some kind of machine to transmit the vote cast confidentially.[2] But other issues are raised by secrecy, and the technicalities of voting are not fully determined by being defined as 'secret'. Thus polling booths, in order to perform their functions, must be located in polling stations, which are special, politically neutral places where it is forbidden either to observe the political behaviour of others or to flaunt one's own. Similarly there are many different ways of voting secretly, and in particular many different ways of inscribing the voter's choice among available options (assuming that there actually are several of these). It is not exactly the same thing to choose an individual, several people, a party candidate, a party list, a policy option or whatever. Each of these possibilities—all of which are exemplified in mature democracies—makes distinctive demands on the information, political capacity and social capital of the voter. The US case discussed below will illustrate very clearly how the secret ballot, far from being a self-sufficient technique, takes its place in a densely patterned configuration of political technology.

Technical considerations, therefore, suffice to establish that the secret ballot has an indeterminate political meaning until the pattern of institutions and practices to which it belongs has been adequately described. However, the point is reinforced and enhanced by analysis of the complex, and in many ways ambivalent, normative issues underlying the secret ballot. As Alain Garrigou (1992, 1993) has stressed, the 'secrecy' of voting is a piece of democratic common sense that is not just taken for granted (as common sense is by its very nature) but fossilised. Being simply an aspect of democracy as it is, it seems to escape both criticism and justification. Yet the secret ballot was for much of the nineteenth century deeply controversial, in the United States as we shall see, but equally in Britain[3] and in France. The reason was partly that it had a significant role in a major technological shift; but that shift itself reflected,

---

2 Pending the development of reliable and socially acceptable computer-based technology, which might in principle make the whole notion of a polling booth in a polling station obsolete. As we shall see, however, there are significant flaws in the idea that technology might operate in this way (quite different from American-style voting machines, which are located in polling stations), especially if the *normative* basis of the secret ballot is taken into account. A portable, online 'polling station' might well guarantee one aspect of secrecy—that it should be impossible to ascertain the vote of any particular citizen. It fails to deal, on the other hand, with the second aspect of secrecy: that the social context of the vote should, at least for an instant, be hidden from the voter.

3 See O'Gorman's chapter in this volume.

and also reinforced and to some extent caused, a profound normative change—in effect, a whole new common sense regarding what, for modern purposes, the ancient word 'democracy' was to mean.

It is a familiar observation that from the middle of the nineteenth century an ideological crisis gradually engulfed the Enlightenment reinterpretation of politics in terms of public virtue—and thus of democracy as a horizon of education and progress.[4] What gradually emerged in its place, and was entrenched as a set of principles in the aftermath of the Second World War, dispensed with public virtue and replaced it by a certain view of regulated social conflict.[5] At the heart of the crisis lay the very basis of democratic citizenship and, as the US example shows very clearly, the secret ballot was of central significance in this respect. Strikingly, however, the secret ballot encapsulates *neither* fundamental model of democracy. Rather its meaning is at stake in both. As we shall see, it was crucial to the history of the secret ballot during the American Age of Reform that it should be promoted by an *ad hoc* coalition comprising very diverse ideological agendas. While a full theoretical discussion of the underlying issues would be quite out of place in this chapter, a brief sketch will clarify the deep-seated ambivalence that made it possible for the secret ballot to be used and abused in such a variety of manners.

A basic principle of democracy is that for certain purposes, including many of vital importance, decisions should be based on the expressed will of the majority (in most cases of the electorate or of an assembly). An equally basic question is why the majority—the mere 'more-than-ness'—should matter: not simply in the crudely practical sense that a law, say, rejected by more people than accept it is unlikely to be enforceable (though this is both true and important), but also in distinctively *moral* terms that make civil obedience a matter of *prima facie* obligation. No sophisticated democrat has argued that the numerical majority is always right.[6] The point is rather that, subject to certain procedural constraints, the balance of power will tend to reflect the balance of judgement. And the relevant constraints are those that prevent vested interests from simply combining to enforce their will and, more positively, encourage or even force citizens to act politically at one remove from their immediate (or apparent) interests. As Habermas and others have stressed, the liberal bourgeois age formulated these constraints in two distinct and indeed opposite ways. On the one hand the basis of political judgement was *individual*: it was by detachment from affiliation, clientage and depend-

---

4 One of the best-known developments along these lines is Habermas (1990).

5 I have expanded on this theme in Crowley (1999a, 1999b).

6 Not even Rousseau, whose well known claim that the people cannot harm itself (*Contrat social*, II, chapter 12, section 2) has much more complex implications than crude majoritarianism. In particular, the people is strictly speaking not a majoritarian concept at all; and indeed the whole cast of Rousseau's thought is in fact unanimist.

ency that a social being could become a citizen.[7] Hence the liberal preoc-
cupation with the independence of elected representatives; the suspicion
of 'factions', and later of parties; the exclusion from active citizenship
of those whose socio-economic status made them subservient, *ex offi-
cio*, to their masters, landlords, employers, fathers or husbands. On the
other hand the basis of political judgement was *collective*: it lay in the
participation of the citizen in the movement of informed public opinion. Especially in English, 'opinion' long remained a loose synonym of
'reputation'. It was exposure to the gaze, wit and reason of others—and
to their possible sarcasm and ridicule—that was formative of genuine
citizenship.

The bourgeois public sphere was capable, at least at an ideal level, of
reconciling these apparently contradictory requirements. It offered, in
effect, a socially neutral arena of political engagement where dependence on public reciprocity was premised upon private independence. In
such an arena it would be a matter of complete indifference whether
the ballot was secret or not. However, one of the implications of the
'structural transformation of the public sphere', in Habermas's phrase,
is that such a socially neutral arena ceases to exist. Affiliation, clientage
and dependency—possibly unconscious, in the form of ideology—are
part and parcel of politics. If they are to be neutralised at all, it must be
within the structures and procedures of politics, not by virtue of some
background social condition. But then the secret ballot appears to be the
site of an irresolvable tension. Private dependence removes the basis for
public independence (i.e. the secret ballot guarantees crude majoritarianism), but public dependence simply entrenches private dependence (i.e.
the public ballot guarantees crude class rule). Yet in a specific phase of
American history practical considerations cut through the theoretical in-
determinacy of the secret ballot. That story is the subject of this chapter.

II

It is not an easy task to locate the distinctive position of the secret ballot
within US debates on democratic institutions. A long-standing peculiar-
ity of US federalism has been to reject in principle the Federal definition
of voting rules. In practice the system remained profoundly fragmented
until the 1960s and was indeed unified at that time only with respect
to certain features, specifically those relating to blatant forms of racial
discrimination. Although the question has periodically been raised in
recent decades, no systematic attempt has been made to address it, as
the world—and doubtless many sections of the American public—found

7 Conversely the historical development of liberal thought was connected in a range of
complex ways with the struggle of an emerging intellectual class against, but at once inescapably within, clientage (Dunn, 1985).

out with *Schadenfreude* or horror during the Presidential election of 2000. One does not need to be an utter cynic to believe that no technical apparatus of voting is immune to abuse, manipulation and downright fabrication. Nonetheless, the discovery of the antiquated and distinctive apparatus used in Florida[8]—dating indeed from precisely the period discussed in this chapter—was something of an eye-opener. And even more striking was the revelation that voting in Florida was not simply different but internally diverse. Furthermore, while the diversity had something to do with historical patterns of racial discrimination, it owed more, in 2000, to a range of random factors than it did to any deliberate design.

Quite apart from any theoretical considerations, the diversity of US voting rules creates some awkward practical difficulties and effectively almost defies exhaustive analysis. Such an analysis, if it were to be attempted at all, would require consideration of multitudinous local debates and issues, often unconnected to each other and extending over more than three centuries since the early colonial period. Furthermore the secret ballot has never been a major strand of political debate around which opposing ideological camps have coalesced. To find any trace at all of a secret ballot debate, it is necessary to excavate at the margins of a series of cleavages structured around a very diverse range of topics. For that reason alone this chapter makes no attempt to offer a comprehensive archaeology of the secret ballot in the United States and covers only a brief period, overlapping roughly with what is canonically called the 'Age of Reform',[9] during which a multifaceted national debate crystallised on the fundamental features of American democracy. At this juncture, which involved proponents both of what might broadly be called 'aristocratic' principles and of enhanced democracy, the secret ballot played a subsidiary but significant role. Moreover this is not merely of historical interest. The secret ballot, for the reasons discussed earlier, might appear—not least because we are so familiar with it—to be a self-evident requirement of democracy, about which only opponents of democracy itself might express scepticism. The way in which the American opponents of democracy latched on to the secret ballot for their own purposes, in a specific historical context, shows that things are much more complicated. John Stuart Mill was an important influence on American voting reform, and quite apart from cynical and circumstantial considerations, clear traces are perceptible in US debates of his own concerns about the compatibility of universal suffrage with democracy in the true sense of the word (*Considerations on Representative Government*, chapter 10). The role played by the technical details of the material organisation of suffrage in the shifting ideological configuration sketched here also has

---

8 See Lacorne's chapter in this volume.
9 The classic study is Hofstadter (1955).

a deeper theoretical significance. Democracy is undoubtedly an idea, but it is not something that exists simply in the minds of democrats—or, polemically, of their enemies—nor does it develop simply under the pressure of conceptual tensions. Democracy is equally a form of political institutionalisation, with its practices, habits, techniques and material structures. They shape the ideas that in turn assess, justify and challenge them. No account of what it means to be a citizen is complete without detailed consideration of what citizens actually do.

The late-nineteenth-century debates studied in this chapter incorporated the institutional and ideological legacy of the colonial period. The colonies were characterised by considerable institutional diversity, of which voting rules were merely one aspect.[10] Indeed their very structure was profoundly uneven and in many cases ostensibly non-political: Massachusetts was legally a religious community (Merriam, 1926), for instance, and Virginia a commercial company (Chute, 1970). British rule never sought to impose uniformity in this respect: indeed division was convenient in many ways. One of the many consequences of this situation was to introduce the constitutive tension between aristocratic and democratic 'parties' that Tocqueville was later to place at the heart of his analysis.

The colonial legacy was taken over into the foundation of the Republic. The 1776 Bill of Rights, for instance, mentions suffrage only in stipulating that 'the right of suffrage in the election for members of both houses shall remain as exercised at present.' In so far as it at least countenances Federal intervention in such matters,[11] the Constitution of 1787 may seem to mark a change of direction or emphasis. However, the authorised commentaries of Madison, Hamilton and Jay—written during the ratification campaign in the State of New York—point to a measured assessment, at least as regards the intentions prevalent at the time. Congressional intervention in matters of suffrage, according to the *Federalist Papers*, would be a serious violation of the Federal principle and would be acceptable only in exceptional circumstances, and only with respect to Federal elections.[12] Indeed subsequent reforms were the work of constitutional amendments rather than Federal legislation: the prohibition on restrictions of voting rights on grounds of race (Fifteenth Amendment, 1870) or sex (Nineteenth Amendment, 1920) and the lowering of the minimum voting age to eighteen (Twenty-sixth Amendment,

---

10   For examples of debates from the colonial period explicitly relating to the secret ballot, see, for instance, Seymour and Frairy (1918: 218–23) and Chute (1970: 21–3).
11   'The times, places, and manner of holding elections for senators and representatives, shall be prescribed in each state by the legislature thereof: but the congress may at any time by law make or alter such regulations, except as to the places of choosing senators' (Constitution, article 1(4)(i)).
12   See in particular *Federalist Papers*, 52 (8 February 1788) and 59 (22 February 1788).

1971). Congress has admittedly been more concerned with campaigns, and particularly with finance, than with the moment of voting itself, but there is to this day no national 'electoral code' as in countries like France that have a tradition of legal codification, nor is there any equivalent of the uniform British Representation of the People Act, operating within the common-law tradition. This does not mean that the secret ballot was never a political issue,[13] but the institutional requirements for a truly national debate never obtained.

The moment of foundation also entrenched the constitutive ideological ambivalence of the American polity. The Constitution derived from a compromise between the quite different views of Madison, Hamilton, Adams, Jefferson and others, driven in part by the divergent interests within the Confederation, and while Jefferson's presidency (1801–8) led, in practice, to the ascendancy of a predominantly 'democratic' interpretation, the 'aristocratic' alternative was never eradicated. In line with the prevailing historiographical shorthand, we may regard the re-election of Andrew Jackson in 1829 as the culmination of a distinctively democratic phase of American political history. Jacksonian democracy was certainly a social form as much as an ideology, and Tocqueville, in *De la démocratie en Amérique* (vol. 1, pt II, chapter 2), was prescient in pointing to its basis in social egalitarianism. Each of the factors Tocqueville stressed was to prove crucial in the shifts and realignments of the latter half of the nineteenth century: the predominantly rural nature of American society, the vast and for these purposes empty territories of the West, inheritance laws unconducive to the entrenchment of property in land, the influence of Protestantism etc. In the favourable ideological climate of the period, the principle of universal male suffrage (for 'Whites') was entrenched, along with the principle of election to a wide range of judicial and other offices. What the two principles have in common is a refusal to regard the holding of public office as something requiring specific competence beyond the capacity of the average citizen (Williamson, 1960; Merriam, 1926: 143–7). In practical terms, politics was about sharp but unideological party competition and pervasive fraud (Seymour and Frairy, 1918: 247–9). However, precisely because it was unrelated to ideology, fraud was widely tolerated.[14] Those excluded from the Jacksonian consensus—Southern Blacks and to a lesser extent the emerging industrial

---

13 For an example from the late eighteenth century, see Pole (1950: 275–84).
14 Following Tocqueville, we should, however, beware of generalising about a vast and in many respects fragmented country. Jacksonian democracy was never hegemonic, and the secret ballot indeed played a role in challenges to it in the first third of the nineteenth century. In an interesting reversal of the North Atlantic circulation of ideas discussed later in this chapter, American experience, particularly from New York, was extensively referred to in the early phases of British debate about the secret ballot (about this debate, see Jaffrelot [1993]).

proletariat—were written out too effectively to be able, at this stage, to disturb the balance. Of more significance for present purposes was what Tocqueville himself called the 'aristocratic party'. As the heir to the Federalist movement of the Constitutional moment, it was opposed, on fundamental ideological grounds, to the very principle of equality as enshrined in Jacksonian democracy. The social context made aristocracy subservient to the 'tyranny of the majority', but could not by its very nature remove the cleavage for which it spoke. As Tocqueville put it (*De la démocratie en Amérique*, vol. 1, pt II, chapter 2):

> Beneath this habitual enthusiasm and in the midst of this obsequious submission to the dominant power, the contempt of the rich for the democratic institutions of their country is unmistakable. The people are a power they fear and despise. If, one day, democratic misrule were to bring a political crisis, if ever monarchy were to seem practicable in the United States, the truth of my analysis would become very clear.

As it happens monarchy never did seem practicable. Tocqueville's prophecy of anti-democratic reaction, on the other hand, was strikingly accurate. The social basis of Jacksonian democracy was undermined by four fundamental shifts, all of which were either consummated or clearly perceptible by the end of the third quarter of the nineteenth century: the Civil War and emancipation; urbanisation and industrialisation; growing immigration; and finally the closing of the frontier, which had been predictable since the 1848 gold rush and was officially declared in 1890. Taken together they fundamentally transformed both the social and the ideological structures of the United States. In terms of explicit political thought, the first was the starkest, the earliest and the most influential—although, as we shall see, one should not underestimate the extent to which consideration of it was filtered through perceptions shaped in less explicit ways by the others. Emancipation exploded the Constitutional fiction of the natural freedom and equality of 'all' human beings. With the end of slavery it was no longer possible to skirt around awkwardly crucial questions about the meaning of freedom, equality and the American political community (Pole, 1978). In addition emancipation was the result of war and reflected a complex balance of power: for the 'Whites' of the Confederacy it threw up the challenge of maintaining privileges for which the ultimate legal basis had been removed. And, at the very same time, the ideologies of the industrial age were imported and Americanised: capitalism (particularly in its vulgarised Darwinian-Spencerian interpretation), socialism and 'scientific' racism.

This complex set of sociological and ideological shifts undermined and eventually destroyed the social basis and the political common sense of Jacksonian democracy. Whether democracy, as a result, was to be purified, extended, restricted or suppressed was very much an open question. What is important for present purposes—although not entirely surprising, in theoretical and comparative terms—is that the secret ballot had a significant place in the ensuing debates. An adequate account of the transformation of American democracy must tie together social dynamics, political technology and the history of ideas.

III

Jacksonian democracy was, in its way, highly corrupt. Whether the American polity became *more* corrupt as it became more industrialised and urbanised, and socially and racially polarised in new ways, is a moot point. What matters is that corruption came to acquire a new meaning and was transformed into a polemical resource for new purposes. The urban party machine, in particular, with its close connections to immigrant community networks and political patronage, flaunted vote-buying, manipulative campaigning, physical intimidation and other familiar techniques of political mobilisation, and the very power of its social base made it difficult to dismiss as an aberration or temporary anomaly. For many observers the new urban politics discredited democracy itself; but even those who continued to subscribe to the democratic ideal in principle were led to the conclusion that democracy could survive, and be justified, only by being *purified*.

It is by no means self-evident that the secret ballot is a technique conducive to a 'purer' form of democracy. Indeed, as Habermas has stressed, early bourgeois liberalism took it for granted that 'publicity' was the only secure basis of political virtue. The scope of the idea of publicity was undoubtedly much broader than voting technology; nonetheless, it was generally believed that to be seen to vote, and to be accountable for one's choice, were necessary components of citizenship. Conversely, as John Stuart Mill put it very explicitly, secrecy has something to do with selfishness.

The spirit of vote by ballot—the interpretation likely to be put on it in the mind of an elector—is that the suffrage is given to him for himself; for his particular use and benefit, and not as a trust for the public. ... Instead of opening his heart to an exalted patriotism and the obligation of public duty, it awakens and nourishes in him the disposition to use a public function for his own interest, pleasure, or caprice; the same feelings and purposes, on a humbler scale, which actuate a despot and oppressor.[15]

The key word here is trust. To be a citizen, as discussed in theoretical terms in section I, is not to be the beneficial owner of some portion of the common wealth (or public good); it is, on the contrary, to act politically without regard to personal benefit or inconvenience. A popularised ver-

---

15 J.S. Mill, *Consideration on Representative Government*, chapter 10.

sion of Mill's liberalism was widely familiar in the United States in the latter part of the nineteenth century, and the language of trusteeship—often without reference to its source—was a commonplace of early objections to the secret ballot in the name of democratic purification. Indeed the spirit of the argument was far more widespread than the language itself. As the Virginian politician John Randolph put it pungently in 1847: 'I scarcely believe that we have such a fool in all Virginia as even to mention the vote by ballot, and I do not hesitate to say that the adoption of the ballot would make any nation a nation of scoundrels, if it did not find them so' (quoted in Seymour and Frairy, 1918: 247). What is remarkable for present purposes is that within a few decades common sense should have been turned on its head. By the turn of the twentieth century it was taken for granted that, on the contrary, *only* the secret ballot could make a racialised urban industrial society safe for democracy. By then common sense was on the side of Senator John Bidwell, speaking in 1891: 'The Australian ballot system is to me the most important .... I believe that if the people can ... exercise the intelligence ... the intelligence itself will grow .... Under the Australian ballot a Man is obliged to exercise his intelligence. ... He goes into a room by himself, and he exercises his own good judgment in regard to the Man he wants to vote for' (quoted in Fredman, 1969: 67–8).

As discussed in section I, there is arguably no such thing as 'the' secret ballot. Depending on how the issue of secrecy interacts with other concerns, there are many different ways of making voting secret. For practical purposes US debates of the period covered here, starting in the 1870s, took it for granted that the secret ballot was to be implemented under the so-called Australian system referred to by Bidwell, the main additional feature of which was to provide the voter not merely with a booth but also with a single uniform ballot paper, printed at public expense, covering all posts up for election and all candidates.[16] Indeed some strands of the debate put more emphasis on the uniform ballot, which was regarded as equalising access by reducing the cost of campaigning, as precluding fraud, and by facilitating split-ticket voting, as breaking the machine stranglehold on local politics. Part of the astonishingly protean nature of the 'Australian' ballot derives precisely from its technical duality.

Why, then, might the secret ballot come to be seen as an instrument of enlightened citizenship? Mill himself was ambivalent. Despite his strong objections at the theoretical and symbolic level, he was prepared to recognise pragmatic grounds for secrecy, in a social context where the ability of the powerful to put pressure on their fellow citizens would otherwise be unchecked. Especially in the early phases of US debate there are

---

16 Subject to write-in provisions, which were the creation of a slightly later period.

numerous indications of such a view of the secret ballot, combined with (indirect) regulation of campaign finance, as the lesser of two evils.

Since the ballot is the only means by which, in our republic, the redress of political and social grievances is to be sought, we especially and emphatically declare for the adoption of what is known as the Australian system of voting, in order that the effectual secrecy of the ballot, and the relief of candidates for public office from the heavy burdens now imposed upon them, may prevent bribery and intimidation, do away with practical discriminations in favour of the rich and unscrupulous, and lessen the pernicious influence of money in politics.[17]

It is possible to take a step beyond pragmatic accommodation. Assume, with all the theorists of bourgeois liberalism, that democracy is viable only so long as the citizenry is virtuous. Assume further—also fairly consensually—that there is some connection between virtue and competence, in other words that it is possible to learn to be a citizen. It follows logically that while universal suffrage lies inescapably on the horizon of democracy, the purification, and thereby the preservation, of democracy necessarily require, at least as an interim measure, some form of restricted suffrage. This view was widely aired in the period covered here and was advanced in terms both of robust common sense and of mainstream political theory.

The [theory] that suffrage ought to be universal on the assumption that it is a natural right has been very generally condemned by publicists as erroneous in principle and dangerous in practice. ... Since it was they who put us on the downward slope to perdition, the State governments [should] now put on the brakes, by restricting the privileges of the ballot to persons qualified by intelligence to use without abusing it ... (Scruggs, 1884: 492, 500)

Having gone this far, to take a further step is easy. Certainly citizenship must be learned, one might say, but that does *not* mean that all are capable of learning to be citizens. Equality of fundamental moral capacity is an additional assumption that requires independent justification; and basic common sense suggests that no such justification is in fact available. It is at this point that the purification of democracy shades into its replacement by something else: something that is best called, following Tocqueville, *aristocracy*. For understandable historical reasons, the word itself is rare in American debates of the period, but the sentiment is transparently expressed.

There seems to be no doubt but the government of the best men [quite literally, aristocracy] is really the best government; and, since this is so, that a democratic government, where the people are corrupt, is necessarily a bad government, because the vicious will not only not elect the best, who will not stoop to their level,

---

17 Presidential platform of the United Labor Party for the election of 1888, reprinted in Porter and Johnson (1966: 85).

but, by virtue of the law of affinity, will choose the baser sort of men. (Spalding, 1884: 203–4)

The steps that lead from the desire to purify democracy to the desire to dispense with it are made, as quoted here, without reference to the secret ballot. The following section will elucidate the circumstances that made it possible to connect such arguments with a defence of the secret ballot that a Millian liberal would scarcely recognise.

IV

To vote, as noted in section I, is not simply to form and to express a political opinion. It is, inseparably, to participate in a technological process. In the US case the details are complex, important and in some respects unusual. In the nineteenth century, as today, American voters were called to choose a large number of office-holders, from the President (every four years) through state and county officials to the proverbial dogcatcher. They must therefore select, very quickly, dozens of names. One obvious way of simplifying the problem would be to rely on the party affiliation of the minor candidates and to vote for a party 'ticket'. Whether that is possible, however, depends on the layout of the ballot and the rules for expressing one's preference. If, for instance, one votes by choosing a pre-printed ballot paper and marked papers are considered void (this is the case in France for many elections), it may be literally impossible to vote a 'split' ticket. Even if marked papers are not considered void, it may be difficult to 'mix and match' as the French call it (*panacher*) if the rules require each chosen candidate to be marked separately. Conversely, if party affiliations are absent from the ballot paper (as was required by law in Britain as late as the 1960s), it may be impossible to vote for a party ticket, except in the unusual case of a voter with reliable information on all levels of politics from the national to the local. Between these two extreme cases an infinite range of variants is imaginable, with all kinds of effects on the possibility of ticket voting.[18]

In such a context, one of the most important practical issues is the illiterate vote, and in the late-nineteenth-century United States illiteracy was widespread, among both recent immigrants and former slaves. In the Jacksonian period, as Tocqueville emphasised, the social context was different, and in any case Jacksonian democracy had developed practical mechanisms to mobilise the illiterate. Ballot papers were printed by party machines and used symbols (such as the still familiar elephant and donkey) and colours to facilitate identification, and assistance was available outside, and often even inside, polling stations. Needless to say, opening the suffrage to the illiterate was an ambivalent process. It genuinely

---

18 For a contemporary discussion, see Allen (1910).

made it possible for people to participate who would otherwise have been unable to cope with the political technology, and thereby gave their interests, which were not those of the dominant groups within society, some chance of being taken into account. But, equally, it was created and maintained by party machines for their own purposes, namely to entrench political domination. The objective of the machine 'boss' was to lock in an ethnic or class vote that was premised on the kind of patronage and clientage that bourgeois liberalism was ideologically and socially committed to eliminating from the public sphere. And, of course, it worked very effectively, as Tammany Hall New York and, later, Daley Chicago famously illustrate. The idea that the conditions that make practical citizenship possible are inseparably those that negate the normative basis of citizenship is a familiar one from critical political sociology.[19] What is important for present purposes is the crucial significance of the mechanics of voting as a mediating factor.

What was at stake normatively is fairly obvious and can be summarised briefly. Far from reflecting enlightened consideration of the public good by each voter, or rational choice between competing programmes—or even, *à la* Schumpeter, between competing fractions of the governing élite—an electoral majority was a mechanical translation of the balance of power between party machines. Furthermore that balance of power had to do with the ability to distribute favours (such as public employment and housing) conditional upon party loyalty. The mobilisation of consent was thus inherently coercive, since it depended on reliable information about voters' actual behaviour (as distinct from their promises) and on the ability to exact punishment for disloyalty. No nineteenth-century defender of the democratic idea could view such a situation with equanimity. Nor, for somewhat different reasons, could any liberal aristocrat suspicious about the social and moral implications of the reign of the common man and about the democratic propensity to misrule. However, the differences between the commitments underlying these two critical stances came to seem less important than the common diagnoses. Tocqueville had perceptively analysed the uneasy balance of the Jacksonian period in terms of a passion for equality underwritten by a genuine basis of social equality. Once the balance had unravelled there were good practical and theoretical reasons for an American democrat (in the non-party sense) to be an élitist. And specifically, both the defenders and the opponents of 'true' democracy could applaud the idea of the Australian ballot, which would erode the coercive capacity of the party machines, effectively reduce the illiterate to a choice between abstention and random voting and thus, to all intents and purposes, introduce an

---

19 Notably in work inspired by Pierre Bourdieu. For a concise statement, see Bourdieu (2000).

educational qualification for voting that was judged intellectually requisite but politically impracticable.

One can of course also take a more cynical view. Broadly the balance of power between party machines was, in the postbellum period, a structurally unequal one. A Democrat who was also a democrat might be ambivalent, but for, say, a New York Republican or Socialist, things were fairly simple. 'Purification' of voting would be a good deal for *both* democracy and the party. Clear traces of such debates are in fact perceptible, but it was fairly easy to be an idealist in New York. Opportunistic partisan commitment to the Australian ballot was mainly a feature of the very peculiar politics of the postbellum South. Before we pass the Mason-Dixon line, however, it is important to note that none of this should be read in terms of some kind of tension between idealism and opportunism. The whole point, which is of general application and starkly illustrated in the American case, is that it is perfectly possible in practical politics to be a cynical idealist or an idealistic cynic. The only, easily met, condition is that what is normatively desirable should also be in one's personal interest or, equivalently, that one's opponents should have an objective interest in something judged to be bad. The main risk to which idealism is exposed is that it should decay into 'extreme views weakly held'.[20] Being interested in the implementation of one's ideas is a very useful 'commitment booster'.

The political peculiarities of the postbellum South are traceable not just to emancipation and to its direct social consequences, particularly for the poorer 'Whites', but also to the way in which the broader implications of the Civil War were addressed. Partly for ideological and partly for partisan reasons, the initial policy of the Union, under Republican leadership, was to punish the Confederacy. In the event, the policy proved harsh, inconsistent and short-lived. During the period of so-called 'Reconstruction'—a term that shows the scale of the ideological ambitions in Washington—the former Confederate States were initially expelled from the Union and placed under military government, then directly administered from Washington. The so-called 'carpet-bagger' administrators sought to use their guaranteed 'Black' constituency to organise an alternative political hegemony. This radical Republican project had begun to evaporate long before the Hayes-Tilden compromise of 1877, which formally closed the Reconstruction period, but its consequences were nonetheless far-reaching. Having alienated the South, Reconstruction virtually guaranteed that emancipation—its primary supposed *raison d'être*—would fail.[21] From the moment of its ratification,

---

20 Which is what the British historian A.J.P. Taylor reportedly claimed in response to being called an 'extremist' by a senior colleague. The anecdote, which may or may not be apocryphal, is given by Watkins (1982: 178).

21 For reasons that Tocqueville had very presciently anticipated, the North's position on

the cornerstone of mainstream Southern politics was the undoing of the Fifteenth Amendment, which had, in principle, entrenched the political rights of former slaves in 1870.

However peculiar, Southern politics was not disconnected from national politics. Specifically two ideological factors were of general significance. First, as we have seen, the questioning of democracy as ideal and practice was related to social transformations of which emancipation was only one aspect. Secondly, ideas of 'race' were themselves undergoing transformations as Darwinian evolutionism and Mendelian genetics became popularised.[22] Undoubtedly pre-scientific ideas remained powerful, especially in the South, and shaped the way in which the new 'racial science' was incorporated into ordinary social practices and into political language. As a result there were complex interactions—not just in the South—between considerations of supremacy, for which 'Whites' were in principle at least a uniform political category, and considerations of aristocracy, in terms of which the illiterate 'White trash' was as repugnant as the average former slave. From both viewpoints, given the practical impossibility of explicitly discriminatory legislation (whether on educational or 'racial' grounds), the Australian ballot was to become the indirect strategy of choice. Thus local issues of 'Negro' suffrage were intimately and technologically connected with general concerns about democracy.

In intellectual terms, the aristocratic current of ideas was dominant throughout the period. A superficially paradoxical reason was that outside the South the new 'scientific' racism was inimical to supremacy in the traditional sense. This was due to the shift, already alluded to, from a straightforwardly hierarchical conception of race—which makes all the more sense in that it is legally and culturally entrenched—to a more bio-

---

emancipation had in any case always been ambivalent and ultimately self-contradictory. As early as the 1820s the 'Negro' population in the non-slave states was in steady decline and the idea of an 'integrated' society (a phrase Tocqueville himself uses), without which emancipation was meaningless, was therefore largely devoid of any practical social basis (*De la démocratie en Amérique*, vol. I, pt 2, chapter 10).

22 This statement assumes a judgement in the long-running debate about the genealogy of 'race' and racism that cannot be justified within the compass of this article. Suffice it to say that it implies disagreement with those specialists who claim a high degree of continuity, traceable at least to the earliest phase of contact between Christian Europe and Africa and the Americas. The competing argument is that two major turning points can be identified, which cumulatively redefined both the ideological and social meaning of 'race' by the middle of the nineteenth century. First, the (mainly eighteenth-century) development of the colonial plantation economy and the corresponding shift towards an increasingly unilateral slave trade; and secondly, the development, in the early nineteenth century, of a 'science of life' (biology) that gradually superseded older taxonomic-religious approaches to 'race'. For overviews on the lines sketched here, see, for instance, Banton (1987) and Malik (1997).

logical form of racism in which miscegenation is the primary matrix.[23] What is important for present purposes is the relation between this ideological development and social and legal trends. Naturally the ostensibly egalitarian thrust of 'differentialism', to borrow Taguieff's term (1987), was rarely taken seriously, especially in the postbellum South. It was indeed affirmed in the 'separate but equal' doctrine propounded by the Supreme Court in the famous *Plessey v. Ferguson* case of 1896, the date of which, as we shall see, has considerable political significance. Nonetheless, while the fact of the affirmation is of great interest in terms of the history of ideas, it was transparent, long before the Supreme Court reversed its doctrine in 1954, that the equality referred to was devoid of any practical significance. But this does *not* mean the new doctrine was vacuous. On the contrary, to abandon the traditional hierarchical conception of 'race', in which the lowliest 'White' would stand above the loftiest 'Negro', was to open up new possibilities. Henceforth an imperfectly correlated additional dimension of intelligence, moral capacity and biological fitness was introduced. The groups into which it divided the population—say, the enlightened and the others—did not quite coincide with the 'races', since many 'Whites' would be lumped together with the vast majority of 'Negroes' on the wrong side of the line.

Conversely, a few 'Negroes' might, on grounds of personal capacity, possibly combined with appropriately mixed ancestry, be admitted, by a precarious and one-sided courtesy, to the favoured group. This is not to say, obviously, that the new racism blurred the colour line in the Jim Crow South. In practical terms the opposite was the case. What did happen, however, is that segregation, even more than slavery, failed to make sense at the ideological level. At the very moment when the 'one-drop' rule was being adopted as a coercive administrative technique for policing the new colour line, the explicit discourse used to justify the new settlement was subtly undermining the terms of its implementation. The essential role that murderous violence played in the segregationist South had to do, undoubtedly, with the highly unequal social patterns within the dominant group, but also, and to some extent correlatively, with the underlying ambivalence of the principle of group demarcation itself. 'Dead certainty', in Appadurai's evocative phrase, needed to be actively produced precisely because nothing in the background conditions pro-

---

23 To take just one representative quotation: 'Fusion is forbidden by natural laws, and white repugnance has a permanent and scientific basis. The human family is marked off by colour into three grand divisions—white, yellow and black. It is altogether probable that fusion between varieties of the same colour is beneficial, but that fusion across the colour line is lowering. The blending of different white bloods makes, in every way, a stronger race; but every instance of blending between white and black has proven adverse, creating, in the end, a half-breed race below the pure African ancestry.' (Gilliam, 1884). On similar lines, see, for instance, Gardiner *et al.* (1884) and Page (1892).

vided it.[24] Textual evidence for the combination of practical certainty and conceptual vacillation is extremely widespread. Space permits just one typical excerpt.

There never was any question more befogged with demagogism than that of manhood suffrage. Let us apply ourselves to the securing of some more reasonable and better basis for the suffrage. Let us establish such a proper qualification as a condition for the possession of the elective franchise as shall leave the ballot only to those who have intelligence enough to use it as an instrument to secure good government rather than to destroy it. In taking this step we have to plant ourselves on a broader principle than that of a race qualification. It is not merely the negro, it is ignorance and venality which we want to disfranchise. If we can disfranchise these we do not need to fear the voter, whatever the color. At present it is not the negro who is disfranchised, but the white. We dare not divide. (Page, 1892: 412)

From the 1880s aristocratic reformers came to realise that the Australian ballot, which they had traditionally opposed, could serve the purposes of the anti-democratic reaction. As a result the debate about the issue became increasingly complex. Left-wing parties and movements were still demanding the ballot in the name of democracy, and Southern supremacists were agitating for it for their own purposes. The aristocratic party being, structurally, in the minority, it could achieve its objectives only by establishing an *ad hoc*, and in many ways rather improbable, coalition. Having given a rough sketch of the background conditions that made such a coalition thinkable, by establishing connections between the diverse reasons for the ballot, it remains to be seen how the politics actually played out. However, even the indications offered here suffice to show that it would be far too simple to claim that the Australian ballot, which was introduced in thirty-eight states between 1888 and 1892 (Fredman, 1969), was an anti-democratic reform, despite the undoubted fact that its adoption restricted the scope of American democracy and was widely defended as such.

The national picture may have been complex, but things were much simpler in the South. There the Australian ballot was, for the most part, explicitly and straightforwardly racist:

The Australian ballot works like a charm / It makes them think and scratch /And when a Negro gets a ballot / He has certainly got his match.[25]

The compendium of techniques used, especially in the South, to turn the Australian ballot into a means of manipulating and restricting the suf-

---

24 See, among other developments on this theme, Appadurai and Holston (1996: 187–204). For more detailed development of the analysis sketched here, see Crowley (1999c and 2000). For a broader historical and cultural perspective on some of the implications, see King (1991 and 1992).

25 Democratic Party campaign song from 1892 Arkansas, quoted by Kousser (1974: 54).

frage—in the name, ostensibly, of 'pure democracy'—would be comical if it were not tragic (Bishop, 1891; Wilson, 1910; Allen, 1910; Kousser, 1974). In some cases candidates were placed on the ballot in alphabetical order with no indication of party affiliation. Each ballot, remember, comprised dozens of names. In one famous case the entire ballot was printed in medieval Gothic lettering. Some states imposed time limits for voting with a view to precluding mature reflection. The rules for ballot marking also left unlimited scope for creative manipulation. Several states hit on the astute principle that voters should strike out candidates they did not wish to see elected by drawing a line through three-quarters of the length of their names. Contemporary observers of 'chad pregnancy' will not miss the connection: anything as vague as 'three-quarters' effectively makes the validity of the ballot a matter for the discretion of the counter, who is called upon to guess what might have been the voter's intention. Whereas in many Northern states the polling booth was initially introduced as a facility for the voter, who could also choose to request help from the polling-station officials, Southern states typically either made it compulsory or introduced discriminatory restrictions on the option to request help. In many cases this took the form of the infamous 'grandfather' clause, later used to restrict the suffrage as such. The option to dispense with the booth was thus made available only to those who could have voted, or whose father or grandfather could have voted, before the Civil War. Furthermore, in the absence of any requirement that suffrage must be uniform, and given a political and ideological context in which the Federal government chose to turn a blind eye to Southern peculiarities, the ballot was often introduced only in certain districts within a state. In such cases the districts chosen correlated very neatly with the percentage of the 'Negro' population.

All this may seem remarkably crude, but it was certainly effective (Kleppner, 1987; Kousser, 1974). Immediately after the Civil War the 'Negro' electorate had been in a majority throughout the South—all the more so as many former Confederate soldiers and officials had been temporarily disenfranchised. By the first years of the twentieth century that electorate had virtually disappeared. Jim Crow ruled and the great migration north had started. In the Presidential election of 1896, by which time most Southern states had adopted the Australian ballot, the Republican and Populist parties collapsed throughout the former Confederacy and sixty years of Democratic hegemony began. Even the states that seem at first glance to be exceptions in fact support the analysis. In Georgia and South Carolina, where the Australian ballot was not adopted until much later, the poll tax served the same purpose. As for North Carolina, where the ballot was introduced in certain districts only in 1909, it had for historical reasons an unusually powerful Republican party which, uniquely, was able to compete with the Democrats even at their zenith.

The destruction of democracy by the implementation of the ostensibly democratic secret ballot was not the only paradox of the age. It fits with the others to form a complicated pattern that reveals the true character of the Age of Reform. It was equally the time of restrictions on capitalist enterprise (through anti-trust laws and the first forms of social insurance) and of the darkest forms of racialisation. Under the bipartisan aegis of Theodore Roosevelt and Woodrow Wilson the whole system of government was transformed with a view to restricting the politicisation of the civil service and enhancing direct democracy. It was also the golden age of American socialism. Yet the promotion of what both Roosevelt and Wilson called 'good government' effectively undermined the democratic ideal. This may appear to have been a coincidental consequence of federalism and Southern peculiarities. However, while the Age of Reform undoubtedly had a different character in New York and California, to say nothing of the Socialist strongholds of Wisconsin and Minnesota, there is nonetheless a sense in which the 'liquidation of political democracy in the name of good government' (Kleppner, 1987: 230) was at least implicitly present in the whole logic of the reform project. The evidence for this view is provided by the transformation of racial discourse at the turn of the century, by the growing critique of the idea of 'rights' and by the form of the debates about women's suffrage. It is, in particular, no coincidence that female suffrage was primarily defended in terms of the supposedly beneficial influence of women on a corrupt polity rather than as a consequence of any fundamental or natural equality of right.[26]

V

It is not possible, within the limited compass of this essay, to prove the claim that debates about the secret ballot and the practicalities of its implementation reveal one aspect of a fundamental transformation, between 1880 and 1910, in the basic common sense of American democracy. By way of support and illustration, some pointers are offered from the analysis of a convenient and fairly homogeneous textual source: national party presidential platforms.[27] The secret ballot itself is barely present in the platforms. There are only four explicit references, three of which are unambiguously democratic (the United Labor Party in 1888 and the Socialist Labor Party in 1892 and 1896); the fourth, while not formulated as a demand, is in the same spirit: 'Most of the states have been compelled to isolate the voters at the polling places to prevent universal intimidation and bribery' (Populist Party, 1892).[28] After 1896 the

---

26 For example, Pitman (1884) and Sutherland (1910).

27 Collated in Porter and Johnson (1966).

28 Porter and Johnson (1966: 89). The convention at which this platform was adopted also adopted a resolution, omitted from the platform, that made the same point in a more ex-

issue disappears entirely from the national political agenda, as reflected in these rather stylised documents. Even those parties that had a vested interest, in both ideological and partisan terms, in confronting the Democratic ascendancy henceforth ignored this key feature of its political technology. In itself this evidence is sketchy and inconclusive. However, when set within the broader pattern of suffrage debates the silence about the ballot begins to look very much like Sherlock Holmes' dog that did not bark. Before 1880 suffrage is absent from national party platforms, except for the Prohibition Party's constant demand, from its creation in 1872, for female suffrage. Furthermore, when the first echoes of the reaction against democracy finally appear in 1880 (the Republican Party and Greenback Party), they are still unambiguously hostile. In the words of the Greenback Party platform: 'We denounce as most dangerous the efforts everywhere manifested to restrict the right of suffrage' (Porter and Johnson, 1966: 160).

During the following two decades the Democratic Party is alone in its indifference to suffrage. Having implemented suffrage restriction very vigorously throughout the South, it mentions the issue only once in passing (in 1892 in the rather ambivalent words, 'popular education being the only safe basis of popular suffrage...' [Porter and Johnson, 1966: 89]). Of course such issues were among those that—as the liberal North and illiberal South drifted apart—the Democratic Party had to fudge for its very survival. Other references are numerous and, with one exception, uniformly hostile to the principle of suffrage restriction, however ostensibly or sincerely justified: Greenback Party (1880), United Labor Party (1888), Socialist Labor Party (1892 and 1896), People's Party (1896 and 1900), Republican Party (1888, 1892, 1896 and 1900). The single exception is, however, an interesting and important one. The Prohibition Party, more than any other political movement, spoke for the idea of democratic purification. The outlawing of alcohol, which was of course its main demand, was at once one practical step towards public virtue and a metaphor for the very idea of an unperverted public sphere. The parallel demand for women's suffrage—which, as noted earlier, goes back to the origins of the party—further reflected the nature of the kind of political purity that was at stake. The language was that of the public good, rather than of women's rights, and the party's position on suffrage restriction was ambivalent from an early stage. Thus in 1888 the presidential platform rejected suffrage restrictions that were not based on impartial educational requirements.

---

plicit way: 'We demand a free ballot and a fair count in all elections, and pledge ourselves to secure it to every legal voter without federal intervention, through the adoption by the states of the *unperverted* Australian or secret ballot system' (quoted in Pollock [1967: 64; emphasis added]). The single word 'unperverted' carries the whole weight of the contemporary debate.

After 1900 matters become much more complicated. No longer is there a straightforward divide between proponents and opponents of suffrage restriction, however convoluted their arguments. As late as 1908 the Socialist Party unequivocally demands universal suffrage (to demand it is of course to recognise that it does not exist), but the case is very unusual. Political rights disappear entirely from the platforms of the Socialist Labor Party in 1900, 1904 and 1908. The Populist Party, which fails to mention suffrage in 1904, demands in 1908 the extension of direct democracy (specifically initiation and ratification of laws by popular referendum and recall of elected officials) without referring to suffrage at all—at the very time when steps taken in the previous decade had finally excluded from suffrage the whole 'Negro' population of the South, to say nothing of large numbers of other potential voters. The Socialist Party eventually followed this lead: by 1912 and 1916 demands for direct democracy, which the Socialists had been instrumental in achieving in their California and Mid-West strongholds in the previous decade, cease to be related to any consideration of the background question of access to suffrage. The question 'direct democracy *for whom?*' simply drops off the agenda.

The Left's surprising promptness in embracing the reshaping of American democracy is present in heightened form in the Republican and Prohibitionist movements. When the Republicans, in 1904, demand the effective implementation of the Fourteenth Amendment, it hardly counts as a ringing endorsement of universal suffrage.[29] In 1908 their position clearly implies support for the general principle of suffrage restriction: 'We condemn all devices that have for their real aim [the Negro's] disfranchisement *on grounds of colour alone* ...' (Porter and Johnson, 1966: 160; emphasis added). After 1908 suffrage simply disappears from Republican Party platforms. The Prohibition Party is much more explicit in demanding in 1904 'the recognition of the fact that the right of suffrage should depend on the mental and moral qualifications of the citizen' (Porter and Johnson, 1966: 137). Thereafter, in Prohibitionist platforms as elsewhere, the demand for direct democracy takes centre stage, in a context where the suffrage question has been answered in a fundamentally anti-democratic way.

There seems therefore to be fairly clear evidence that a major ideological shift occurred between 1880 and 1910, by which time the principle that some kind of suffrage restriction based on considerations of

---

29   The Fourteenth Amendment (1868) was intended to modify the representation of the states in the Federal House of Representatives. In principle each state was to have a number of seats strictly proportionate to its population. However, the Amendment stated that those states that excluded from the suffrage certain adult males (in historical context, the reference was of course to former slaves) would lose seats in proportion to the proportion of adult males thus excluded.

democratic 'quality' was legitimate had been very widely accepted. The theoretical significance of this configuration lies in the light it sheds on the relation between the conceptual and social foundations of democracy. Equipped with a set of ideas in which democracy was inseparable from virtue, theorists and practitioners of the late nineteenth century were unable to make sense of universal suffrage in an emerging mass industrial society. Their adoption, in response to this new intellectual challenge, of an aristocratic perspective similar to the one their intellectual forebears had fought against a century earlier indicates that their *demos* had in fact always been implicitly imagined in aristocratic terms. The sophisticated ambivalence of Tocqueville and Mill resolved itself, in cruder thinkers faced with pressing practical requirements, into the unravelling of the very idea of liberalism. However, this is not to invalidate liberalism or to endorse the Reformist critique of democracy. No doubt the new common sense quickly became intellectually respectable. 'From the standpoint of political science the slaveholders were right in declaring that liberty can be given only to those who have political capacity enough to use it' (Merriam, 1926: 250). 'In spite of its services to direct representation and to parliamentary government the theory that every man has a natural right to vote no longer commands the support of students of political science' (Seymour and Frairy, 1918: 13). Nonetheless the anti-democratic reaction was viciously incoherent and ultimately transitory.

In terms of the history of political theories, the period of Jim Crow and Samuel Gompers and high-minded reformers deliberately dissolving messy, unpredictable democracy in neat and tidy 'good government'[30] looks like an anomaly. Not, of course, that technocrats have ceased to regard democracy as unacceptably messy and to develop theoretical arguments in support of their suspicions. Nonetheless the whole theoretical configuration changed with the intellectual invention of pluralism, which is a way to cope with scepticism about the political virtue of the common man by developing a model of democracy as regulated competition between organised interests. It is one indication of the incoherence of the dominant ideas of the Age of Reform that the theory of pluralism was, to a large extent, a distinctively American contribution to political science. In Schumpeter's famous theory of democratic competition the

---

30 See Kousser (1974) and Kleppner (1987). It is noteworthy in comparative terms that the European intellectual path to pluralism was very different. In response to the same theoretical challenge as sketched, what developed in Europe was the strongly institutional élitism of Michels and Weber. Distinctive forms of class conflict and dynamics of statehood, as well as Catholicism, do much to explain the transatlantic contrast, which is also reflected in the powerful corporatist tendencies at work in both the theory and practice of twentieth-century European democracy (and, one might add, non-democracy too). European pluralism is more closely related to the critique of corporatism than it is to the collapse of nineteenth-century liberalism.

defence of universal suffrage and party mobilisation is inseparable from the rejection of any form of direct or participatory democracy. Strikingly this is a theoretical mirror image of the Socialist and Populist positions of the early twentieth century that were summarised earlier. The essential reason, as contemporary theorists of strong or participatory democracy have stressed, is that the question to which pluralism is an answer is itself a mirror image of the traditional question of democracy—the one with which, precisely, nineteenth-century American liberalism struggled so unsuccessfully.

The political context in which the secret ballot was generalised in the United States may have been anomalous, but the technology itself survived and prospered. Having served as both a symbol and a practical guarantee of a certain kind of (oddly perverted) political virtue, it performed equally well, at the symbolic and practical level, within the framework of pluralism—which offers reasons to regard the privatisation of citizenship as conducive to, rather than destructive of, the public good. This, however, points to a paradox, which requires some consideration in concluding. Hitherto the whole argument of this chapter has emphasised the importance of political technology, including the most mundane and apparently trivial features of the apparatus of voting. Yet the ability of a given piece of technology to fit into radically divergent ideological contexts suggests that, on the contrary, technology makes no difference. Ideas, one might conclude, drive politics and the machinery merely keeps step. In a sense this is no doubt true. The secret ballot, for instance, could undoubtedly operate in almost any political system, and it would certainly be compatible with highly individualised forms of political-social control so long as powerful background coercive capacities were available. But the key phrase here is 'so long as'. The secret ballot, like any other political technology, has a logic that can be counteracted, but that nonetheless points in a certain direction. Furthermore ideas, especially ideas that operate as theories—i.e. with supposedly explanatory and predictive rather than merely prescriptive force—do not develop independently of institutional and technological political configurations. On the contrary, these are precisely what they are ideas *about* or theories *of*, and the internal dynamic of ideas is therefore inescapably symbiotic.

In the case discussed here, therefore, the remarkable flexibility of the secret ballot cannot be attributed to features of political technology in general. It points us, rather, in two complementary directions. First, as discussed in some detail in section I, the secret ballot is profoundly ambivalent in normative terms. Secondly, and partly as a consequence, the divergence between what I have called the 'aristocratic' interpretation of democracy, *c.* 1910, and mainstream pluralism is less radical than one might think. They are, as suggested, mirror images—at once opposite and inseparable. They provide the poles between which our ideas about democracy—élitist, populist, participatory, representative, radical, institutional, agonistic, consensual etc.—tend to circulate and cross-fertilise. There are many reasons to be dissatisfied with this rather one-dimensional polarity and indeed much theoretical activity has been devoted to attempts to break out of it. Whether this might be possible, and if so in which direction, is quite beyond the scope of this chapter. What this sketch of some of the issues raised by the secret ballot does show, however, is that political technology is among the things at stake. How exactly one might cast a vote in 'another kind of democracy' is not some trivial detail that can, in theoretical terms, be left until later, to be dealt with by mere 'technicians'. It is a question of fundamental importance.

Allen, Philip L., 1910, 'The Multifarious Australian Ballot', *North American Review*, no. 191, pp. 602–11.

Appadurai, Arjun and James Holston, 1996, 'Cities and Citizenship', *Public Culture*, no. 8, pp. 187–204.

Banton, Michael , 1987, *Racial Theories*, Cambridge University Press.

Bishop, Joseph B., 1891, 'Genuine and Bogus Ballot Reform', *The Nation*, no. 52, pp. 491–3.

Bourdieu, Pierre, 2000, *Propos sur le champ politique*, Presses Universitaires de Lyon.

Chute, Marchette, 1970, *The First Liberty: A History of the Right to Vote in America 1619–1850*, London: J.M. Dent.

Crowley, John, 1999a, 'Ecrire l'histoire de la démocratie? Quelques remarques en guise de conclusion' in Jean-Paul Bled (ed.), *La démocratie aux Etats-Unis d'Amérique et en Europe, 1918–1989*, Paris: SEDES, pp. 441–6.

——, 1999b, 'Le Royaume-Uni: stabilité des institutions, mutations des idées' in Jean-Paul Bled (ed.), *La démocratie aux Etats-Unis d'Amérique et en Europe*, Paris: SEDES, pp. 389–440.

——, 1999c, 'The Politics of Belonging: Some Theoretical Considerations' in Adrian Favell and Andrew Geddes (eds), *The Politics of Belonging: Migrants and Minorities in Contemporary Europe*, Aldershot: Ashgate, pp. 15–41.

——, 2000, 'L'identité collective comme configuration politique: l'exemple du racisme', *Cahiers politiques*, no. 5, pp. 9–30.

Dunn, John, 1985, 'Individuality and Clientage in the Formation of Locke's Social Imagination' in *Rethinking Modern Political Theory*, Cambridge University Press.

Fredman, L.E., 1969, *The Australian Ballot: The Story of an American Reform*, East Lansing, MI: University of Michigan Press.

Gardiner, Charles A. *et al.*, 1884, 'The Future of the Negro', *North American Review*, no. 139.

Garrigou, Alain, 1992, *Le vote et la vertu. Comment les Français sont devenus électeurs*, Paris: Presses de la Fondation nationale des sciences politiques.

——, 1993, 'La construction sociale du vote. Fétichisme et raison instrumentale', *Politix*, no. 22, pp. 5–42.

Gilliam, E.W., 1884, 'The African Problem', *North American Review*, no. 139.

Habermas, Jürgen, 1990, *Strukturwandel der Öffentlichkeit. Untersuchungen zu einer Kategorie der bürgerlischen Gesellschaft*, Frankfurt: Suhrkamp, 2nd edition. (English translation: *The Structural Transformation of the Public Sphere: An Inquiry into a Category of Bourgeois Society*, Cambridge, MA: MIT Press, 1991).

Hofstadter, Richard, 1955, *The Age of Reform*, New York: Random House.

Jaffrelot, Christophe, 1993, 'L'invention du vote secret en Angleterre. Idéologie, intérêt et circulation des arguments', *Politix*, no. 22, pp. 43–68.

King, Preston, 1991, 'Modernity: All "Niggers" Now? Or New Slaves for Old?', *New Community*, no. 4, pp. 489–509.

——, 1992, 'Modernity: Prisoners' Dilemma in Colour', *New Community*, no. 2, pp. 229–49.

Kleppner, Paul, 1987, *Continuity and Change in Electoral Politics, 1893–1928*, New York: Greenwood Press.

Kousser, J. Morgan, 1974, *The Shaping of Southern Politics*, New Haven, CT: Yale University Press.

Malik, Kenan, 1997, *The Meaning of Race: Race, History and Culture in Western Society*, Basingstoke: Macmillan.

Merriam, Charles E., 1926, *A History of American Political Theories*, New York: Macmillan.

Page, Thomas N., 1892, 'A Southerner on the Negro Question', *North American Review*, no. 154, pp. 401–13.

Pitman, Robert C., 1884, 'Woman as a Political Factor', *North American Review*, no. 139, pp. 405–16.

Pole, J.R., 1950, 'Constitutional Reform and Election Statistics in Maryland', *Maryland Historical Magazine*, no. 55, pp. 275–84.

——, 1978, *The Pursuit of Equality in American History*, Berkeley, CA: University of California Press.

Pollock, Norman (ed.), 1967, *The Populist Mind*, New York: Bobbs-Merrill.

Porter, Kirk H. and Donald B. Johnson (eds), 1966, *National Party Platforms 1840–1964*, Urbana, IL: University of Illinois Press.

Scruggs, William L., 1884, 'Restriction of the Suffrage', *North American Review*, no. 139.

Seymour, Charles and Donald P. Frairy, 1918, *How the World Votes: The Story of Democratic Development in Elections*, Springfield, MA: C.A. Nichols & Co.

Spalding, J.L., 1884, 'The Basis of Popular Government', *North American Review*, no. 139.

Sutherland, Rosamund, 1910, 'The Appeal of Politics to Woman', *North American Review*, no. 191, pp. 75–86.

Taguieff, Pierre-André, 1987, *La force du préjugé. Essai sur le racisme et ses doubles*, Paris: Gallimard.

Watkins, Alan, 1982, *Brief Lives*, London: Hamish Hamilton.

Williamson, Chilton, 1960, *American Suffrage from Property to Democracy 1760–1860*, Princeton University Press.

Wilson, Woodrow, 1910, 'Hide-and-Seek Politics', *North American Review*, no. 191, pp. 587–601.

'CHAD WARS'

VOTING MACHINES AND DEMOCRACY IN THE UNITED STATES

Denis Lacorne

'Admittedly the present scenario is surreal: all the king's horses and all the king's men could not get a few thousand ballots counted. The explanation, however, is timeless. We are a nation of men and women and, although we aspire to lofty principles, our methods at times are imperfect.' (*Per curiam* opinion, *Supreme Court of Florida*, 22 December 2000)

The 2000 US Presidential Election raised an important question for the specialist of comparative politics. Why did one of the oldest representative democracies, a highly educated and highly advanced technological country, fail to properly count the votes of its two leading presidential candidates? Why did it take more than a month to find out who the winner of the Presidential Election was, and only after the surprising intervention of the US Supreme Court? The answer is paradoxical: too much democracy and not enough modern technology.

TOO MUCH (CORRECTIVE) DEMOCRACY

The closeness of the 2000 Presidential Election was not due to chance. It resulted from the remarkable skills of highly sophisticated pollsters, party organisers and spin-doctors, who were able to invest the most resources in the few critical states where the outcome was likely to be decisive. It was the anachronistic structure of the Electoral College and the winner-take-all system of election that allowed party workers to single out a few critical states, among them Florida (Lacorne, 2001). Contrary to common belief, the Electoral College did not favour small states. As aptly demonstrated by Lawrence Longley and Neal Peirce (1999: 134–61), it favoured large states capable of delivering more than twenty-one electoral votes.[1]

Florida, with twenty-five electoral votes, was just such a large state and a victory there would give the election to one of the two leading contenders. At first glance Bush was the winner of the Florida election.

---

1 For two excellent analyses of the 2000 Presidential Election, see Ceaser and Busch (2001) and the special issue of the *Revue française d'études américaines* (2000).

So why did the first official count not give him the election? For a simple reason ignored by most commentators: Florida's electoral outcomes were complex, because local elections had often been disrupted by flawed and corrupt electoral procedures. Past political corruption and the manipulation of absentee ballots had provoked a democratic reaction: the organisation, at the urging of the state legislature, of counting and re-counting mechanisms to 'clean the vote' and expose dubious counting practices. The introduction of such 'cleansing' mechanisms had already produced a striking result: the overturning of the 1998 election of the mayor of Miami when court proceedings revealed that a large number of absentee ballots had not been legally valid votes. An appellate court settled the municipal vote fraud by throwing out the disputed ballots altogether. That was enough to change the outcome of the election and in the end the loser of the election, Joe Carollo, was declared the winner. Such voting irregularities filled the humorist columns of the national press. For example, the *Washington Post*, reporting on the 1998 Miami election, published an article appropriately entitled 'Welcome to the Jungle':

Two years ago Miami Mayor Xavier Suarez—affectionately called 'Mayor Loco' because of idiosyncrasies that included late night visits to constituents in his bathrobe—lost his job when it was revealed that his election involved many absentee ballots cast by persons who were technically dead or in other ways unaware that they had voted. And so Suarez's opponent became the new mayor. That would be Joe Carollo—affectionately called 'Crazy Joe' because of past idiosyncrasies that included publicly challenging a political rival to a duel. (Weingarten, 2000)

To prevent the reoccurrence of such irregularities the Florida legislature chose to democratise the electoral process by permitting complicated recount procedures in cases of contested elections. Both machine and manual recounting procedures were created to guarantee the fairness of future elections in a noticeably corrupt state. The new electoral code adopted in the 1990s thus permitted a candidate whose name appears on a ballot to file a written request with a local county canvassing board for a manual recount. This request, if accepted by the board, must include at least three precincts and at least one per cent of the total votes cast for the candidate. Should the limited manual recount indicate an 'error in vote tabulation which could affect the outcome of the election', the county canvassing board 'shall', among other options, 'manually recount all ballots'.[2] An 'error in vote tabulation', according to the Supreme Court of Florida, includes 'errors in the failure of the voting machinery to read a ballot' as revealed by, among other things, 'a discrepancy between the

---

2 See Sections 102.166(4) and 102.166(5), Florida Statutes as cited in Supreme Court of Florida, *Palm Beach County Canvassing Board, Petitioner v. Katherine Harris etc.*, 21 November 2000, reprinted in Dionne and Kristol (2001: 29–30).

Table 1. VOTING TECHNOLOGIES USED IN
THE UNITED STATES, 1998

Voting method	Number of counties	Voter (%)	Precincts (%)
Paper ballot	410	1.6	2.9
Lever machine	480	18.6	21.8
Punch-card	635	34.3	37.4
Optical scan	1,217	27.3	24.7
Touch-screen	257	9.1	7.3
Other/mixed	141	9.1	5.9

Source: Eric Fischer, Congressional Research Service, RL30773: *Voting Technologies in the United States*, 11 January 2001, p. 3.

number of votes determined by a voter tabulation system and the number of voters determined by a manual count of a sampling of precincts pursuant to section 102.166(4)' of the Florida Statutes (reprinted in Dionne and Kristol, 2001: 31).

Why should an error in vote tabulation change the outcome of a presidential election? One could assume that the error, because it was mechanical, was random in nature and therefore equally distributed among the candidates. This interpretation was favoured by Republican leaders who did not see any reason to proceed with a recount: 'Machines are neither Republicans nor Democrats, and therefore can be neither consciously nor unconsciously biased', argued former Secretary of State James Baker in Florida (cited in Merzer and Keough, 2000). But the opposite argument was defended by Democrats who noticed that the most unreliable voting machines were almost always located in large, urban, predominantly Democratic counties.[3]

As indicated in the two electoral maps of Florida (Figs 1 and 2), the percentage of discarded votes was unevenly distributed and directly related to the type of ballot system used. On average the percentage of nonvotes was 3.92 per cent in counties using a punch-card system, whereas the rate of error in counties using the more modern optical-scan system was only 1.43 per cent.[4] As Justice Breyer noted in his dissent in *Bush v. Gore*—the Supreme Court decision that reversed the decision of the

[3] 'When computerised vote tabulation first became feasible in the 1960s, the more populous counties adopted it first because hand counting is slower the more votes there are to be counted, and the only system of computerised vote tabulation available at the time was the punch-card system. The counties that adopted that system were loath to switch later on, when new and better technology came on the market, because of the cost of buying new equipment when the old was still serviceable' (Posner, 2001: 90).

[4] See Justice Stevens' dissenting opinion, *Bush v. Gore* (U.S. 12 December 2000), reproduced in Dionne and Kristol (2001: 119). In fact 3,718,305 votes were cast under punch-card systems and 2,353,811 under the optical-scan systems.

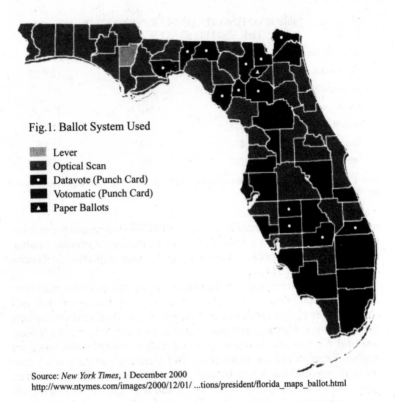

Fig.1. Ballot System Used

- Lever
- Optical Scan
- Datavote (Punch Card)
- Votomatic (Punch Card)
- Paper Ballots

Source: *New York Times*, 1 December 2000
http://www.ntymes.com/images/2000/12/01/ ...tions/president/florida_maps_ballot.html

Florida Supreme Court and put an end to all recounting procedures—'in a system that allows counties to use different types of voting systems, voters already arrive at the polls with an unequal chance that their votes will be counted' (reprinted in Dionne and Kristol, 2001: 134).

There was nothing unique about Florida's electoral system. In a federal system of government such as the United States, elections, including presidential elections, are administered at the state and local levels. In Florida, as in most states, elections are administered at the county level. The small size and limited resources of state electoral jurisdictions have had a direct impact on the choice of voting technology. For reasons of convenience, paper ballots have progressively been replaced by punch-card systems (first introduced in 1964), optical scanners in the 1980s and touch-screen systems in the 1990s. However, the system most commonly used in the United States remains the punch-card machine (see Table 1).

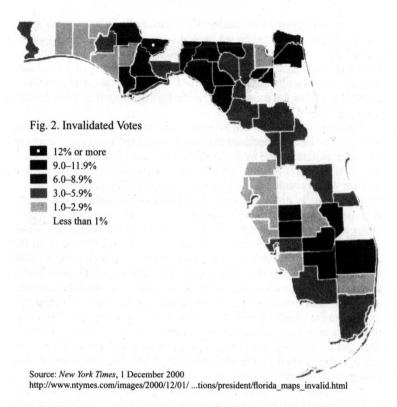

Fig. 2. Invalidated Votes

- ▪ 12% or more
- ▪ 9.0–11.9%
- ▪ 6.0–8.9%
- ▪ 3.0–5.9%
- ▪ 1.0–2.9%
- Less than 1%

Source: *New York Times*, 1 December 2000
http://www.ntymes.com/images/2000/12/01/ ...tions/president/florida_maps_invalid.html

NOT ENOUGH MODERN TECHNOLOGY

Since American elections are a matter of state law, it is the responsibility of state courts, and state courts alone, to construe the law and to regulate the election process in situations mentioned by states' election codes. A state court, for instance, can order a manual recount; it can also create safeguards or establish procedures that minimise the risk of arbitrariness during a recount. This risk is real and has two common forms: partisan bias and lack of consistency.

The remedy to the risk of partisan bias is simple enough. It consists of making sure that counties' canvassing boards are truly multipartisan: each party sending at least one representative. The problem of lack of consistency is more serious and requires the intervention of state legislatures (or state courts if the law is silent) to impose uniform rules for counting discarded votes and determining the true intent of the voter. In the Florida Presidential Election about 175,000 ballots had been rejected (i.e. not counted) as either 'undervotes' (failure to properly mark a ballot on a paper form read by an optical scanner or failure to punch out a chad on a computer card fed into a computer reader) or 'overvotes' (selecting more than one candidate or writing the name of a candidate already chosen with another method). 'Undervotes' raised a particularly difficult problem for county canvassing boards located in counties that used punch-card ballots.

The boards were supposed to enforce a 2000 Florida statute specifying that 'no vote shall be declared invalid or void if there is a *clear intent* of the voter as determined by the canvassing board.' But what is the 'clear intent' of the voter if the punched chad (a perforated square punched in a ballot with a pointed metal tool—a stylus—to mark the voter's preference) is partially dislocated from the surface of the ballot? Each county canvassing board could come up with a specific rule; some counties even chose to change the counting rule in the middle of a counting procedure. The choice of a counting rule was not foolproof and depended on the accuracy of the observation. A skilful observer examining a ballot could ascertain the intent of the voter in three different ways. He could notice a 'dimple', sometimes called a 'pregnant chad', i.e. a visible impression, best seen from the back of the ballot, that has failed to detach the chad from the computer card. He could observe a 'pinprick': a tiny hole through which light can be seen, which suggests that some pressure has been put on the chad, but not enough to detach it fully. Finally he could see a 'hanging chad', i.e. a chad that has clearly been detached at one, two or three corners.[5]

Recovering a vote from an 'undervoted punch-card ballot by a hand recount' could have been done in seven distinct ways, ranked in ascending order of liberality, as demonstrated by Richard Posner in his attempt to reconstruct the new voting science of 'chadology':

1) Count dangling (that is, hanging or swinging) chads but no dimpled chads. 2) Count any chads if light can be seen through the chad hole. 3) Count dangling chads plus dimpled chads if but only if none of the chads in the ballot is fully or partly punched through. 4) Count dimpled chads only if there are no fully punched chads. 5) Count dangling chads, plus dimpled chads, provided there are several dimpled chads. 6) Count dangling chads plus dimpled chads. 7) Count dangling chads plus all dimpled chads that are near indentation or other mark (maybe made in pen or pencil rather than with the stylus that the voter is given to vote with). (Posner, 2001: 56)

---

5 The measure of a 'voter's intent' varies from state to state. In Illinois a one-corner hanging chad signals a voter's intent, but not a dimple; in Michigan a chad must be detached at two corners to be considered a valid vote; in Massachusetts and Texas dimpled ballots are accepted; California and Virginia require a two-corner hanging chad… Overall, nearly half the states have no state-wide standard. How to determine the nature of a 'legal vote' in hand counting procedure is up to local authorities. See Silva (2001).

'The problem', as noted by Justice Wells in *Gore v. Harris*, is 'how a county canvassing board translates [the search for the voter's intent] to these punching cards?' Some county boards saw a voter's clear intent in a 'dimpled chad', others only counted hanging chads with at least two corners detached, yet others accepted as a valid vote a one-corner hanging chad. As Wells prophetically concluded: 'Continuation of this system of county by county decisions regarding how a dimpled chad is counted is fraught with equal protection concerns which will eventually cause the election results in Florida to be stricken by the Federal courts or Congress.'[6] And yet the solution to Wells' problem was simple enough: to impose a single state-wide uniform standard on all undercounted votes in Florida—a solution that was indeed considered 'practicable' and 'necessary' by the majority in *Bush v. Gore*, but not retained on the (very questionable) ground that there was not enough time to establish a uniform standard and proceed with a full hand recount.[7]

We know the result: on 8 December 2000 the Florida Supreme Court ordered a state-wide hand-recount of Florida undervotes; on 9 December the Supreme Court of the United States stayed the recount; on 12 December it reversed the Florida Supreme Court's decision and halted the manual recounts entirely and the next day Gore conceded the election to his opponent. Two Justices—Souter and Breyer—had sought a remand, permitting the Florida Supreme Court 'to require recounting all undercounted votes ..., and to do so with a single uniform substandard' (reprinted in Dionne and Kristol, 2001: 134). But the majority of the Court refused to permit such a remand on the ground that there was not sufficient time. Critics of the decision have argued that there was in fact ample time to organise a recount and that it was up to Congress to resolve disputes arising from the certification of presidential electors.[8]

Assuming there was indeed enough time to proceed with an orderly hand-recount of all the 'undervotes' of the Florida election, who would have won in that state? The answer has been provided by a systematic review of all the contested ballots undertaken by a consortium of nine media organisations together with the University of Chicago's National Opinion Research Center.[9] This large-scale political science experiment, the largest ever undertaken in the United States, took nine months to complete and consisted of reviewing each of the 175,010 ballots that

---

6 Justice Wells, dissenting, Supreme Court of Florida, *Gore v. Harris*, reproduced in Dionne and Kristol (2001: 87).

7 *Bush v. Gore, per curiam* decision, in Dionne and Kristol (2001: 104).

8 For a thoughtful criticism of the Supreme Court decision, see Fiss (2001) and Dworkin (2001: 53–5).

9 The media consortium included the *New York Times, Washington Post, Wall Street Journal*, CNN, Tribune Publishing and *Palm Beach Post*. For further details, see NORC Florida Ballots Project (www.norc.uchicago.edu/projects).

had been discarded by machine counting (i.e. uncounted votes—'non-votes'—or ballots not registered as votes) at the cost of $1 million. The results were ambivalent, depending on three basic hand-counting scenarios:

1. Scenario one assumed the Supreme Court would not have intervened to stay the vote counting ordered by the Florida Supreme Court. In that case Bush would have won the election by a majority of 493 votes (instead of the official, state-certified 537 votes).

2. Scenario two assumed the imposition of a uniform state-wide standard to determine the voters' intent, based on all the counties' under-votes—a uniform rule considered 'necessary' by the Supreme Court but inapplicable for reasons of time constraint. In this scenario Gore would have won the election by a razor-thin margin of 'less than 200 votes', irrespective of the 'chadology' involved: counting either only two-corner hanging chads (the Republicans' preferred choice), or one-corner and dimpled chads (the Democrats' preferred solution).

3. Scenario three assumed that a uniform voting standard would have been imposed on all county canvassing boards and that both under-votes and overvotes would be counted after being examined by three independent coders. In this case, according to the *Wall Street Journal*, Gore would have won 'an unrestricted multistandard state-wide recount that included overvotes' (Calmes and Foldessy, 2001).[10] Had a uniform, restrictive standard been applied, including 'only clean punches and properly filled-in optical-scan ballots', Gore would still have won the election (Calmes and Foldessy, 2001).

The most disturbing finding of the media consortium study is that 'counties with the most black voters had the highest rates of ballot rejections. While Florida's overall rate of spoiled ballots was just below 3 per cent, in precincts that are home mostly to blacks, the percentage was nearly four times as high' (Calmes and Foldessy, 2001). This disparity was attributed by the media consortium to crowded urban precincts, low educational levels and the failure (or lack) of voter-education programmes.

In many ways the media consortium study contradicts the findings of the Supreme Court expressed in *Bush v. Gore*. It suggests that a hand recount based on a state-wide uniform standard is feasible (coders, according to the *Wall Street Journal*, agreed among themselves in more than 95 per cent of the cases) and it points to a serious disparity of results (in the rates of ballot rejection) between predominantly black precincts and predominantly white precincts. This in turn suggests that it is not the hand count *per se* that creates a disparate treatment of citizens and a

---

10 The results of the study contradict the title of the article: 'Late Results are in from Florida: Bush Beat Gore after All'.

possible violation of the principle of equal protection as assumed by the Supreme Court, but the use of different voting systems within a single state, the types of precinct geographical locations (urban *v.* suburban, crowded *v.* uncrowded) and an unequal distribution of voter information and error-correction mechanisms, particularly lacking in large urban areas. The only possible remedy to the blatant injustices of the Florida electoral system is not the imposition of a uniform state-wide hand-counting standard, but the adoption of a single, modern voting technology[11] combined with equal access to voter information, irrespective of race and geographical location.

Calmes, Jackie and Edward Foldessy, 2001, 'Late Results are in from Florida: Bush Beat Gore after All', *Wall Street Journal*, 12 November.

Ceaser, James W. and Andrew E. Busch, 2001, *The Perfect Tie: The True Story of the 2000 Presidential Election*, Lanham, MD: Rowman and Littlefield.

Dionne, E.J. and William Kristol (eds), 2001, *Bush v. Gore: The Court Cases and the Commentary*, Washington, DC: Brookings Institution Press.

Dworkin, Ronald, 2001, 'A Badly Flawed Election', *New York Review of Books*, 11 January.

Fiss, Owen, 2001, 'Bush v. Gore and the Crisis of Legitimacy', unpublished paper presented at the Centre d'Etudes et de Recherches Internationales (CERI), Paris.

Lacorne, Denis, 2001, 'Sur l'élection présidentielle américaine. Vestiges d'un âge pré-démocratique et antimonarchique', *Le Débat*, January, pp. 15–26.

Longley, Lawrence D. and Neal R. Peirce, 1999, *The Electoral College Primer 2000*, New Haven, CT: Yale University Press.

Merzer, Martin and Caroline Keough, 2000, 'Bush Goes to Court: Halt to Recount Sought', *Miami Herald*, 12 November.

Posner, Richard A., 2001, *Breaking the Deadlock*, Princeton University Press.

Revue française d'études américaines, 2000, no. 90 (October).

Silva, Mark, 2001, 'Most States Follow Tough Rules', *Miami Herald*, 5 April.

Weingarten, Gene, 2000, 'Welcome to the Jungle', *Washington Post*, 9 November.

---

[11] No technology is error-proof, but the consensus is that optical-scan systems are the most efficient, provided they include a 'precinct counter' which tells the voters about possible voting errors (no recorded vote or too many votes) and allows them to correct their mistakes (Calmes and Foldessy, 2001).

VOTING IN INDIA

ELECTORAL SYMBOLS, THE PARTY SYSTEM AND
THE COLLECTIVE CITIZEN

Christophe Jaffrelot

The Republic of India is often described as 'the largest democracy in the world' chiefly because of its ability to organise free elections at regular intervals. In the period from 1951 to 2004 fourteen elections were held to renew the lower house in New Delhi, the Lok Sabha. However, the country's socio-cultural and demographic conditions complicate the electoral process. The electorate grew, in just over three decades, from 173 million in 1952 to nearly 400 million in 1984, and voter participation progressed, during the same period, from 45.7 per cent to 64.1 per cent. In 1989 the right to vote was extended to include young people aged eighteen to twenty-one, increasing the electorate further, to 499 million people, from which a total of 298.3 million cast their vote. Furthermore the electorate grew at each of the following six elections, from 491 million in 1991 to 670 million in 2004. Over the same period the turnout rate peaked at 62 per cent in 1998 and then decreased marginally to 58 per cent in 2004. Still the number of voters remained high, at about 389 million in 2004.

The difficulties linked to the sheer size of the electorate are exacerbated by widespread illiteracy (in 1990 nearly 52 per cent of the population still could not read), which hinders the domestication of the act of voting for the very simple reason that many Indian citizens cannot read the names of the candidates. According to the 2001 census, 34.7 per cent of the population did not know how to read and write. Thirty years earlier—when India was already the largest democracy in the world—that was roughly the percentage of people that were literate (to be precise, 34.5 per cent according to the 1971 census). Matters are further complicated by the huge number of candidates contesting elections. Despite the small size of the lower house—with 543 members it is no larger than the French National Assembly, but represents a population more than seventeen times larger—the number of candidates is incredibly high: it peaked in 1996 with 13,952 individuals. It has decreased since then, but with 5,436 candidates in 2004 the average number of candidates per constituency remained above ten.

India has tried to grapple with this triple challenge—the size and lack of education of its electorate and the large number of candidates—first by employing enormous material means at each election (in 1999 more than 1.7 million ballot boxes were dispatched across the country so that the vote could take place over the space of a few days in 773,708 polling stations,[1] and in 2004 more than 700,000 stations were equipped with electronic voting machines, while 4 million civil servants supervised the electoral process in and around the polling stations); and second, by developing an electoral procedure that allows citizens to cast their vote under auspicious conditions. Voting takes place through the recognition of electoral symbols, whose growing role has in turn contributed to institutionalising the party system. In addition to using symbols, the Election Commission, an independent administrative body responsible for the electoral process, has tried to surround the act of voting with as many guarantees as possible (concerning voting secrecy and measures against outside influences) so as to create the conditions for rational and independent voting. However, the sophisticated measures taken to this effect have had unintended consequences.

THE USE OF ELECTORAL SYMBOLS AND THE PARTY SYSTEM

India inherited its voting system, among many other political institutions and practices, from methods introduced by the British. In the latter part of the colonial era an increasing number of Indians obtained the right to vote through constitutional reforms in 1909, 1919 and 1935 (by which time 30 million Indians, or one-sixth of the adult male population, were enfranchised). The British administration tried to avoid the obstacle of illiteracy, which became increasingly serious as the right to vote spread, by instituting two procedures, depending on the region: either polling station officials 'helped' hesitant voters to write the name of the candidate across their ballot paper (which violated voting secrecy laws), or ballot boxes were painted a different colour for each candidate, enabling the voter to identify the correct box without needing to know how to read the candidate's name (Butler, Lahiri and Roy, 1989: 15). After Independence India tried to build on the second system through the use of electoral symbols, depicted first on the ballot boxes and later on the ballot papers themselves.

---

[1] In 1998 for the first time polling for the Lok Sabha elections was held in five phases, spread over a month in order to give sufficient time for the paramilitary forces to move from one state to another. Hence the cost of the elections: 75 million rupees were spent in organising the general elections, as against 60 million in 1996 (A.K. Sinha, 'The Price of Democracy', *Outlook*, 22 December 1997, p. 68). In 2004 the Lok Sabha elections were held in five phases spread over three weeks between 21 April and 10 May. The cost of the 2004 General Elections was estimated at 120 million rupees for the Indian state (*India Today*, 8 March 2004, p. 34).

From the balloting system to the marking system

In the 1950s the Election Commission considered that 'the percentage of literacy in India being in the neighbourhood of 16.6 per cent only, it would have been impossible for the vast majority of voters who are illiterate to mark their votes on the ballot papers with the names of the contesting candidates printed on it.'[2] The elections of 1951–2 and those in 1957 were organised using the balloting system procedure, which consisted in distinguishing ballot boxes not by colour but by symbols associated with each of the candidates. In 1951 the Election Commission published a list of symbols; each candidate in a constituency was asked to choose three, ranked in order of preference. The local representative of the Election Commission, having assembled the lists, assigned a different symbol to each candidate to use during the campaign (Graham, 1983: 72). Every polling station in the constituency had a room, closed off by a curtain, containing ballot boxes for each candidate. Voters picked up ballot papers at the polling station entrance and deposited them in the boxes of their choice. There were two kinds of papers—green and pink—because elections for the New Delhi Lower House and for the legislative assemblies of the federal states took place simultaneously. Each voter thus had at least two ballot papers to be placed in two different ballot boxes.

In certain constituencies the situation was still more complex as some electoral seats were reserved for members of Scheduled Castes (Untouchables) or Scheduled Tribes. The Constitution of 1950 set aside seat quotas in the electoral assemblies for these disadvantaged populations. These quotas were—and still are—proportionate to the percentage of the national population represented by these communities for the central Parliament, and proportionate to the percentage of the population in each federal state for the state legislative assemblies. In certain so-called double (or triple) constituencies, where these populations were particularly sizeable, voters had to elect one candidate for the 'general seat', one Untouchable and/or one Scheduled Tribe member. Each party could put forward a candidate for each of these seats and independents could also run. The ballot boxes for candidates for the reserved seats were marked with the same symbols as those for other candidates of the same party, but with the symbol circled in black (Election Commission, 1959: 92).

Partly because elections at the national and state level were held simultaneously and partly because of the double or triple constituency system, the electoral procedure, intended to be simple enough to allow illiterate voters to vote, turned out to be too complex. The sheer number of ballot boxes in polling stations led to mistakes: voters confused ballot boxes for the candidates to Parliament with those for candidates to

2 Election Commission, *Report of the First General Elections in India 1951–52*, vol. I (General), New Delhi, 1955: 80 (quoted in Bharadvaja, 1972: 56).

the legislative assemblies, or dropped both ballots into the same box. The same confusion arose with the ballot boxes for Untouchable or Scheduled Tribe candidates. In 1957 in one constituency in West Bengal 133,063 ballots out of 990,800 were declared spoiled because they had been placed in the wrong ballot box (Election Commission, 1959: 164). This electoral system had two other drawbacks. First, candidates could accuse returning officers of switching ballot papers from one ballot box to another after voting was closed, as the papers had no distinguishing marks. Second, a secret ballot was not absolutely guaranteed since the curtain behind which the ballot boxes were placed did not completely hide the movements of the voter in front of the row of boxes. This voting procedure was thus replaced by another at the beginning of the 1960s.

The marking system was used for the first time in the late 1950s in by-elections, then on a regular basis starting with the General Elections of 1962. Ballot boxes with electoral symbols disappeared. Instead symbols appeared on the ballot papers themselves, next to the candidates' names, to help those voters who otherwise could not decipher the ballot. There was one ballot for elections to Parliament and another for elections to the state legislative assembly, printed with the name and corresponding symbol of each candidate (Fig. 1). Voting took place as follows:[3] 1) In a polling station the first voting officer identified the voter's name on the electoral roll, which was annually updated, and wrote the number of the voter's ballot paper for the state legislative assembly elections in a ledger, before passing it on to a colleague; 2) The colleague did the same with the ballot paper for the elections to Parliament and passed both along to a third official; 3) This third official gave the two ballot papers to the voter and marked the index finger of the voter's left hand with indelible ink in order to spot without difficulty any attempts to vote a second time; 4) A fourth official took the ballot papers from the voter and explained how to mark the ballot paper next to the name and symbol of the chosen candidate, using a rubber stamp lent to the voter for the purpose. The official then gave the ballot paper for the legislative assembly back to the voter and passed the ballot for Parliament to a fifth official. The voter went into the voting booth to stamp the first ballot in secret; 5) The voter then collected the second ballot from the fifth official and stamped it as well, before dropping both ballots into a single ballot box.[4]

This method of voting, codified by the Election Commission,[5] has changed little, except that since 1971–2 elections for Parliament and for

[3] For a more detailed description of voting modalities, see Hauser (1986: 951–6).
[4] Double or triple constituencies had disappeared. There was henceforth only one elected representative per constituency; some constituencies were reserved for Untouchables and Scheduled Tribes.
[5] The above reconstitution of the voting procedure comes from the guidelines of the Election Commission (1965: 66–7).

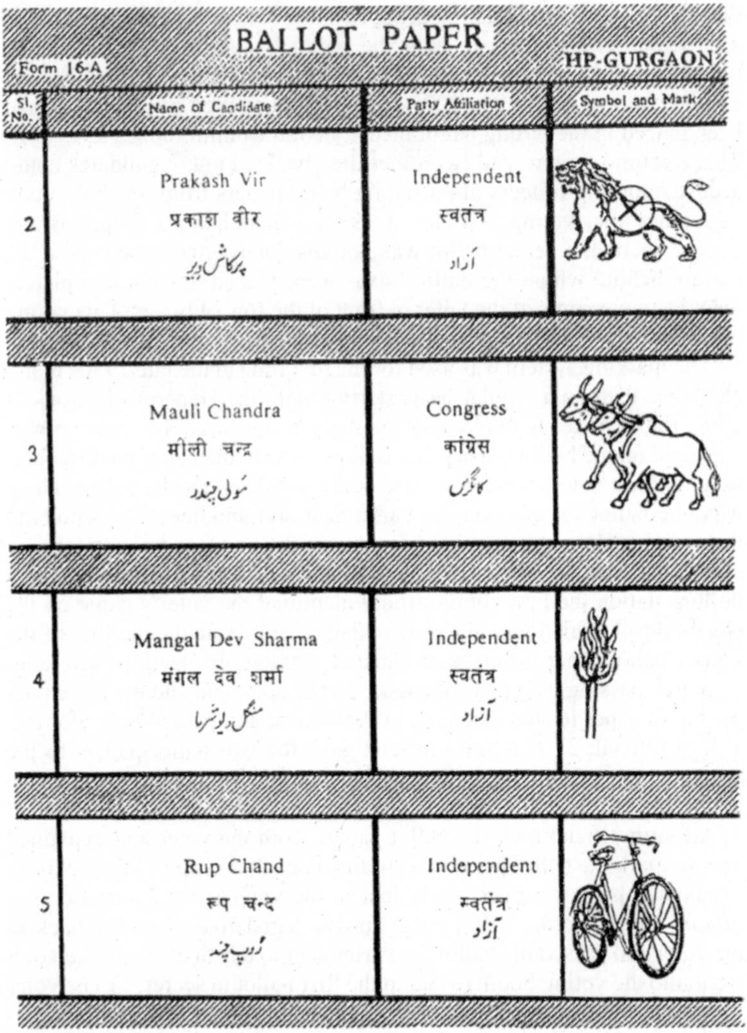

BALLOT PAPER			**HP-GURGAON**
Form 16-A			
Sl. No.	Name of Candidate	Party Affiliation	Symbol and Mark
2	Prakash Vir प्रकाश वीर پرکاش ویر	Independent स्वतंत्र آزاد	
3	Mauli Chandra मौली चन्द्र مولی چندر	Congress कांग्रेस کانگرس	
4	Mangal Dev Sharma मंगल देव शर्मा منگل دیو شرما	Independent स्वतंत्र آزاد	
5	Rup Chand रूप चन्द روپ چند	Independent स्वतंत्र آزاد	

Fig. 1. Ballot paper used during 1957 by-elections

Source: Election Commission, 1959, vol. 1

the state legislative assemblies no longer take place together. The marking system simplified the act of voting, which was the main aim of the Election Commission. However, the use of symbols has had significant repercussions for the political system in that it has contributed strongly to the institutionalisation of political parties.

Electoral symbols and the identification of political parties

The adoption of the system of electoral symbols led parties to demand that they be assigned their own distinctive symbols. Also the Election Commission itself wanted to see all the candidates of a given party use the same symbol, to simplify its own work. In 1951 fourteen parties were recognised as having the right to their own symbols. The headquarters of each party were then required to communicate to the Election Commission the names of the candidates who could be assigned the party's symbol. As Bruce Graham (1983: 74) writes,

... by instituting this procedure the Commission accepted the principle that endorsement by a central party organisation was the essential determinant of party affiliation; in other words the Commission had virtually agreed to accept the appearance of a candidate's name on a party list as adequate proof of his attachment, and took little if any account of other evidence of allegiance, such as the candidate's own views and statements, his endorsement by informal associations and by local party branches and his membership of groups in the outgoing legislature. It was a principle which reduced the complexity of candidatures to two relatively simple categories, mutually exclusive groups of party nominees on the one hand and an undifferentiated mass of independents on the other, and it greatly strengthened the recruiting power of the central party organisations in the process.

The impact of this procedure was reinforced by the 1953 decision of the Election Commission to extend the right to a symbol, at the national level, only to those parties receiving more than 3 per cent of the popular vote in parliamentary elections. Only four parties met this criterion. However, there was a separate list for parties having attained the same threshold in legislative assembly elections, for which these state parties kept the right to their symbol (Fig. 2). Parties which came in under these thresholds lost an excellent means of affirming their existence and making their identity known: their candidates were attributed those 'free' symbols which were not reserved for the recognised parties and which could change from one election to the next. This procedure thus served the purposes of the major parties whose identity, reinforced by unchanging India-wide symbols, grew stronger: all the more so as in 1968 the thresholds were raised from 3 to 4 per cent. The Chief Election Commissioner offered as a partial justification for the symbol system and the new thresholds the fact that they would serve to limit the number of parties (Graham, 1983: 78). However, it did not limit the number of candidates, quite the contrary: parties set up candidates even in constituencies where they had no standing, simply to attain the required 4 per cent.[6]

---

6 Interestingly the introduction of a deposit that each candidate had to pay for contesting and which he forfeited if he could not get a minimum number of the valid votes did not dissuade parties from fielding hordes of candidates. This is one of the reasons for the huge

Fig. 2. Electoral symbols reserved by the Election Commission for the four national parties and for other parties in 1957

Source: Election Commission, 1959, vol. 1

The major parties quickly became associated with their symbols, which they in turn constantly promoted. Party slogans referred, and still refer, explicitly to the party symbol. Ever since the hand was adopted as the symbol of the Congress party, Congress has called on voters to 'give a helping hand' or to 'lend a hand', while the nationalist Hindu party Jana Sangh invited voters to be 'guided' by its long-time symbol, the lamp. Major parties quickly mobilised their workers to teach voters how

amount of money spent by the political parties at the time of elections (for more details, see Jaffrelot [2002]).

to recognise the symbol on a ballot paper. Fake ballots on which only the symbol of the party in question is real are used for instructional purposes (see Fig. 3, a fake ballot used in Bhopal prior to elections in 1989 by militants of the Bharatiya Janata Party (BJP), successors to Jana Sangh, whose symbol is the lotus flower).

The importance electoral symbols had acquired in the functioning of the Indian democracy became clear after the first Congress party split in 1969. The group that seceded from the Congress Party under Indira Gandhi, Congress O (for 'Organisation'), hoped to be attributed the spinning wheel symbol. Congress R (for 'Ruling') protested that this was too close to the national flag, which bears a wheel, the symbol for *dharma* as well as Buddhism. Congress R requested for itself the symbol of a child. The Election Commission's decision was to grant each party its second choice: a woman working at a spinning wheel for Congress O and a cow with her calf for Congress R. Opposition parties objected that this latter symbol had religious connotations attractive to Hindu voters, given the sacred nature of the cow in Hinduism (Election Commission, 1972: 67). In 1977, when four opposition parties (Congress O, the Socialists, the Hindu nationalists and the Bharatiya Lok Dal—BLD, a peasants' party) joined to form the Janata Party (People's Party), they began by using the electoral symbol of Congress O in the Tamil South and the BLD symbol (a ploughman within a wheel) in the North, where it was the best known

क्र	नाम	निशान	क्र.	नाम	निशान	क्र.	नाम	निशान
१	हनीफ खाँ		१४	राधावल्लम		२७	वहीद भाई	
२	चन्द्र मोहन		१५	चुन्नीलाल		२८	प्रकाशचंद्र	
३	अब्दुल सत्तार		१६	सुलेमान		२९	राधेश्याम	
४	शकुन्तला		१७	मधुकांत		३०	महेशकुमार	
५	रामकली बाई		१८	घनश्याम दास		३१	ईश्वर सिंह	
६	अफजल मियाँ		१९	दीपचन्द		३२	हाकम सिंह	
७	बख्तियार		२०	रंजीत कुमार		३३	शिवनारायण	
८	बालाराम		२१	बाबूलाल		३४	चंद्रशेखर	
९	मोहम्मद अली		२२	हीरालाल		३५	रामऔतार	
१०	योगेन्द्र सिंह		२३	श्याम लाल		३६	प्यारे मियां	
११	हरनाम सिंह		२४	प्रेमनारायण		३७	सुशीलचंद्र वर्मा	
१२	रामलाल		२५	रामचन्द्र		३८	सेंट जॉन	
१३	तेजेन्द्र सिंह		२६	ओमप्रकाश		३९	अशरफ खाँ	

Fig. 3. Fake ballot paper used by BJP activists to teach potential voters to recognise their party's symbol, the lotus flower

(Election Commission, 1978: 103). When the party started to splinter in 1979 the Janata Party (Secular) claimed this symbol for itself, but the Election Commission instead assigned it the symbol of a peasant ploughing a field (Election Commission, 1980: 43).

A similar conflict had earlier opposed the two Congress factions created in 1978, the Congress U (named after its leader Devraj Urs) and Congress I (for Indira Gandhi). Both claimed the cow and calf symbol, which the Election Commission withheld. Congress I was finally assigned the hand symbol and Congress U the spinning wheel (Election Commission, 1980: 42). These examples of conflict over electoral symbols reveal the importance of such symbols in identifying political parties; the more so as parties usually manage to obtain symbols reflecting their ideology or their social base, or to introduce relevant elements: for communist parties, for example, a sickle would appear with sheaves of wheat or with a hammer or the Maoist star, while peasant parties always managed to place a ploughman on their electoral symbol. Other cases are, however, more subtle. Congress initially used a pair of oxen as its symbol, alluding both to the use of oxen as draught animals by the peasants and to Hindu respect for the cow. This latter allusion was even more clearly echoed by the symbol of the cow and the calf. The spinning wheel, also favoured by certain Congress factions, recalls the prestige of Gandhi, who liked to spin thread and encouraged India to seek self-sufficiency in this way. The Hindu nationalist party, the Jana Sangh, which was assigned the lamp symbol in 1951, presented it as the instrument used in temples to illuminate the deity within and to carry out morning and evening prayers.

In sum, the electoral procedure which linked a symbol to each candidate and reserved specific symbols for parties overcame the obstacle of illiteracy but was not without political implications: institutionalisation of the party system resulted in large part from this *modus operandi* which, therefore, had rather unintended consequences. The efforts of the Election Commission to develop a procedure to surmount the obstacle of under-education are, however, part of a larger design, the goal of which is to create the conditions for electors to vote in an independent and reasoned way.

SEARCHING FOR AN INDIVIDUAL, REASONED ACT OF VOTING

The Election Commission has always sought to improve voting conditions to ensure that voting is an individual, voluntary act in conformity with the Western model that inspired the Indian Republic. Thus attention has been given to three elements in particular: the secret ballot, the verification of voter identity and the struggle against external influence.

The implementation of the secret ballot

The replacement of the ballot box system by the marking system already constituted progress in ensuring a secret ballot, given that with the former procedure, despite the screening curtain, it was still possible to tell in front of which ballot box the voter paused to vote. The marking system nonetheless also had its weaknesses: the returning officer would note the number printed on the ballot next to the voter's name in the electoral roll, it was thus possible during the count to check the ballot paper against the roll to see how a given voter had voted. Starting with the 1971 elections a ballot book was introduced from which individual ballot papers were detached. The voting officer would detach a ballot paper from the book, write down on the ballot stub the number under which the voter was listed in the electoral roll, ask the voter to countersign the stub, and then underline the voter's name in the roll to indicate that a ballot had been received. After vote counting the stubs and ballots were sealed and stored and could only be unsealed by court order, for instance for a recount. To match votes to voters three documents were thus required, not two: the ballot, the stub (which had the same serial number) and the electoral roll, which had the voter's number that had also been inscribed on the stub at the moment the ballot was distributed (Election Commission, 1972: 203–5). These precautions to ensure secrecy of the ballot were aimed at freeing voters from the control of any external authority. However, more direct measures to protect electors from the influence of local power-mongers were also put in place from the 1950s onward.

The struggle against outside influences

For local notables the most common way to win voters' favour was to convey them to polling stations. The Representation of the People Act of 1951 therefore stipulates that 'the hiring or procuring, whether on payment or otherwise, of any vehicle or vessel by a candidate or his agent or by any person for the conveyance of any elector (other than the candidate himself, the members of his family or his agent) to or from any polling station is a corrupted practice' (quoted in Viraraghavan, 1956: 129). As breaches of this clause continued to take place, in spite of the fines incurred, the Election Commission decided to reduce the risk by increasing the number of polling stations and so reducing the distance the average voter had to travel. In 1962 it was 3 miles, except in sparsely populated areas; in 1971 it was reduced to 1.25 miles. As Untouchables were the most vulnerable to external influence, the Election Commission ensured that polling stations were set up in their neighbourhoods (whether in reserved constituencies or not) to counter any possible intimidation from upper castes (Election Commission, 1965: 35; 1972: 201). In 1980 the Election Commission recommended that this rule be applied even if the

Untouchable neighbourhood in question numbered fewer than 750 voters, until then the minimum size required for a polling station (Election Commission, 1980: 70). For the same reason, it was decided in 1971 that ballots would not be counted in polling stations, but rather would be centralised for counting in district headquarters (the districts roughly corresponded to the constituencies of the state Lok Sabha). The Election Commission explained that this innovation 'eliminated to a large extent pre-election intimidation and post-election victimisation of voters belonging to the weaker, poorer and smaller sections of the community' (Election Commission, 1972: 203). Indeed vote counting in polling stations made clear the voting patterns of large communities in the area in question. Losing candidates—if they came from upper castes or wielded any sort of power (economic or politico-administrative)—could exact reprisals.[7] Removing vote counting from their local base effectively suppressed one of the means of control they exercised over the local voters. This decision was reversed in the late 1970s under pressure from local notables of all the parties, but the Election Commission reimposed a similar *modus operandi* in 1996.

Impersonation and voter identification

The Election Commission also sought to reduce sources of fraud regarding voter identification. The system in place in the 1950s consisted of marking the index finger of the left hand of those who had voted to prevent them from voting more than once. From the outset this procedure proved to be unreliable.[8] After the 1957 elections identity cards (at that point not obligatory) were considered as a solution. The experiment was first attempted in Calcutta, where the administration decided to photograph voters at their own homes, keeping one photo for the electoral roll and putting the other on the identity card. The operation failed three times out of eight: women refused to be photographed and many voters could not be found at home. The cost of the operation was also exorbitant. The only improvement, in 1962, consisted in authorising any polling station official (either independent or from a political party) to question the identity of a voter, at a cost of a deposit of 2 rupees with the president of the polling station (Election Commission, 1965: 73). A further step was taken in the 1971 elections, when the Election Commission recommended the appointment of women officials in voting stations where

---

7 On the victimisation of 'deviant' Untouchable voters by upper castes in Uttar Pradesh, see Maheshwari (1980: 99).

8 In 1957 the idea of replacing ink by a smallpox vaccination whose scar would long remain visible was envisaged (Election Commission, 1959: 106). This suggestion is revealing of the confusion surrounding the official view of electoral activity in India: it is seen as a sign of civic duty, as are vaccinations.

veiled women were numerous (essentially in Muslim neighbourhoods), which facilitated identity checks (Election Commission, 1972: 75). For the 1980 elections the identity card system was introduced on an experimental basis in the state of Sikkim. However, the citizens proved largely suspicious and only 70 per cent of the population of this very small state were registered. Yet the Election Commission still hopes to generalise this system. To try and overcome the distrust of Indian citizens the Commission has proposed that the same card should serve as a social security card, ration card, university admission card and hiring card and for the registry or sale of real estate (Election Commission, 1980: 37). The efforts to make the cards attractive are revealing of the suspicion aroused by the state (which is primarily viewed as a tax-collecting entity in a country where tax evasion is widespread). Above all it confirms the lack of differentiation of separate domains of the public sphere: voting is no more the foundation of citizenship than any other aspect of social life.

The Election Commission has thus in general striven to promote the secret ballot and a safe voting process free of external influence. Its concern for rigour, its perfectionism even, are evident in some very sophisticated recommendations and measures: for instance, because the stamp used to mark ballot papers sometimes left a trace next to another symbol if the paper was folded before the ink dried, a new stamp was introduced in 1971, designed with lines curving in a clock-wise fashion, which permitted the correct mark to be distinguished from any possible imprint (Election Commission, 1972: 202). Other signs of the same attention to detail are evident: polling booths were to be installed, where possible, in public buildings with a courtyard of at least 20 square metres (Election Commission, 1980: 69); polling stations had to offer a waiting line reserved for women; it was recommended that the sale of alcohol be forbidden on the day of the election; and the Election Commission regularly published its advice to voters on posters and in newspapers. Nonetheless there was an obvious contrast between the efforts of the Election Commission to guarantee conditions for reasoned and independent voting, uncompromised by any faults of form, and the actual conditions surrounding the act of voting.

CASTE-ISM, COMMUNALISM AND FRAUD

In the West the act of voting has gradually become more individualistic in nature. Dalton and Wattenberg (1993: 212–13) convincingly argue that there has been 'a shift away from the previous style of decision-making based on social group and/or party cues towards a more individualised and inwardly oriented style of political choice. Instead of depending upon party élites and reference groups, more citizens now attempt to deal with the complexities of politics and make their own political decisions.'

In India, only in the Westernised circles of the largest cities can voting really be considered, sometimes, a personal act.

The myth of the Indian individual voter—or the invention of the rational collective voter

While doing fieldwork in India on the 1980 elections James Manor came to the conclusion:

> ... most rural dwellers seem to have decided how to vote not out of excitement or inspiration by any individual leader, but after careful, and in a great many cases, sceptical deliberation. These deliberations tended to be a group activity, and voting decisions appear in an overwhelming number of cases to have been taken collectively, not individually. A large majority of these choices were very strongly, usually decisively, influenced by 'opinion leaders' who were very different figures from the powerful landed magnates who once used intimidation to dictate to villagers at elections. They tended to be people with a secondary or university education and some appreciation of the workings of government and the legal system. They were very often people who had assisted villagers in dealing with supra-local authority in some way, whether in minor matters like filling in forms or in more serious cases defending villagers' interests in disputes or in gaining them a small share of government largesse. Many opinion leaders lived in or travelled often to towns in the vicinity of the village. They were often school teachers, clerks, voluntary association and co-operative society workers, development board members or employees or—apparently less often—small town lawyers. (Manor, 1983: 98)

This long quote is revealing of two phenomena. First, it testifies to the emancipation of the villagers from the ascendancy that local notables (landlords, money-lenders etc.) exerted over them for three decades after India's independence in the framework of a Congress-dominated clientelistic system. In 1980 this development was mature enough because of the impact of positive discrimination policies and the Green Revolution, as I have shown elsewhere.[9] Second, Manor's analysis is a good illustration of the persisting tendency of political scientists to overlook the role of ascriptive identities in political phenomena, such as the act of voting. Certainly some 'opinion leaders' sometimes led villages to vote *en bloc* for the same party or candidate in order to create a special relationship with the local representative in the assembly. Subrata Mitra (1979: 288–9) recalls that in 1974 three villages of Orissa where he was doing fieldwork 'had coordinated their electoral strategies', an experience which 'had shown them the benefits of making a deal whereby they pooled votes and then shared out resources'. But, for the most part, the collective decision of voting is increasingly determined by collective considerations linked to membership of a caste or a religious community.

9 Jaffrelot (2003).

Religious communities tend more and more to withdraw into themselves when it comes to voting. Muslims have traditionally preferred to vote for representatives from their own community, to ensure representation in Parliament and in the legislative assemblies. They have been especially good at developing a 'tactical vote'. Though they represent, according to the 2001 census, 12.12 per cent of the Indian population, they play a major role in 75 Lok Sabha constituencies (out of 545), where they are concentrated and even, in a few of them, in a majority. This 'tactical vote' has been developed in order to cope with the growing threat posed by the Hindu nationalist Bharatiya Janata Party (BJP). From the early 1990s the Muslims' motto became 'Vote for the strongest anti-BJP candidate' (Fazl, 1996: 19). In some states they have found relevant parties for implementing such a strategy. In Uttar Pradesh (UP), where they represented 20–50 per cent of the voters in 23 constituencies out of 85 in the 1990s, the Muslims have tended to join hands with the Samajwadi Party (SP) of Mulayam Singh Yadav, a low caste Hindu leader, to fight against the BJP. Yadav captured power in 2003 partly because of the Muslims' support. In 2004 62 per cent of the UP Muslims voted for the SP, according to the exit-poll survey of the Centre for the Study of Developing Societies (CSDS).[10]

The same phenomenon holds true for castes. All parties examine the caste composition of a constituency before appointing their candidates. The party leaders tend to select their candidates from the locally dominant caste, that is, the one that is the most numerous (though rarely in the majority); however, it can also be tactically wise to choose someone of another caste who will attract the votes of all the less numerous castes, who may be hostile to the dominant caste. These strategies reflect a larger phenomenon: in many cases, within the sub-caste (the local members of a caste), the vote is subject to deliberation. In Uttar Pradesh G.K. Lieten (1996: 1412) noticed that among the Jats—one of the state's dominant castes—'the vote is decided collectively, according to the general tendency in the Jat *viradari* [local sub-caste].' Lieten even shows that in 1991 the Jats delinked their vote to the state assembly and their vote to the Lok Sabha in order to keep the two main factions of the caste happy: the Jats decided to vote for the Bharatiya Janata Party in the general elections, and for the Congress in the state elections.

Voting appears here to be both a collective and a rational act. Though external influence is still at play, it no longer comes from traditional power sources; it makes itself felt through the advice that the group in question has sought in order to vote in its own best interests. The array of measures implemented by the Election Commission to guarantee a

---

[10] The main results of the CSDS exit poll were published in *The Hindu* supplement 'How India Voted', 20 May 2004. On Uttar Pradesh, see p. AE-5.

secret and reasoned vote has promoted the development not of an individual rational voter but of a collective and rational voter. However, one
must go a step further by looking simultaneously at the two conclusions
we drew from Manor's quote. Indeed, the procedures implemented so
strictly by the Election Commission for creating an *individual voter* exerting his free will are largely responsible for the political emancipation
of the lower castes and their capacity to exert *collective voting*. This
paradoxical outcome is well illustrated by many testimonies—including that of Viramma, a woman of the Pariah caste (the largest caste of
Untouchables in Tamil Nadu) from Pondicherry. To begin with she voted
for the Communist party, but the local notable, the 'Grand Reddi', came
to know about it and she had to vote for him. She explained this shift to
the Communist candidate:

'The party has good ideas, but I've got children to feed. I need work, my son does
as well. All my family are serfs at the Reddiar's and we eat the *kuj* he gives us.
I depend on him completely. I have to run to his house to borrow when we've
got nothing to eat, or when we have to celebrate an important event. I don't want
to provoke his anger and we must vote for him.' (Viramma and Racine, 1997:
263)

The Communist local leader replied that all he asked her was that one
person in the family give him his vote. Viramma's family acted accordingly and the whole Untouchable neighbourhood where she lived did
the same. As a result the area received electricity, running water and
ration cards thanks to the intervention of the Grand Reddi, their patron
who was returned repeatedly from their constituency. This clientelistic
arrangement translated into ritual-like attitudes and material gratifica-
tions. For instance, before the elections the Grand Reddi distributed fake
ballot papers on which his name and election symbols were highlighted
and then organised a function for 'his' electors: 'There was a big party, a
meal for all the voters and loudspeakers playing music. It was like a wedding!' (Viramma and Racine, 1997: 274) In addition, the Grand Reddi
distributed saris to the women voters (and probably alcohol to the men).
Gradually, however, the patron-client relationships loosened because the
dependents, like Viramma, realised the act of voting was secret:

'We had five parties at one time. The ploughmen's party [that is the party whose
election symbol was a ploughman] gave twenty rupees and a bottle of brandy;
the two leaves party twenty-five rupees and a very brightly coloured factory
sari; the cow and the calf party twenty-five rupees and some groundnut oil; the
spinning wheel party fifteen rupees, and another one gave fifteen as well. We tell
them all we'll vote for them and we take their money. But anyway, everybody's
only got one vote...' (Viramma and Racine, 1997: 275)

However, those who paid for but did not receive the votes of the Untouchables could find out so long as the ballot papers were scrutinised at

the local level. Hence the assaults against the recalcitrant Untouchables' neighbourhoods that candidates who had lost sometimes launched in retaliation.[11] Matters changed when the ballot papers polled in a segment started to be mixed and made into bundles for the purpose of counting at the district level. Then the secret ballot enabled the Untouchables to vote for whom they wanted, but they did it as groups, not as individuals.

The Dalits and the lower castes indeed prefer to remain united in order to use their demographic weight to act as interest groups during elections. In Uttar Pradesh, for instance, the Chamars—shoe makers who form the largest Untouchable caste—support the Bahujan Samaj Party (BSP) almost unanimously. In 2004 71 per cent of the Dalits voted for the BSP (according to a very reliable opinion poll) while 72 per cent of the Yadavs, a caste of cowherds, supported the Samajwadi Party. In Bihar 77 per cent of the Yadavs voted for another regional party, the Rashtriya Janata Dal, in 2004.[12] Naturally voters claim they vote according to programmes, but one of the most determining factors is caste and community. In fact the upper castes also tend to vote *en bloc* for 'their' parties. In 2004 77 per cent of the Vaishyas (merchant caste) voted for the BJP in UP. As a result the Congress could not remain the dominant 'catch-all party' that it was in the 1950s–1960s. It continues to attract voters from different sections of society, but not to the same extent.

Indians tend not to vote as individual citizens but as members of religious minorities or caste groups, be they from the upper or from the lower castes. However, the two last categories must not be bracketed together because they are not on the same footing: if the lower castes can vote for the candidates of their liking, it is because of the procedures established by the Constitution of India and the Election Commission, even though these rules of the game were introduced for promoting an individual voter. The Untouchables' collective act of voting for candidates of their liking is really the unintended consequence of procedures designed for other purposes.

Fraud and violence

The sophistication of the measures taken by the Election Commission to surround voting with the best possible guarantees (as far as a secret ballot and voter identification are concerned) seemed also out of place for years when contrasted with the basic conditions under which elections are held, in terms of fraud and violence around the polling stations. While the act of voting itself may be surrounded by guarantees, the same could not be said for ballot boxes until the 1990s. The most common electoral fraud (for those candidates or parties who sense, on election day, that victory is

11 It happened once in Viramma's village (Viramma and Racine, 1997: 278–9).
12 *The Hindu* supplement 'How India Votes', 20 May 2004, pp. AE-5, AE-6.

not assured) consisted for a long time in hiring the services of an armed gang to grab one or more ballot boxes in a constituency. In 1971 the Commission counted eleven acts of 'booth capturing', including eight in Bihar, a state known for political violence (Election Commission, 1972: 81). In 1980 nearly sixty polling stations—including twenty-one in Bihar, twelve in Uttar Pradesh and nineteen in Kashmir—saw similar incidents or faced tensions that led to the cancellation of voting (Election Commission, 1980: 113–14). In addition to these practices there were often incidents around polling stations, such as clashes between party activists and unrest aimed at interrupting the voting procedure. In 1989 electoral violence caused a hundred deaths. In 1991 460 detachments of the Central Paramilitary Reserve Force were deployed around polling stations after campaign violence had already claimed seventy-five victims, including fifty in Bihar.[13]

The new head of the Election Commission, T.N. Seshan, then reacted with proper firmness. He decided to allow new elections to take place in polling stations that had fallen victim to fraud, in a more systematic fashion than in the past. In 1991 new elections took place in 2,614 voting stations (1,177 in Bihar and 876 in Uttar Pradesh, the two states most subject to political violence). Then the Election Commission did not hesitate to postpone an election in order to deploy additional police personnel to reduce the risk of booth capturing and other forms of violence which generally occurred around the polling stations. In 1996 the Election Commission sent 1,500 observers (an average of three per constituency) to supervise the polls.[14] Approximately 600,000 policemen were deployed to enforce law and order around the polling booths, which were manned by 1.5 million agents of the state, supervising the polls. More than 300,000 people were arrested as a preventive measure (125,000 in Uttar Pradesh[15] and 59,000 in Madhya Pradesh, where 87,000 arms were seized[16]). These measures enabled the state to control unrest around the booths, as elections were countermanded and then reorganised in 1,056 polling booths, as against 1,670 in 1989. A little less than half of them (471) were in Bihar, 231 in Andhra Pradesh, 96 in Assam, 31 in Rajasthan, 43 in Uttar Pradesh and 22 in Orissa.[17] Furthermore the number of violent incidents at the polls declined from 3,363 in 1991 to 2,450 in 1998 and the number of deaths from 272 in 1991 to 213 in 1996, 65 in 1998 and 32 in 1999, including 29 people who were killed in landmine

13 *National Mail*, 8 May 1991.
14 Video cameras were used to film the election campaign in order to exert psychological pressure on candidates and their supporters (*Economic Times*, 14 March 1996).
15 *National Mail*, 2 May 1996.
16 *Madhya Pradesh Chronicle*, 7 May 1996
17 *Madhya Pradesh Chronicle*, 4 and 5 May 1996; *Times of India*, 5 May 1996; and *National Mail*, 30 April 1996.

blasts engineered by Naxalites in Bihar,[18] and 18 in 2004.[19] Election-related violence is geographically concentrated, mainly in Bihar and in Uttar Pradesh. The strict policy of the Election Commission was partly responsible for a higher participation rate (+ 10 points in Uttar Pradesh), the security around the booths attracting more voters, especially those of the Scheduled Castes, whom the party thugs could not intimidate quite so easily as before. A fifty-year-old man from the caste of the Dhobis (washermen) recounts how things have changed in his village in Bihar:

'When I first tried to vote some 30 years ago, I was told by them [the upper castes of the village] that I and other members of my community did not have votes. We realised later that they were casting our votes for their candidate. Then we resolved that we would cast our votes. Initially we used to go to the polling booth only to be beaten up and were forced to run away. But our resolve grew stronger with each election and we started reacting to their physical assaults in their own coin. I have been voting without getting beaten up in the last four elections [which include both Assembly and Lok Sabha polls since 1996].' (Quoted in Ramakrishnan, 2004)

ARE ELECTRONIC VOTING MACHINES GOOD FOR DEMOCRACY?

The Indian culture of voting underwent a significant change in 2004 with the systematic use of electronic voting machines (EVMs) during the general elections. The Election Commission first contemplated instituting an electronic voting system in 1977. The experiment, conducted in several by-elections from 1982 onwards, was abandoned in 1989 for reasons of cost (Butler, Lahiri and Roy, 1989: 16) and because of the objections of the opposition, who feared being tricked by the government. The Election Commission nonetheless announced, after the 1991 elections, that this method of voting would enter into force for the next elections. The whole process was delayed but by the end of the decade, in 1999, EVMs were introduced in forty-six Lok Sabha constituencies spread over seventeen states. And in 2004 they dislodged ballot papers everywhere. This new technology obliged the parties to adjust and even to reinvent their campaigns: they even ordered model EVMs to conduct demonstrations of their functioning during their house-to-house visits.

Indeed the citizens needed to be initiated into this new act of voting. According to the website of the Election Commission of India, 'instead of issuing a ballot paper, the Polling Officer in-charge of the Control Unit will press the Ballot Button. This will enable the voter to cast his vote

18 *The Hindu*, 30 August 1999 and *National Mail*, 19 September 1999.
19 Among these eighteen casualties—all of which occurred during the first phase of polling—were seven Maoist militants and four paramilitary personnel in charge of a polling station (*The Hindu*, 21 April 2004).

by pressing the blue button on the Balloting Unit against the candidate and symbol of his choice.'[20] The symbol system has been retained by the Election Commission for an obvious reason: to cope with the persistently high rate of illiteracy. This modernisation of the act of voting has been hailed 'as a bold and progressive decision' in the media. But things may not be as positive as the zealots of this technological modernisation expected. According to the Election Commission, the EVM has four main advantages:

The EVMs will reduce booth capturing in the case of 'miscreants intimidating the polling personnel and stamping the ballot papers on the symbol and escaping in a matter of minutes ... because the EVMs are programmed in such a way that the machines will record only five votes in a minute.'

The EVMs will dispense the state from the printing of millions of ballot papers since 'only one ballot paper is required for fixing on the Balloting Unit at each polling station instead of one ballot paper for each individual elector.'

The EVMs will quicken the pace of polling since the voter has simply to press the button next to the symbol and name of his or her chosen candidate for registering his vote, instead of having to 'unfold the ballot paper, mark his preference, fold it again, go to the place where the ballot box is kept and drop it in the box'. Because of this long process, in the 1990s the voters queuing to cast their votes were sometimes counted in hundreds.[21] The EVMs also make the counting of votes faster.

Use of EVMs will reduce the number of invalid votes due to the stamping in between two candidates on the ballot paper. According to the Election Commission, 'in every General Election, the number of invalid votes is more important than the winning margin between the winning candidate and the second candidate, in a number of constituencies' (In Karnataka on an average there were 30,000 invalid votes for each parliamentary constituency and 5,000 for each Assembly constituency [Raghava, 2004]).

While the EVMs were supposed to go some way toward remedying some of the most blatant frauds, like booth capturing, in fact during the 2004 elections gangs were able to take away some of the machines. Snatching of EVMs was especially prominent—though residual in terms of numbers—in states where Maoist groups tried to enforce some boycott of the elections: Andhra Pradesh, Bihar, Jharkhand, Chhattisgarh etc. For instance, in Andhra Pradesh Maoist activists from the People's War Party 'kidnapped' two EVMs.[22]

Besides, the EVMs introduced new kinds of fraud. For instance, the ballot papers, which are inserted underneath the machines' glass-panes,

---

20 Election Commission of India, 'Frequently asked questions—Electronic Voting Machines (EVMs)' (http://www.eci.gov.in/faq/elecvtmach.htm).

21 Some parties have been known to send underage activists, who cannot in fact vote, to swell the queues in polling stations where candidates are vulnerable, in the hope of making legitimate voters lose patience and leave before voting.

22 'EVMs become the target', *The Hindu*, 27 April 2004.

with the names and symbols of the candidates—different in each constituency—had been printed in such a way, in some parts of Andhra Pradesh, that the election symbols of the Congress and other opposition parties were unduly hazy and small in size compared to the ruling party, the Telugu Desam Party. As a result, and in reaction to complaints lodged by Congress supporters, the Election Commission had to withdraw 45,000 'ballot papers'.[23] In addition to these defects the use of sophisticated technology, instead of reassuring the ordinary citizens, aroused new fears. In Andhra Pradesh, again, 'opposition parties, especially the Congress, and citizen groups' questioned the safety of votes recorded by the EVMs:

> Their worst fear is about the software part of the machine which, they allege, can be 'pre-set' or influenced by polling officials or anybody for that matter to favour a party/candidate. The Congress leaders have been contending that the machine, depending on the type of pre-setting, can ensure every fourth vote being cast to a rival party, say, Telugu Desam, and open up to vulnerability after ensuring that a certain number of votes go to different parties. (Rao, 2004)

Unsurprisingly a scientific innovation, instead of inspiring trust, is perceived as opaque and conducive to manipulations. However, in addition to irrational fears the EVMs are an objective cause for concern for one reason at least: the counting of the votes is now made at the level of the polling station. As a result voting patterns EVM-wise and, therefore, polling station-wise are revealed in the EVMs themselves at the time of counting of votes, and are known by the contestants immediately through their agents since they take part in the counting operations. The victimisation of hostile voters—including Untouchables—by frustrated candidates with muscle power may once again become the order of the day, all the more so as EVMs can record a maximum of 3,840 votes. Today the total number of electors in a polling station is even less—it does not exceed 1,500—which means it is very easy to identify the voting pattern of very precise groups, who can therefore be readily harassed, except in the many regions where low-caste people and Dalits have organised themselves.

India developed an electoral procedure to overcome the widespread problem of illiteracy: the symbol system, perfected over the course of many elections, which allows voters to cast their ballot under conditions guaranteeing independence, adequate information and secrecy. This procedure had unintended consequences since it contributed to institutionalising the party system, which is an important illustration of the effects

---

[23] 'EC withdraws 45,000 "ballot papers"', *The Hindu*, 16 April 2004.

the procedural aspects of elections can have. But the perfection, or even refinement, of the electoral procedure promoted by the Election Commission and inspired by Western practices has had other unintended consequences: while the whole array of measures taken by the state aimed at ensuring an individual act of voting, they also enabled the crystallisation of a collective vote among the lower strata of society, including the Dalits who sometimes dared to vote against the local notables only because the ballot was strictly secret.

By Western, liberal standards the community or caste dimension of voting contradicts democracy since this political system relies on the free will of individual citizens. Certainly members of the group—women for instance—may be forced to vote for candidates they would not have selected, but otherwise the collective dimension of voting strengthens democracy inasmuch as community-based or caste-based aggregations of individual preferences enable dominated religious minorities and lower castes to gain some leverage in the public sphere. This ethnicisation of politics is in fact a major factor in the democratisation of Indian democracy.[24] Similarly one need not worry too much about the degradation of the electoral procedures given the growing watchfulness of the Election Commission. This vigilance has already borne fruit, as the declining intensity of violence at the time of elections testifies. However, the new EVMs may not be the panacea for remedying the plague of booth capturing, and they may even help local notables to regain their lost influence over recalcitrant voters—though such a regression may only happen in the few places where the lower castes are not yet organised.

Bharadvaja, B., 1972, 'Election Symbols in Politics', *The Indian Political Science Review*, vol. 6, no. 1 (October).

Butler, D., A. Lahiri and P. Roy, 1989, *India Decides: Elections 1952–1989*, New Delhi: Living Media.

Dalton, R.J. and M.P. Wattenberg, 1993, 'The Not So Simple Act of Voting' in A.W. Finifter (ed.), *Political Science: The State of the Discipline*, Washington, DC: APSA.

Election Commission, 1959, *Report on the Second General Elections in India, 1957*, New Delhi.

——, 1965, *Report on the Third General Elections in India, 1962*, vol. 1, *Narrative*, New Delhi.

——, 1972, *Report on the Fifth General Elections, India, 1971–72. Narrative and Reflective Part*, New Delhi.

——, 1978, *Report on the Sixth General Elections to the Lok Sabha*, New Delhi.

---

24 This is one of the main arguments of my last book: Jaffrelot (2003).

———, 1980, *Report on the General Elections to the House of the People*, vol. 1, *Narrative*, Jaipur: Government Central Press.

Fazl, O., 1996, 'Muslims need better Strategy for next Polls', *Radiance*, no. 2 (June).

Graham, B., 1983, 'Electoral Symbols and Party Identification in Indian Politics' in P. Lyon and J. Manor (eds), *Transfer and Transformation: Political Institutions in the New Commonwealth*, Leicester University Press.

Hauser, W. and W. Singer, 1986, 'The Democratic Rite: Celebration and Participation in the Indian Elections', *Asian Survey*, vol. 26, no. 9 (September), pp. 951–6.

Jaffrelot, C., 2002, 'Indian Democracy: The Rule of Law on Trial', *India Review*, vol. 1, no. 1 (January), pp. 77–121.

———, 2003, *India's Silent Revolution: The Rise of the Lower Castes in North Indian Politics*, London: Hurst.

Lieten, G.K., 1996, 'Inclusive View of Religion: A Rural Discourse in Uttar Pradesh', *Economic and Political Weekly*, no. 8 (June).

Maheshwari, A.C., 1980, 'Uttar Pradesh: Rigging in Practice', *Economic and Political Weekly*, no. 19 (January).

Manor, M., 1983, 'The Electoral Process amid Awakening and Decay: Reflections on the Indian General Elections of 1980' in P. Lyon and J. Manor (eds), *Transfer and Transformation: Political Institutions in the New Commonwealth*, Leicester University Press.

Mitra, S.K., 1979, 'Ballot Box and Local Power: Elections in an Indian Village', *Journal of Commonwealth and Comparative Politics*, vol. 3, no. 17 (November).

Raghava, M., 2004, 'EVMs May Eliminate Invalid Votes, Vhange Poll Outcome', *The Hindu*, 9 March.

Ramakrishnan, V., 2004, 'A Dalit Village's Struggle to Vote', *The Hindu*, 26 March.

Rao, M., 2004, 'EVMs Continue to Raise Hackles', *The Hindu*, 20 April.

Viramma, J. and J.-L. Racine, 1997, *Viramma: Life of an Untouchable*, London and New York: Verso.

Viraraghavan, V.C., 1956, 'Election Law and Procedure' in R.V. Krishna Ayyar (ed.), *All India Election Guide*, Madras: Oriental Publishers.

IMAGINING ELECTIONS

MODERNITY, MEDIATION AND THE SECRET BALLOT IN LATE-COLONIAL TANGANYIKA[1]

Peter Pels

In September 1952 three British administrators organised the first election by secret ballot to be held in the chiefdom of Uluguru in Eastern Tanganyika. Their experiment was part of the post-war attempt to move towards political modernisation and economic development, also known as the 'second colonial occupation'. In the context of the Uluguru Land Usage Scheme—a development project aimed at soil conservation, resettlement of the population and improvement of local agriculture—British administrators tried to modernise indirect rule by introducing local government. In his report on the 'democratic progress' achieved by the election of a leader for the Luguru subchiefdom of Mgeta by secret ballot, District Officer Alan Linton intimated that such political innovation faced serious obstacles. The system of the secret ballot was, he thought, not something most Waluguru understood easily. Seeking to put across the meaning and mechanics of this technology of election to Waluguru, Linton and his subordinates had recourse to theatrical performance: in a 'short but very lively sketch' they impersonated a 'moronic voter being instructed in the system of voting by a somewhat resigned Administrative Officer'. Afterwards, in commenting on the 'highlights' of this election, Linton singled out:

The man who had never heard of any of the three main claimants [to the position of subchief]; the man who imitated faithfully Mr Duff's original imitation of a moronic voter; [and] the woman who brought her husband's tax ticket and, after gazing longingly at the recording officer, finally cast her vote according to her husband's instructions, resisting the temptation to behave as in another District's election and vote for Bwana Shauri [the Swahili term for a British District Officer].[2]

1 The research for this paper was made possible by the Netherlands Foundation for the Advancement of Tropical Research (WOTRO, grant no. WG52-699) in the context of its programme, 'Globalization and the Construction of Communal Identities'. It encompassed fieldwork in Tanzania in the summers of 1996 and 1997 and archival work in Dar es Salaam, Oxford and London, and also relies to a large extent on material gathered in the context of an earlier project (Pels, 1999).
2 Tanzania National Archives (TNA) 26/238/H/1: Linton for DC to PC, 8.10.52.

Like his fellow-officials, Linton had no doubt that the ballot implied democratic progress, and he interpreted the lack of appreciation by Waluguru as illiteracy and ignorance, marking the conservatism of the 'traditional' Waluguru.

Surprisingly those 'conservative' Waluguru—in so far as they were allowed to vote—flocked to the polling booths only six years later, in September 1958, to vote for candidates for seats in the Legislative Council, in the first territorial election by secret ballot in Tanganyika. Under the influence of the rapid changes forced on the British administration by international agencies and the rise of the African nationalist movement, the Legislative Council elections were in many ways the turning point of the decolonisation process because they gave the Tanganyika African National Union (TANU), the official opposition party, an overwhelming majority in the Council. Waluguru, and their fellow-voters in the constituency of Eastern Province, turned up in large numbers (74 per cent of registered voters).[3] They elected the TANU president, the late Julius Nyerere—later, of course, the first president of newly independent Tanganyika—into office with a three-quarters majority over his opponent Patrick Kunambi, the Deputy Chief of the Luguru local government. Beforehand doubts whether the African electorate was already sufficiently responsible to acquire the vote were widespread among colonial administrators, but the election went off smoothly. Official and expert comments on the introduction of this mode of democratic representation spoke of a 'watershed' from local government to centralised nationalism, and remained mostly silent about the obstacles that ignorance, illiteracy and tradition might possibly have put in the way of successful implementation of the method of election by secret ballot (Hucks, 1960; Young, 1959).

The attitude of the British administrators during the first event shows how they interpreted it in terms of tradition and conservatism obstructing modernity's progress, or conversely, as modernity disrupting a way of life that—as many argued—was not yet 'ripe' for a modern political form like the secret ballot. In contrast their attitude was drastically altered after the events of 1958: now British administrators (and American observers relying on their testimony) saw successful modernisation—in terms of the capture of the rural areas by centralising agencies like the victorious African nationalist party—brought about, in part, by the modern apparatus of party politics and campaigning, and the smooth introduction of the secret ballot as a technique for registering popular favour. Taken together these distinct attitudes form a typically modernist pat-

---

3 In the 1952 elections for the Mgeta subchief less than 20 per cent of the enfranchised taxpayers showed up—as one of the officials remarked, not much less than in the average English local government elections.

tern: a supposition of two diametrically opposed entities—tradition and
modernity—in which the transition from the first to the second is made
by the introduction of the techniques and forms of organisation of the
latter, to which the former can only put up obstructions. In the imagination of officials like Alan Linton, modernisation would be successful if
it was not hampered by 'local' tradition and ignorance; this implied that
whatever went wrong with modernisation could not be the fault of modernity. In this way modernity was immaculately conceived: it produced
itself by the introduction of its own institutions, without outside help. As
Bruno Latour (1993) has argued, modern thought postulates purified categories, but neglects the mediations and translations that produce these
categories. Yet we need these mediations to understand how in only six
years' time Waluguru successfully adopted these new political forms for
their own political goals.

FROM INTROVERSION TO EXTRAVERSION

One way of thinking about such translations is to allow for the possibility
of divergent cultural interpretations of something like the secret ballot.
This is what struck me when—doing research for a different project
(Pels, 1999)—I first came across Alan Linton's description of the 1952
experiment with the secret ballot in Mgeta in the Tanzanian national
archives. I felt that, contrary to Linton's assessment of conservatism,
the individualised secrecy of the ballot might have been perceived by
Waluguru in culturally different but nevertheless pragmatic, creative and
rational ways. Despite all the political changes wrought by the colonial
period, Luguru political routines still associated secrecy with the privilege of closely-knit groups of initiates, power-holders who were supposed to guard politically sensitive communications against premature
public discussion and interference by outsiders. Indigenous political
culture was marked by initiation into a group of politically responsible
or authoritative adults. During initiation one embodied political responsibility through the receipt of secret information, instead of empowering
someone else by parting with and thereby disembodying one's individual
secret vote.

Initially I merely guessed at what Waluguru thought about these matters, but it seemed plausible to allow for such potential cultural incom-
mensurability and to reinterpret Linton's 'highlights' of the 1952 local
government election in Mgeta in a different, subaltern way. The man who
never heard of the three claimants may have doubted or even suspected
the way in which the administrators established or denied the claim of
African candidates to stand for election. The faithful imitation of the
imitation of a moronic voter may be seen as an expression of uncertainty
about the kind of performance expected by colonial rulers: one might,

for instance, be punished in the same way as one would when failing to pay tax. Lastly, the woman's hesitation to vote for Bwana Shauri can be interpreted as an indication of resistance to the colonial predicament by Luguru women, who had lost much of their political power by the implementation of indirect rule, who were not represented by themselves but by tax-paying husbands, and who still had to vote for only male candidates put forward by only male lineage heads and approved by only male British officials (see Pels, 1996a). This raised the issue of what kind of trajectories of local interpretation and political practice enabled the shift from reluctance to participate in the secret ballot towards the widespread success of the 1958 elections. Modernity—in the form of the secret ballot or other forms of novel political organisation—might have been perceived and enacted by Waluguru in ways quite different from those imagined by the colonial administrators. In fact this lack of cultural reciprocity seemed, at first, a sufficient explanation of the latter's inability to think of a transition from tradition to modernity except by a miraculous leap out of a state of 'ignorance'. This was the basis on which I formulated the core questions of a research proposal in 1995, which sought to reconstruct Luguru trajectories of interpreting the secret ballot, to explain why the 1958 election went off so smoothly.

When researching these questions in Uluguru in 1996 and 1997 I was sorely disappointed, in the first place because the memories of participants in the elections turned out to be very erratic, and I had to reconstruct the trajectory by which the secret ballot was adopted by Waluguru on the basis of circumstantial evidence rather than direct testimony. But I also discovered that my own research expectations were flawed: they started from the essentialising assumption that because the secret ballot could be experienced as alien by the Waluguru on whom this political form was foisted, they therefore should have interpreted or imagined it in 'their own' discourse. Put differently, I implicitly assumed that Waluguru would deal with a new political form in a culturally introverted, 'local' way. I only later learned from Jean-François Bayart that many African political practices are, instead, characterised by extraversion (Bayart, 1993: 20ff.): a pragmatic eagerness to use and experiment with novel and alien forms. Waluguru were actively and consciously globalising themselves: they eagerly adopted technologies like the car and the radio, and modern political forms like the political party, the cooperative production society and the secret ballot, and fitted them into their cultural routines even though they often lacked a clear and conscious articulation of how these particular forms operated. I failed to consider that possibility because I assumed that the adoption of the secret ballot by Waluguru was determined by 'local' interpretations: a postcolonial version of the colonial administrator's assumption that the failure to adopt the secret ballot by Waluguru was caused by 'local' conservatism. To understand the spread of the secret ballot I had to move away from 'culture' in terms of some kind of 'native point of view' and towards a less conscious and more pragmatic cultural interaction—one that was more analogous to the way one would describe the spread of cars, radios or any other technology. Yet the culturally 'thin' world of modern technology and discipline was, of course, also parochial, and as my research progressed I came to see that this technological parochialism, however globalised, could never completely escape the exigencies of the culturally specific situations in which it was deployed.

TECHNOLOGY AND PERFORMANCE

The advantage of thinking about the secret ballot as analogous to a technology is not only that it allows one to think of its unreflective, pragmatic use as a relatively autonomous element of colonial and postcolonial culture: it also reflects the mode of thinking of the colonial administrators themselves. Western interpretations of the introduction of a new technology usually waver between two positions: the 'neo-Luddism' that opposes the technology because its introduction to a novel situation is seen to be disruptive and disastrous, and the 'technophilia' that, conversely, expects that its introduction will effect immaculately conceived and miraculous transformations for the better.[4] The distinction between neo-Luddites and technophiles exactly replicates the two attitudes to the secret ballot voiced by British administrators in the two cases recorded earlier: the fear (in 1952, but also later) that Waluguru were not ripe for democratic institutions and that the latter would disrupt their life; and the optimistic faith that the secret ballot would help centralise politics and overcome local obstacles to the transition towards democratic progress (voiced after the 1958 operation). This is no coincidence: these latter interpretations of the introduction of the secret ballot arose at the same time that a global discourse of 'development' emerged which expected miraculous transformations by technological innovation in the newly invented 'Third World'—a discourse that was, therefore, equally based on a kind of technophilia (Escobar, 1995: 36).

However, emphasis on technology would fail to address a crucial site of cultural contest identified above: the secret ballot's particular notion of secrecy, which seemed difficult to relate to the practices of secrecy employed by Waluguru in their initiatory forms of politics. While technology seems to promise a kind of commodification and instrumentalisation that also allows it to be more easily transferred across cultural boundaries, there seems to be little room within a phenomenology of technological diffusion for the secrecy that characterises both the secret

4 For an elaboration of the distinction between neo-Luddites and technophiles, see Gordon Graham's discussion of the philosophy of technology (1990: chapter 1).

ballot and Luguru politics of initiation. This aspect seems to be better served by emphasising that the secret ballot is also a performance, a public display that, at the same time, produces a secret realm within which proper individuals—voting citizens—should be generated. However, the specific form of individuality generated by the secret ballot is mediated by the cultural background that voters embody. As the contrast between the secrecy of the ballot and the secrecy of initiation suggests, embodied culture and commodified technology may not correspond to each other. By recognising, through a phenomenology of political technology, that the secret ballot is itself a culturally parochial construct, we may be able to move away from the classical attitude of colonial administration and modernisation theory, which regard the political technology introduced as self-evident unless local ignorance and tradition prevent it from being so. By doing so we may be able to show that no form of 'modern' discipline can be realised without engaging with forms of mediation and translation that are, culturally speaking, non- or anti-modern.

These issues might be illustrated briefly first, by discussing some features of the 1958 election entry conditions, the franchise and the procedures of registration in particular; second, by considering the secret ballot as performance, as material culture and as disciplinary mechanism, through the example of the preparations for the 1958 elections; and lastly, by examining how the commodification or technologising of the secret ballot in Uluguru may have resulted in a different appreciation of its role, especially when seen against the background of the lack of an electoral culture and the embodiment of a different, more initiatory and corporate form of political organisation.

FRANCHISE, REGISTRATION AND COLONIAL CULTURE

The franchise for the 1958 elections was limited: just as the franchise for the 1952 elections was restricted to taxpayers, now only Native Authority officials, people earning over sh. 3000/- a year (which was a lot) or people who had finished Standard VIII were allowed to vote: around 1 per cent of the population of Tanganyika. This automatically included all those who had a vested interest in colonial rule (settlers, traders, Native Authorities) and minimised the participation of the less privileged, especially Africans. (However, this did not help in keeping the African nationalists at bay.) A propaganda film showing how to register emphasised the multiracial scheme thought up by the British: all voters had to choose a European, an Asian and an African candidate to represent him (very rarely her) in the Legislative Council. If a voter had not chosen one of these *mataifa matatu* ('three races', but also translatable as 'three tribes' or 'three nations'), the ballot paper would be invalid. This shows one of the principal ways through which an embodied culture of colo-

nialism—expressed as 'race'—cut across the individualised (and therefore; in its statistical aspect, disembodied) performance expected from
modern electoral procedure. As is well known, the African nationalist
party (TANU) vehemently opposed voting by multiracial parity, since
it might mean the party would not be able to profit from the country's
vast African majority; in November 1957, a month before the closing of
the registration procedure, the party's secretary made known that adherents should register anyway, despite the protest against the multiracial
scheme—a move that turned out to be hugely successful.[5]

But it was especially before TANU urged its adherents to register that
the culture of colonialism pervaded the seemingly anonymous registration procedure. People had to register almost a year in advance of the
actual election in September 1958, and this temporal distance from the
actual act of voting itself, and the colonial culture in which one had to
register, made the registration procedure itself difficult to interpret (and
not only for Africans). Although administrators were prohibited from
ordering any prospective voters to register, fears of this were apparently
so habitually voiced by Africans that the Superintendent of Elections had
to stress time and again that there was no obligation to register. Africans
rumoured that filling in the registration form meant voting for the UTP,
the party of European settlers and Native Chiefs (it was a public secret
that UTP was supported by the government). Other people thought registration implied that they had to vote.

The Superintendent of Elections not unnaturally thought that Africans associated registration with taxation, as yet another form of control
with unforeseen but probably nasty consequences (this was, as indicated
above, a likely mode of interpretation in the case of the Mgeta subchiefdom elections in 1952). This interpretation becomes the more likely
given that the African nationalist party was perceived as a rival of the
state (rather than as an entity within the contested public sphere coordinated by the state)—an interpretation that was not only advanced by
African nationalists and their followers, but also by the anxieties of senior colonial officials themselves. This was reinforced by the fact that the
nationalist party also collected money—a commodity that was widely
perceived as alien by Africans and that could easily be interpreted as
a rival tax (in Uluguru most rumours had it that the party would abolish tax after receiving initial financial support from the populace). This
was all the more logical since, for Africans, one's tax chit was, in local
government elections, the marker of being enfranchised for an election
(whether by secret ballot or by other methods, such as lining up behind
one's preferred candidate). In any case, some people at least withdrew

5   TNA 26/L5/70: Hucks to all DCs, 31.7.57; Circular, CS to all PCs and DCs, 20.11.57;
Z.M.M. Mtemvu to Wakuu Wote wa TANU, n.d. [November].

from the registration after having been registered first.[6] Registration for the elections therefore produced much insecurity and doubt about the kinds of demands people had come to expect from what they perceived as a hostile and taxing state. As a North American observer argued, the neutrality which administrators had to maintain while instructing people how to register and vote was 'a change' from their 'usual function' (Young, 1959: 7). For Africans the state had never been neutral and they had little reason to believe the secret ballot would be.

MATERIAL CULTURE, FRONT- AND BACKSTAGE

Yet it was neutral, at least in the more obvious political sense of administrative officials not taking sides or committing fraud. However, that does not mean the secret ballot was culturally innocent. The secret ballot is (part of) a form of enumeration, and like all other forms of enumeration practised by the state, it combines learning about people with justifying state policy and disciplining state subjects (Appadurai, 1996). In the practice of preparing the performance of the secret ballot of 1958 the disciplinary aspect came furthest to the fore. However, it is the secret ballot's material aspect in particular that demonstrates that the public produces the private in a number of ways. The material culture of the secret ballot was made subject to tremendously careful attention: the ballot box should be positioned in view of the polling officer and the polling booth was to be so placed that screens (here of grass or reed or 'any local material') hid the voter's act of marking the ballot paper while openly displaying the voter's back to the polling officer. (This parochial, that is, British, way of constructing a polling booth is in marked contrast to the French polling booth which, rather than being open to official scrutiny, was closed off on all four sides by the use of a curtain, preventing the polling officers from seeing what the voter was doing inside [see Garrigou, 1988: 43]). Public buildings without walls, into which the police could not keep people from peeking, were unsuitable as polling stations. Private houses were 'entirely wrong', because they might be associated with a specific party. Even the space around a building should be kept neutral: printing kanga cloth that said 'vote for TANU'—a kind of dress that was worn particularly by women, whose role in the mobilisation of African nationalism in Tanganyika was crucial (Geiger, 1997)—was allowed, yet it was forbidden to wear these wrap-arounds when coming into the voting arena. Entry into this arena—the polling station and its immediate surroundings—was carefully policed: only voters, candidates

---

6 TNA 26/L5/70: Hucks to PCs Northern, Eastern, Tanga, Western and Southern Highlands Provinces, 30.9.57; Hucks to all PCs and DCs Northern, Eastern, Tanga, Western and Southern Highlands Provinces, 10.10.57; Minutes, 2nd Provincial Meeting of Eastern Province Native Authorities, 4.6.58; TNA 26/L5/72: Kerr to Chief RO, 20.1.58.

and polling staff on duty were to be allowed. Instructions extended to the colours and symbols to be printed on the ballot paper (for the benefit of illiterate voters), what to do with a spoilt ballot paper, and the actions of displaying the sealing of the box and presenting it to the next legally empowered official for transport.[7]

All these instructions worked together to limit the space for voters' agency and independent initiative to a minimum: the only freedom voters were allowed was contained within the secret moment produced by all this discipline, when they were to mark their ballot papers in the isolation of the polling booth—but even there their backs were supervised by the polling officer. In this way the secret ballot produced, if only momentarily, the required privacy of the citizen, marked by its reduction to a single individual function of marking a piece of paper. Yet even in this meticulously orchestrated performance cultural mediations intervened, for in the privacy of the polling booth no voter could escape reading the ballot paper. As we know from literary studies, no reading, of either verbal or visual signs, can be controlled by the author of the signs themselves. Thus even the translation of the names of the candidates on the ballot paper into visual symbols—a hoe, a house, a maize cob—for the benefit of illiterate voters gave (according to many people I spoke to) reasons to vote for the one or the other (the hoe, as an agricultural implement, being the most popular among those who favoured the slogan of the nationalists: *uhuru na kazi*, 'freedom and work').

The secret ballot is identifiable as a carefully orchestrated performance not just by the detail and discipline: it is apparent from its own theatrical language. In Tanganyika the 1958 ballot procedure had to be 'rehearsed' not once but time and again, shown by film, performed in practice, or both, the last rehearsal being on election day, only an hour before the polling station became operative. As we have also seen, the 1952 local government election needed a 'short but lively sketch' to put across the meaning of the ballot. One rehearsal in Tanga confused the elder Africans on whom it was tried out (the younger ones were at work): they mistook it for the actual election. But if people could confuse the imitation with the 'real thing', they could also suspect the real thing of being mere mimicry. When the Superintendent of Elections finally announced that 'the stage is set' and 'the curtains are about to go up', he felt he had to reassure his audience: 'Do not imagine I am behind the stage. I know no more than you do about who the candidates will be.'[8]

---

7 TNA 26/L5/70: Notes for the Guidance of Returning Officers, by G.W.Y. Hucks, 6.2.58; Notes for the Guidance of Presiding Officers, by G.W.Y. Hucks, n.d. [March 1958]; Hucks to PCs and DCs, 14.4.58; Hucks to Organising Secretary General TANU, 26.6.58.

8 TNA 26/L5/70: Notes for the Guidance of Returning Officers, by G.W.Y. Hucks, 6.2.58; Notes for the Guidance of Presiding Officers, by G.W.Y. Hucks, n.d. [March 1958]; Returning Officer Eastern Province to all DCs, 28.3.58; Hucks to PCs and DCs, 23.5.58;

This shows that a performance—including that of the secret ballot—can always create uncertainty about whether what is publicly displayed is the actual thing, and raise the question of whether the performance has not been doctored 'behind the stage' in some way. As the theatrical metaphors show—in evoking a comparison with scripts drawn up elsewhere and realised on stage—we need to acknowledge that in its essence a secret ballot has been doctored behind the stage by state officials, though that does not necessarily mean the result of the election has been doctored as well.

Thus we see that to treat a political form like the secret ballot as a performance immediately implies speculations about the type of operation that has gone on behind the stage to make the performance possible—an operation that in itself produces the space for both speculation about and real occurrence of fraud and deception. We have become disconcertingly familiar with (the accusation of) such secret machinations in the usual Western commentaries on non-Western democratic practices ever since decolonisation. Worse, the second coming of 'democratisation' to Africa in the 1980s has shown that an uncanny amount of creativity can be employed in turning the results of elections—at the levels of party mobilisation, of delimiting the franchise (by 'autochthony'), of the actual act of voting and of manipulating its result—to the rulers' advantage. However, the US Presidential Elections of 2000—especially their results in the state of Florida—show how little of this is peculiarly or essentially 'African'. On the contrary, they confirm that this space of performative uncertainty is inherent in the cultural form of the secret ballot itself; it is part of its modernity as a political technology.

Yet even this observation reinforces a culturalist reading of the secret ballot as a parochial performance, guided by the insight that, however disciplined it is supposed to be, a performance always carries a potential for multiple interpretation and subversion (Fabian, 1990). The secret ballot's performance not only produces a public individuation of electoral choice (with all the attendant possibilities of manipulating what happens backstage), it also generates multiple ways of interpreting what this public appearance means—in terms of power, of being forced to vote for someone one doesn't want to vote for, or in terms of secrecy, of one's act of voting being taken up in a kind of orchestration that invalidates one's voice. More important, this public performance can always potentially turn into a riot, as was usually the case with the ritual subversions in British elections before the introduction of the secret ballot (O'Gorman, 1996: 22–3), or with the elections in the Indonesian city of Solo during the Suharto years (Pemberton, 1986 and this volume). The point to be made here is that such sometimes transgressive ritualisation of elections

---

Hucks to all PCS and DCs, 27.6.58.

did not take place in Tanganyika in 1958, neither on the part of the administrators (who regarded the secret ballot largely as a technical and legal problem, in the commodified and instrumental terms by which one also regards a technology), nor on that of the Waluguru (whose only riotous conduct took place in the context of the political campaign of the rival of the African nationalist's candidate, the rival being stoned). The absence of ritualisation does not mean that the introduction by the secret ballot was culturally uncontested—we have seen above how many doubts, withdrawals and different interpretations it could generate—but that it was remarkably smoothly integrated into African political practice at the time. What, then, is the significance of this?

INITIATION AND ELECTORAL CULTURE

The introduction of the secret ballot in England took place against a background of an earlier electoral culture in which both voters and non-voters were a relevant audience for political activity, and such activity occurred, around election day, in a festive and 'carnivalesque' public sphere, which brought voters and non-voters together in some sort of shared political realm. This more or less informal mode of political communion was subsequently broken up by the discipline, commodification and mass enumeration of the secret ballot, which fragmented the audience and emphasised the distinction between voter and non-voter in, for instance, restricting access to the voting area (see O'Gorman, 1996). As a result of his study, Frank O'Gorman suggests that one should study not merely the forms of an electoral system but also the cultural patterns that underpin it: role-playing and performance, family and kinship (rather than the atomistic individual), ritual community and culturally enhanced forms of popular participation beyond those who are on the electoral roll. This surely applies to the study of elections in late colonial Tanganyika, but the discipline, commodification and enumeration that transformed the political landscape in England were introduced into Tanganyika in rather different ways. While the carnivalesque and festive elections in England provided—even after the disciplinary effect of the introduction of the secret ballot—a background that tied non-voters to the act of voting as such, the culture of colonialism in Tanganyika, with its ingrained suspicion of the state, made such an electoral culture of popular participation well-nigh impossible. Whatever ritualisation of politics took place in Tanganyika was not based on any individualised ideal of political participation, but articulated by the African nationalist party—a corporate body.

This was at least partly a result of the way in which the administration introduced the ballot. Local district officers—usually those responsible for translating modern forms to Waluguru—refused in 1958 to shoulder the burden of explaining the election mechanism to Africans. The central government and the Superintendent of Elections in particular detected in these ways of translating modern political forms to Africans—in the language of the period, of 'putting across' unfamiliar messages—a whiff of paternalism, and seemed to assume that Africans would work out the use of this political technology for themselves.[9] The result was that if the secret ballot was indeed 'put across' to Africans, it was portrayed as if it was a neutral technology. But as we have seen, Africans had little reason to suppose it was.

Moreover, culturally the secret ballot was never a neutral technology (even if Africans too tried to employ it as such). The contrast between the secrecy of the ballot and the secrecy of initiation shows that they not only deal with very different notions of secrecy but also very different notions of power. While the ballot divests a person of information, handing it over to a superior agency, an initiation, in passing on powerful and secret knowledge to the initiand, gives a person power from a superior agency and thus incorporates him or her in the body politic. While the secret ballot divorces the body from power in the act of individualising the voter—as in all forms of modern discipline—initiation works by embodiment: by transforming the body of the initiand so that it can enter a new political sphere. (As Walter Benjamin might have said: while the vote divests the person of her political aura, an initiation invests her with it.) In such a situation the individuation characteristic of the act of secret voting could be interpreted in terms of suspicion of what the superior agency was going to do with one's vote—a suspicion that might explain part of the Luguru reluctance to vote during the 1952 subchiefdom elections. Conversely it could also be interpreted as an act subject to the kind of empowerment that Waluguru were already familiar with, which is what may have happened in 1958.

This second, non-technological and 'cultural' appreciation of the secret ballot was not possible among Waluguru without a prior transformation of political routines that provided, if not an electoral culture, at least a cultural innovation allowing for a ritualisation and publicisation of modern mass politics that could accommodate the African nationalist party, the one that was to receive most of the votes. Between 1952 and 1958 Waluguru had rebelled against a soil conservation scheme imposed upon them by the British, a culmination of interventions by the state that had long been experienced as predatory by Waluguru (Pels, 1996b). The rebellion was organised along the lines of the politics of initiation, in secret, away from the public performance of authority that the British had institutionalised in the form of the Native Authorities and local government. Indigenous valley politics used to be directed by incorporating

9   TNA 26/L5/70: Moore to Duff, 16.8.57; Hucks to DC Morogoro, 20.2.58.

all adults into a group of responsible inhabitants by initiation, and subsequently organising this group (which met in public council), through the secret council of a group of senior initiates of higher rank, along family or kinship lines. In starting the rebellion, Waluguru had to move from valley politics (of a few hundred inhabitants) to a much larger scale of political organisation, encompassing at least half of the mountain area and ending in a demonstration of about 4,000 people in July 1955. This was organised along similar lines to those of valley politics: the mass meeting in July 1955 was classified (at least retrospectively) as a public council (or *mtingano*), turning the leaders of the protest—the core of what was to become TANU in Uluguru—into the equivalent of a secret council (or *mtsengwe*). The big difference was, of course, that this form of mass political organisation bore the names of kinship-based initiatory politics but was no longer organised along (fictive) kinship lines—except, eventually, those of race, or 'African' nationalism.[10]

Initially this organisation of protest arose from Luguru political practice itself, and it is doubtful whether nationalist consciousness was the main factor in lifting it to a more encompassing, mass political scale. However, not long after the rebellion the leaders solicited TANU membership cards from the capital, Dar es Salaam (apparently ignorant of the fact that a TANU branch had already been started in the nearby provincial town, Morogoro) and distributed them among all those who were willing to join the rebellion. These cards were handed over in secret and kept in secret, even though party membership was not officially prohibited.[11] All in all one gets the impression of a kind of secrecy—very much akin to that working among initiates—protecting a corporate group. In this context party membership may have been more a way of empowering a person (*vis-à-vis* a state perceived as predatory), rather than the expression of an individual electoral choice. Membership of the party may have meant that one was required to do one's duty and vote as an instrumental, 'technological' way of bringing one's corporate group—the nationalist party—to power, as an 'African' alternative to (rather than a political party within) the existing state. Thus it seems the secret ballot was commodified and treated as a neutral technology by Africans, just as the colonial administrators wanted, but without reproduction of the private person that the late-colonial state hoped to see emerge in the individual voter. Instead the act of voting may have been 'de-commodified' in the context of the embodied culture of TANU membership.

---

10 For a detailed account, see Pels (2000).
11 In this connection it is interesting that the word *chama* ('party') is also the term used for a witches' coven, which also meets in secret.

Appadurai, Arjun, 1996, 'Number in the Colonial Imagination' in *Modernity at Large*, Minneapolis, MN: University of Minnesota Press.

Bayart, Jean-François, 1993, *The State in Africa: The Politics of the Belly*, London and New York: Longman.

Escobar, Arturo, 1995, *Encountering Development*, Princeton University Press.

Fabian, Johannes, 1990, *Power and Performance*, Madison, WI: University of Wisconsin Press.

Garrigou, Alain, 1988, 'Le secret de l'isoloir', *Actes de la recherche en sciences sociales*, no. 71–2, pp. 22–45.

——, 1993, 'La construction sociale du vote', *Politix*, no. 22, pp. 5–42.

Geiger, Susan, 1997, *TANU Women: Gender and Culture in the Making of Tanganyikan Nationalism, 1955–1965*, Portsmouth, NH: Heinemann.

Graham, Gordon, 1999, *The Internet*, London and New York: Routledge.

Hucks, Geoffrey W.Y., 1960, 'The Territorial Elections—1958', *Tanganyika Notes & Records*, no. 54, pp. 38–47.

Latour, Bruno, 1993, *We Have Never Been Modern*, Cambridge, MA: Harvard University Press.

O'Gorman, Frank, 1992, 'Campaign Rituals and Ceremonies: The Social Meaning of Elections in England, 1780–1860', *Past and Present*, no. 135, pp. 79–115.

——, 1996, 'The Culture of Elections in England: From the Glorious Revolution to the First World War, 1688–1914' in E. Posada-Carbó (ed.), *Elections before Democracy: The History of Elections in Europe and Latin America*, Institute of Latin American Studies, University of London, pp. 17–31.

Pels, Peter, 1996a, 'The Pidginization of Luguru Politics: Administrative Ethnography and the Paradoxes of Indirect Rule', *American Ethnologist*, vol. 23, no. 4, pp. 738–61.

——, 1996b, 'Kizungu Rhythms: Luguru Christianity as Ngoma', *Journal of Religion in Africa*, no. 26, pp. 163–201.

——, 1999, *A Politics of Presence: Contacts between Missionaries and Africans in Colonial Tanganyika*, Chur and Reading: Harwood Academic Publishers.

——, 2000, 'Creolization in Secret: The Birth of Nationalism in Late Colonial Uluguru', The Hague: WOTRO Programme on 'Globalization and the Construction of Communal Identities', working paper.

Pemberton, John, 1986, 'Notes on the 1982 General Election in Solo', *Indonesia*, no. 41, pp. 1–22.

Young, Roland, 1959, 'The Tanganyika Elections, 1958–1959', unpublished manuscript, Evanston, IL: Northwestern University archives, Roland Young papers 35/5.

THE ENGINEERS OF DEMOCRACY

ELECTION MONITORING AGENCIES AND POLITICAL CHANGE IN POST-SUHARTO INDONESIA

Romain Bertrand

Taking into account both the popular success of the 2004 General Elections and the rise of army-backed and village-based violence in Java, one is led to wonder where the process of 'reform' (*reformasi*) in Indonesia stands today. Not long after the forced resignation of President Suharto in May 1998 a number of critics, such as the columnist Goenawan Mohamad, were already wondering what was to be understood by the omnipresent term *reformasi*, brandished both by the radical student movements and by discredited sycophants of the *ancien régime*. The combination of the word *reformasi* with antithetical qualifiers provided a way of tracking the conflicting interpretations of the term. While the National Mandate Party (PAN) of Amien Raïs called for 'peaceful reform' (*reformasi damai*), the militants of the People's Democratic Party (PRD) favoured 'total reform' (*reformasi total*). The *reformasi* referred therefore to a process of political liberalisation which some thought should culminate in the holding of free elections and others considered a means to eliminate the defects of the political system, commonly referred to as KKN (corruption, collusion and nepotism). In the eyes of the ordinary voter it was above all a question of 'moralising' the public sphere, of making certain that, both in the struggle for power and in the day-to-day administration of the country, virtues such as honesty and impartiality would win out.

The *reformasi* has been a success as far as the transformation, on a technical level, of the functional rules of politics are concerned. The return to a multi-party system and to a free press, the dismantling of the repressive state structures inherited from the New Order regime and the military's loss of influence in legislative assemblies all point to an obvious turn towards greater political freedom. But as far as the sense of belonging in terms of citizenship and nationality is concerned—i.e. the way in which people feel bound as individuals to the state and bound as members of a community to a single nation—the record of the *reformasi* is, to say the least, ambiguous. The confidence citizens had placed in public institutions and elected assemblies quickly evaporated, and the number of lynchings and of conflicts labelled 'inter-ethnic' rose dramatically.[1] To understand how the process of democratic reform and the spread of political violence, far from being mutually exclusive, increasingly fed on each other, one must return to the founding act of the *reformasi*: the *trompe l'oeil* elections of 7 June 1999. In so doing, one particular aspect of the electoral process that has as yet received little attention can be brought to the fore: the role played by the engineers of democracy, those experts from large-scale international agencies specialising in 'democracy-building' and 'electoral monitoring'.

The purpose of this is by no means to place undue emphasis on the influence exercised by non-Indonesian actors on the process of political change, the roots of which are strictly endogenous—a pro-*demokrasi* movement that gained in momentum from 1996 onwards, the financial crisis of 1997 that severely limited the regime's ability to distribute the country's wealth among its cronies, the student demonstrations in the spring of 1998. It is rather to explore how the professional expertise of the 'engineers of democracy' affected the way the new rules for institutions were formulated, with particular reference to the drawing up of the new electoral laws; and, in doing so, to redirect attention to those issues that were sidetracked by the fetishistic focus on elections and their accompanying rituals: issues such as the as yet very limited widening of social sources of recruitment for parliament members, the relations between the executive and the legislative powers, and the spread of violence-prone party militias.[2]

ON THE ROLE OF EXPERTS IN DEMOCRACY: THE *TROMPE L'OEIL* ELECTIONS OF JUNE 1999

A multi-party political system was reintroduced in Indonesia by Laws 1, 2, 3, 4 and 5 dated 1999,[3] adopted at the instigation of B.J. Habibie, the country's provisional president from 22 May 1998 to 20 October 1999. To draw up the texts of these laws Habibie had named a team of experts known as the 'Team of Seven', presided over by the secretary-general for Administrative Affairs and Regional Autonomy attached to the Ministry of Home Affairs, a law professor by the name of Ryaas Rasyid

[1] For a chronological presentation of the main sequences of political violence in Indonesia since 1998, see Tornquist (2002).

[2] This article is based on a series of research missions undertaken in Java since 1998, and in particular a period spent in Jakarta and Surabaya during the first *reformasi* General Elections (April–June 1999).

[3] To be more precise: Law 1/1999 concerned political parties, Law 2/1999 general elections, Law 3/1999 the make-up and status of the legislative bodies (MPR, DPR, DPRD) and Laws 4/ and 5/1999 the participation of state employees in political party activities. These election laws are to be found in English translation in National Elections Commission, 1999.

(Bourchier, 2000). These laws put an end to the tripartite system set up in 1973 by Suharto, instituted through a forced 'simplification' of the party system. Only the Indonesian Democratic Party (PDI), the United Development Party (PPP) and Golkar (a government-backed body) were authorised to take part, every five years, in the 'festival celebrations of democracy' (*pesta-pesta demokrasi*), and only Golkar ever emerged as winner, with results that usually exceeded 60 per cent of the vote.[4] All political activity in the villages between elections was banned, and state employees were automatically made members of Golkar (which presided over a network of corporatist associations).[5] The 'Habibie laws' of February 1999 fully re-established freedom of assembly and of political association, rights that had been cut back by the 1966 anti-subversion laws.[6] Groups of fifty adult citizens (over twenty-one years old and in possession of their civil rights) could now create political parties without the slightest fear of being harassed by the police or by security agencies. This was a real break with the past. In 1997, less than one year before the end of the New Order, Golkar, relying as always upon a deep-reaching coercive state apparatus, had once more gathered 74 per cent of the votes (Antlöv, 2004). But even if an unusually high number of violent incidents took place during the 1997 campaign, few political analysts would have dared predict the collapse of the whole political system.

In the course of the second half of 1998, after the new president had reiterated his intention to organise 'free and fair elections', more than 200 new political parties sprung up. Admittedly most of them consisted only of cliques drawn from the ranks of the old regime élites, anxious to delay their eviction from power, or else of organisations closely linked to religious networks (either *pesantren*-based[7] or church-oriented) or to large-scale interest groups in search of increased media visibility and privileged access to public financing. For example, the vice-president of the aptly named 'PAY' party (Partai Abul Yatama, Father of Orphans Party) could thus state openly that he had 'no hope of winning a single seat in parliament', but that he intended to take advantage of the media time allotted all candidates by the public TV channels to promote his private foundation.[8] Another party, the Partai Nasional Bangsa Indone-

---

4 The best introduction to recent historiography concerning the New Order is the biography of Suharto by Robert Elson (2002). For an ethnographic treatment of the *pesta-pesta demokrasi*, see Pemberton (1986).
5 For the ideological origins of the corporatist system of the New Order, see the masterful synthesis by David Reeve (1985).
6 These laws had been adopted during the massacres of Communists in 1965–6 as a means of providing a pseudo-legal basis for the arrest, deportation and murder of those suspected of being PKI militants.
7 In Java the *pesantren* are Islamic boarding schools run by religious scholars (*kyai*).
8 Interview with the author, Jakarta, May 1999.

sia, brought together three New Order 'charity foundations' (the *yayasan* Hodondento, Ganesha Muda and Wanita Padma) known for their unscrupulous way of managing public funds. Another example, the 'Unity in Diversity' party (Partai Bhinneka Tunggal Ika), was a creation of powerful Jakarta industrial lobbies, who accordingly campaigned in favour of huge tax remittances for large-scale firms (Bertrand, 2001a). This blossoming of new political parties, rooted in the self-serving interests of higher social groups rather than in genuine individual democratic commitments, nevertheless hastened acceptance of the new political order by the élite, at a time when the possibility of an authoritarian, army-led backlash was not yet fully out of the picture.

To handle the organisation of the election in practical terms and monitor the balloting, a National Elections Commission (Komisi Pemilihan Umum, KPU) was created through Law 3/1999 (further elaborated by the Presidential Decree 16/1999). As defined by Article 8, Paragraph 2 of the law, the KPU was to be a body 'free and independent, made up of [representatives of] the political parties taking part in the elections as well as of government representatives accountable to the president'. Further, Article 9 stipulated that the KPU must consist of party representatives (one per legally recognised party) and government officials, with a system of 'balanced weighing of votes' between the two groups.[9] The KPU set up strict rules to limit the number of parties that could compete. The new parties had to have branches in at least half of the archipelago's twenty-seven provinces, refrain in their campaign platforms from coming out against the 'fundamental principles of the state' (the Pancasila)[10] and not 'endanger the unity and integrity of the nation' (which meant, not serve as a sounding board for separatists or radical Islamists). In addition they were to render public their campaign budgets. Donations by individuals and corporate entities were limited to 15 million rupees (approximately £1,000). At the close of a series of auditions held by the KPU 'screening committee' forty-eight parties were 'accredited'. They represented a fairly wide spectrum of ideological orientations, including 'Sukarnoist' parties (nationalist-republicans, such as Megawati Sukarnoputri's PDI-P), Muslim parties (whether traditionalist like Gus Dur's PKB or reformist like the neo-Masjumi), worker parties (such as the People's Democratic Party) and the *ancien régime* pseudo-parties.

9 The KPU was finally made up of forty-eight party representatives and five government officials.
10 The Pancasila ('Five Principles') were proclaimed by Sukarno as a form of compromise to settle differences between the republicans and religious groups. They were included in the preamble to the 1945 Constitution. They concern: 1. belief in a single almighty God; 2. a just and civilised form of humanity; 3. the unity of Indonesia; 4. democracy through the quest for unanimity by means of a process of collective deliberation; and 5. social justice.

Towards the judicialisation of political practices

Contradicting the pessimistic forecasts of most Western embassies and ministries of foreign affairs, the 7 June 1999 elections were held in an atmosphere of calm and without any major technical hitches, despite the colossal scale in both territorial and demographic terms (250,000 polling stations for more than 130 million voters, with a 87.4 registration percentage).[11] The political stakes were also far-reaching. As set down in Law 4/1999, 462 seats of 'mandatories of the people' (*wakil rakyat*) in the lower house (DPR) were to be filled by direct universal suffrage, while 135 seats in the upper house (DPR-D) were to be filled by representatives chosen by elected provincial and regency councils (the DPR and DPR-D making up the MPR: People's Consultative Assembly). Thirty-eight seats in the DPR were still reserved by decree for representatives of the armed forces and the police, and within the ranks of the MPR a joint parliamentary commission was to nominate sixty-five non-elected 'representatives of contributive groups' (workers, peasants, students, ethnic minorities, physically-disabled persons etc.). The system was still a mixed one, for it combined the liberal principles of multi-party elections and mutually accountable assemblies with authoritarian, corporatist 'top-down' designation devices.

Moreover the legion of agencies engaged in poll-watching made frequent reference in their 'progress reports' to attempts to bribe voters with gifts of food, money, t-shirts or even karaoke cassettes, and mentioned isolated cases of strong-arm intimidation.[12] These reports make for instructive reading. In the first place, all the political parties were involved in these illegalities: the PDI-P, headed by Megawati Sukarnoputri, and Hamzah Haz's PPP were no more innocent than Golkar headed by Akbar Tandjung. Given the degree of control it exercised under the former regime, Golkar could count on a wider base of financial and administrative patronage, but newcomers in the field were quick to adopt the same vote-buying techniques. The province of South Sulawesi serves as an example: it appears the local Golkar authorities 'gave money to village leaders meeting in assembly at Janepot', the PAN delegates in the district of Banggai promised to 'give a goat to those who voted for the party', and

11 Statistics obtained from the Ministry of Home Affairs and from the KPU, Jakarta, September 1999.
12 These cases of strong-arm intimidation have also been reported in a scholarly publication (Sulistyo *et al.*, 2000). For an analysis of some cases of vote-buying and 'money politics' (*politik uang*), see Sulistyo and Kadar (2000). According to these authors, the 'price' of a vote fluctuated between 10,000 and 50,000 rupees. Party agents also frequently distributed rice, cooking oil and sugar to poor families, expecting them to make the 'right choice'. All these activities were forbidden by KPU decrees (if not by Law 2/1999), but in many cases it was difficult to draw the line between conscious and unconscious cheating, all the more so since many parties were linked to wider charity networks whose aim precisely was to provide the needy with food and clothes.

in the Biringkanaya district both the PDI-P and Gus Dur's PKB 'offered people clothes (in particular clothes bearing party insignia), with a preference for *becak* [rickshaw] drivers' (Solidarity Center [ACILS], 1999). Secondly, most of the pre-election misdeeds reported can be considered traditional clientelistic practices rather than political crimes. In fact the distribution of essential goods in return for the promise to vote for a given ticket does not in itself mean election results are skewed, since the privacy of the polling booth guarantees that the voter's actual choice remains unknown. Providing potential voters with t-shirts (a scarce commodity in shantytowns and remote villages) is by no means equivalent to threatening them with knives. We can discern here the influence of the approach adopted in the past two decades by political scientists in Western universities when analysing election fraud, for the criminalisation of incidents of vote trafficking is the by-product of a recent (but ongoing) public debate in Western democracies. Before the mid-1980s very few Western countries equated clientelistic trade-offs or minor abuses due to local cronyism with unlawful or morally objectionable practices. Laws making the public recording of private donations to parties compulsory were passed only recently, after the scandalous dimension of under-the-table dealings became a favourite target of the media (Briquet and Garraud, 2002). In that respect the 1999 General Elections in Indonesia received much more attention than those held in Corsica or in southern Italy in the 1970s.

The pervading presence of election watchdogs, both before and after the voting took place, added—in and of itself—a new dimension to the electoral process. The number of representatives of non-Indonesian election monitoring agencies was unusually high (approximately 600). The US Chamber of Commerce sent 26 field agents, the Asian Network for Free Elections (ANFREL) 69, the Australian Council for Overseas Aid (ACFOA) 17, the International Republican Institute (IRI) 15, the Carter Institute and the National Democratic Institute 100, the Japanese government 20 and the European Union 130 (Election Facilitation Center, 1999).[13] Former US President Jimmy Carter himself junketed to Jakarta (and Bali) to underscore the degree of importance the American political establishment as a whole (still spellbound by Samuel Huntington's theory of 'third-wave democracies') attached to the transition to democracy in Indonesia. In fact, in the eyes of the Clinton administration, the shift of the largest Muslim country in the world onto the side of liberal regimes would necessarily set off a chain reaction of democratisation in South Asian countries and beyond—possibly as far as the Middle East. The United Nations Development Programme (UNDP) also set up a bureau

---

[13] The document states that the numbers cited do not include 'the non-official observers from the diplomatic corps'.

of election assistance in Jakarta. Thanks to gifts received from Japan (more than $35 million), the UNDP financed the total costs of printing 400 million election bulletins and 2.8 million instruction manuals for election personnel, as well as the cost of 600,000 bottles of indelible ink (intended to prevent multiple voting) and 1,000 radios for polling booths located in remote areas (UNDP-Jakarta, 1999: 2). The importance to the United States, Japan and Australia, for reasons of global strategy, of political stability in Indonesia was reflected in financial terms by the high level of investment in the material organisation of the first free elections to be held after the demise of the authoritarian New Order regime. Given the vast financial and technical resources made available by multilateral agencies and foreign governments, we can conclude that, to put it mildly, the international community intended to keep a tight watch on the election.

The influence of US electoral doctrines and the pre-selection of prominent political figures

The massive presence in the first half of 1999 of engineers with 'doctorates in democratisation', whether senior UN officials or private advisers, also had an effect, marginal perhaps but certainly tangible, on the way a legitimate political process could be defined—that is to say, on the very idea of what constituted successful political change. The reluctance, expressed from the start by members of the National Elections Commission, to allow an unlimited number of parties to take part in the poll, and the fact that the Commission campaigned in favour of rules designed to reduce the number of party organisations in the hope of instituting a stabilised system of governmental alliances, point to their close acquaintance with US centres of expertise in democracy-building. Indeed it may be no coincidence that one of the most sought-after members of the KPU, Andy Mallarangeng, obtained his Masters degree in sociology (1991) and subsequently his PhD in political science (1997) from Northern Illinois University.[14] His thesis, largely influenced by the work of Dwight King, was devoted to 'a contextual analysis of Indonesian electoral behaviour'. Dwight King, a well-known scholar of Indonesian affairs, and specialist in elections held under the New Order regime, had served as consultant to the World Bank for Indonesia (in March 1989, February and May 1990, January 1991, November 1992 and January 1997). He was also one of the senior advisers of the Carter Center from February to June 1999, at the very time of the Indonesian General Elections, before becoming a monitor in East Timor for the election of the constituent assembly in 2001. Describing his role as a political con-

---

14 Information taken from his *curriculum vitae*, www3.niu.edu/acad/polisci/faculty/king.

sultant in Jakarta, Dwight King wrote, in an inimitable bureaucratic-academic style:

Duties: provided weekly analysis and background papers on political developments and the transition process in Indonesia, wrote press releases, gave oral briefings to Carter Center personnel, including former President and Mrs Carter, participated in high level interviews (as translator and/or co-questioner) between Jimmy Carter and high level Indonesian government officials, including President, Foreign Minister and Commander in Chief of the Armed Forces, and leaders of major political parties. Recruited and helped screen/select members of the election monitoring delegation.[15]

Andy Mallarangeng's decided preference for a 'major party' system can thus be traced to the influence on his thinking of the American model of 'two and a half parties', considered by US-based theorists as a guarantee of long-term governmental stability. Prior to the election this doctrine had circulated among a wide public. By the end of 1998 the major works of the 'transitology' thinkers, including the joint studies edited by Philippe Schmitter, had been translated into Indonesian. Thanks to Guy Hermet's critical analyses of this school of thought, it is now crystal-clear that the 'transitology' in vogue in the 1970s and 1980s evinced a marked preference for elections that would produce a clear-cut majority, on the grounds that the non-violent shedding of an authoritarian regime required adoption of 'peace pacts' between ideological opponents, and that 'catch-all parties' were best suited for these sorts of transactions (Hermet, 1996). Within the Elections Commission itself, however, there was a deep split between party representatives (the 'political' members of the Commission who favoured increased proportional representation) and the 'technocrats' (law professors and experts who opted for major-party elections). As one member of the latter group put it, 'the *politikus* only want DPR seats, while what we need is a strong government.'[16] The intensity of the quarrel that then broke out inside the KPU over the issue of proportional representation can be guessed simply from the use of the term *politikus* (politician); for in popular parlance, the word is ironically often taken to mean 'political rats', 'corrupt politicians'—since *tikus* (rat) designates a corrupt official.

The media-orchestrated diplomatic pre-selection of prominent political figures prior to the electoral process constitutes another form of outside 'interference'. Take, as an example, the event organised by the Asia-Europe Foundation (ASEF) in Jakarta three weeks before the elections. The ASEF is an intergovernmental organisation financed by both European and Asian countries to implement the 'cultural chapter' of the political dialogue process known as the Asia-Europe Meeting

---

15 Text taken from Andy Mallarangeng's *curriculum vitae*, June 1999.
16 Interviews with members of the KPU, Jakarta, April 1999.

(ASEM).[17] From 12 to 14 May 1999 the ASEF, in close partnership with the Jakarta British Council, held a 'colloquium for journalists' entitled *A Preview of the Indonesian Elections.*[18] Held in the lounges of the Gran Melia, a four-star marble-and-orchids hotel, it was presided over by the then ASEF Director Tommy Koh, an influential Singapore diplomat. This 'colloquium' was intended to 'help Asian and European journalists better understand the dynamics and complexities of the Indonesian elections of June 7', and to this end tried to provide participants with 'a summary view of contemporary Indonesian politics'. The second session of the 'colloquium', named for the occasion 'Meeting the Major Parties', featured speeches by five party delegates: Mochtar Pakpahan, a member of the advisory committee of the National Labour Party (PBN); Marzuki Darusman, Vice-President of Golkar; Abdillah Toha, member of the executive committee of the National Mandate Party (PAN); Fadjrul Fallah, member of the executive committee of the National Awakening Party (PKB); and Mochtar Buchori, assistant secretary-general of the Indonesian Democratic Party-Struggle (PDI-P). Each of the speakers gave a brief presentation of his party (sometimes accompanied by slides), concentrating on a minimal ideological platform made up of the catchwords from the language of democratic correctness of international agencies: respect for 'democracy and the rule of law', promotion of 'corporate (or good) governance' through the war on corruption etc. The audience was composed of members of the Western diplomatic corps and some sixty newspaper and television reporters, both national (the press agency Antara, the magazines *Gamma, Panji, Tajuk* and *Warta Ekonomi,* the daily newspaper *Kompas* etc.) and international (*Asiaweek, The Asian Wall Street Journal, Xinhua News Agency*, AFP, Reuters, *Deutsche Welle, Asahi Shimbun, The Star, The Nation* etc.). Most of the foreign correspondents had only just flown into the capital. They had only second-hand knowledge of the political situation and had not as yet established contacts and made arrangements for interviews.

The ultimate purpose of the event in terms of 'networking' was from the start all too obvious. In the foyer of the meeting hall a wicker basket was set up as a receptacle for visitors' name cards, which were then photocopied and distributed on demand. It seems unlikely that the selection and the mediatisation of only five of the forty-eight competing parties derived from a Machiavellian plot to discredit the others. Nonetheless this ASEF and British Council 'colloquium' had its effect on media coverage of the campaign, giving these five political formations an unprecedented publicity bonus and convincing foreign observers that the crux of the election consisted of a competition between a limited number of

---

17 For a fuller description of the ASEF, see www.asef.org
18 Quotations taken from the handouts distributed to participants in the colloquium.

prominent figures. For example, despite the degree of interest shown by the Indonesian press in the parties labelled as 'Islamist' (such as the Crescent Moon and Star Party or the Justice Party), none were invited to attend the event. Furthermore, Pakpahan's party failed to send one single deputy to the DPR: the only explanation for his appearance alongside the big wheels of the PDI-P and Golkar was in all probability the moral credit he enjoyed internationally—stemming from his imprisonment under the New Order regime. Last but not least, the fact that the five chosen party representatives were perfectly fluent in English, whereas the majority of the candidates for the DPR could not speak it at all, proves that the understanding of the new political landscape promoted by foreign experts was already a largely distorted and misleading one.

Polling-booth fetishism: dictating a narrow approach to the political process[19]

The purpose of these remarks on the role, during the election period, of international agencies specialising in helping and recording the 'transition to democracy' is by no means to minimise or ignore the endogenous character of political change in Indonesia.[20] Nor is it to point up the unexpected consequences that inevitably go hand-in-hand with all forms of 'interference' linked to cases of multilateral technical assistance, or to overemphasise the oddities of the democracy-building business and its curious language, full of suggestive neologisms. Rather it is to call attention to the limited nature and narrow scope of the interpretation of the political process that these agencies promulgate—an interpretation that, given its terms and methods, cannot take underlying social dynamics into consideration. For what these agencies have in common is celebration of the election itself as the alpha and omega of political transition—something that could be expressed by the motto 'when the elections work, then everything works'.

In other words, if no large-scale acts of violence are committed on election day, then the country is deemed to have successfully entered the democratic phase—no need to pursue things any further. Indeed KPU sponsors took an almost fanatical interest in the slightest indication of violence directed at voters by 'uncontrolled elements'. The latter were almost always referred to as *preman*, neighbourhood thugs (often thought to be in cahoots with the police). In the 'checklist for poll watch-

---

19 The remarks that follow concerning the electoral 'fetishism' of the engineers of democracy owe much to Alain Garrigou's work on the invention of universal secret suffrage and the image of the ideal citizen in France during the late nineteenth and early twentieth centuries (Garrigou, 1992).

20 The importance of this endogenous process of political mobilisation is emphasised in Bertrand (2003a).

ing' distributed to all observers by the election monitoring network set
up by the Rectors' Forum, the great majority of questions relative to
'conditions prevailing at the time of ballot casting' henceforth had to
do with acts of 'intimidation' ('violent physical threats', 'non-physical
threats', 'intimidation by security personnel', 'intimidation by unknown
individuals') (HONEST, Rectors' Forum Indonesia, 1999: sections E
and F). In a handbook edited in comic strip style, financed by the International Republican Institute (IRI) and distributed in polling stations
to all party representatives, this obsessive fear of violence on the part
of 'uncontrolled elements' took graphic form in a series of vignettes in
which a group of ugly mugs surreptitiously make off with the ballot box
or threaten an honest housewife who is about to enter the polling booth
(International Republican Institute, 1999: 23–4).[21] The artist, Harnaeni
Hamdan, as a way of lending a note of humour to the nightmare of an
electoral disaster that never ceased to haunt the analysts of the Carter
Center and the IRI, had obviously taken as a model the gangsters that
figure in the highly popular *komiks*.

Questions concerning the balance of power between institutions, the
role of political groups challenging the parliamentary system and operating outside its legal reach, or the degree of legibility of the political process for ordinary citizens are questions that electoral fetishism rendered
irrelevant. Proof: during the week following the 7 June 1999 elections
almost every single poll-watching agency, having awarded Indonesia a
'certificate' of democratisation, promptly quit the country. But subsequent events were to prove that electoral choice was only one among the
many aspects of boisterous national politics, and that the legitimacy of
the power in the hands of the parliament or the presidency was not determined solely by the ballot box, even if the exact dimensions of these
ballot boxes had been fixed by a KPU decree in the hopes of avoiding
fraud. Indeed, an entire chapter of the instruction manual published by
the National Elections Commission for its poll-watching agents (KPPS)
was devoted to the design of the ballot box (to be equipped with a hinged
lid), to the exact measurements of the polling booth (1.5 m by 1.5 m by 2
m high), and to floor plans of the polling stations (exhibiting the location
of entrances, exits, polling booths, registering and observation tables).
The bureaucratic taming of the voter went even further, since his moving
inside the polling station was also given a prescriptive significance in
official documents, thanks to the use of small direction signs mapping
his zigzagging journey through the flawless world of democracy in the
making (National Elections Commission [KPU], 1999: 20–5).[22]

---

21 Note also that the Indonesian term *saksi* is usually employed in Java with reference to
a witness (for a marriage or a trial).
22 These prescriptive details were reiterated in the KPU decree 1/2004 (23 January 2004),
which figured a detailed map of a standard 'polling station layout' (this map is reproduced

Hence, the material culture of voting was deemed a priority target of the state and monitoring agencies' regulatory action. But paradoxically the detail of these technical instructions was to be a source of endless problems for the civil servants in charge of the stations. In a south-eastern neighbourhood of Jakarta a violent quarrel broke out between those who stood for a booth made out of cardboard and those who stood for one constructed of plywood. The official texts said nothing about the kind of raw material that should be used and the Neighbourhood Chief (Kepala RW) was obliged, as a last resort, to appeal to the District Officer (Camat) to settle the matter.[23] Elsewhere the question of the polling station's location engendered dispute. For practical reasons voting booths were, as a general rule, set up in public buildings: schools, dispensaries etc. However, sometimes they were located in the courtyard of the Neighbourhood Chief's house (which often also served as his headquarters), in which case citizens were quick to protest, on the basis that since state employees were traditionally Golkar sympathisers they would exercise undue pressure on voters, and to request that the site where people cast their votes be clearly separated from administrative premises.[24] Given that the local administration had actively supported Golkar for over three decades, the citizens' suspicions regarding the partisan nature of the state servants were fully understandable. The voicing of this criticism, directed at technical problems, is also evidence that ordinary people very quickly appropriated the new political tools and discourse.

Nevertheless the quest for technical perfection seems only to have rendered the process less intelligible for ordinary citizens. First, the complexities of the mode of voting and the merging of electoral lists up to the last day of the campaign (justified as a way of assuring total transparency) created a deep-seated malaise and the suspicion of having been cheated, which considerably reduced the original social impact of the *reformasi*. Secondly, the sociological profile of the parliament that resulted from these elections in no way reflected that of the electorate. An overwhelming majority of MPs were entrepreneurs or came from the ranks of the lower- and middle-urban bourgeoisie. No delegate of the industrial workers or of the 'common people' living in the shantytowns and lower-class neighbourhoods was elected to the DPR. The great majority of representatives of the PDI-P—the party of the 'People's Mother' (Ibu Rakyat, Megawati Sukarnoputri)—were small-time businessmen in the transport and textile sectors, university professors, lawyers, former high-ranking civil servants or engineers. 77.8 per cent of the new MPs

---

in European Union Election Observation Mission [2004]).

[23] Scene witnessed by the author on the eve of the elections.

[24] Paradoxically the dispute took place in Menteng, a posh section of Central Jakarta inhabited for the most part by high-ranking civil servants. The local Neighbourhood Chief was actually known to be dictatorial—in all probability the origin of the quarrel.

had engaged in university studies and 7.6 per cent of them held an MA or a PhD degree—figures far higher than the national average.[25] It is thus not surprising that in almost four years of legislating, this 'Parliament of the Educated' passed none of the major social measures (concerning redundancy compensation or sick leave) that could have improved the everyday living conditions of the lower classes at a time when the country was engulfed by a major economic crisis.[26]

The explanation for the obvious indifference to the social dynamics of politics manifested by the various agencies engaged in smoothing the way for the 'transition to democracy' is not based solely on theoretical or ideological considerations: it stems also from the manner in which these agencies are structured. Most are set up to operate simultaneously in several countries. The Institute for Democracy and Electoral Assistance (IDEA), which maintains a permanent representative in Jakarta, defines its objective as 'helping to develop democratic institutions and a democratic culture', and to this end publishes comparative handbooks on 'financing public parties', 'women in parliament', 'electoral systems design' etc. IDEA is financed by some twenty nations and works in close collaboration with other international organisations (such as the World Bank, the Interparliamentary Union, the International Press Institute and Transparency International). It has offices and finances projects in Nigeria, Burkina Faso, South Africa, Mozambique, Peru, Guatemala, Burma and Georgia.[27] The programme officers of IDEA, like the senior advisers of the IRI and the *chargés de mission* of the European Commission leading the election monitoring teams, work on a rotating schedule and frequently change assignments. IDEA thus operates as an agent of international standardisation of the terminology for the 'transition to democracy'. Its procedural definition of the democratic system lends itself to rapid-fire comparisons between societies that in fact have very different historical trajectories. It insists on a technical, even technocratic approach to political change. Democracy is, in this perspective, a matter for experts: the establishment of sound democratic institutions is supposed to result from the strict application of a set of universal rules.

25 These data on the socio-economic status of DPR deputies have been compiled from *Wajah Dewan Perwakilan Rakyat Republik Indonesia*, 2000. There seem to exist no studies as yet of parliamentary personnel and procedures in the scholarly literature on the *reformasi*.

26 For a useful update on the dramatic social consequence of the 1997–8 economic crisis (often played down by the multinational agencies), see Breman and Wiradi (2002).

27 Information taken from the IDEA website, www.idea.int. Modelled on the North American foundations, IDEA is presided over by a board of directors composed of 'international figures', drawn for the most part from the political world and the ranks of senior UN diplomats. IDEA was founded in 1995; its headquarters are in Stockholm. Information regarding the functioning of the Jakarta branch of IDEA is drawn from discussions held in 2002 with some of its staff members.

THE CRISIS OF THE PARTY SYSTEM AND THE RISE OF POLITICAL MILITIAS

The legacy of the Gus Dur Presidency

The particular conditions in which the 7 June elections took place can provide an adequate, if simplified, explanation of the political crisis that plunged Indonesia into legislative paralysis during the presidency of Abdurrahman Wahid (October 1999 – July 2001). Head of a party that had come fourth in the elections, and thus held only fifty-one of the 462 seats in the DPR, Abdurrahman Wahid (known as Gus Dur) lacked the necessary political means to put his programme into effect. All the more so because he was caught up in a political system in which the prerogatives of the head of government were not clearly established by the text of the Constitution, but exercised *de facto* by a vice-president whose formal attributions were purely honorary. Chosen by parliament not for his leadership qualities but to block the candidacy of Megawati Sukarnoputri—once it was clear that Golkar had lost all relevance following the vote of no-confidence against B.J. Habibie—Gus Dur was incapable of forming a stable parliamentary majority.[28]

Wahid's solitary exercise of power led rapidly to a deterioration in the relations between institutions, relations that had never been clearly spelled out by the Constitution. By listening to the advice of his shadowy mystical cabinet advisers (*pembisik*) rather than to public opinion polls, by treating parliament as if it were a 'kindergarten' (his own word), by alienating the army and the police (meddling in their internal promotion criteria), and above all by treating Megawati, whose party had topped the election results with 33 per cent of the votes cast, with contempt in assigning her a secondary role, Gus Dur set in motion the events leading to his downfall.[29] Latching on to rumours of corruption in the handling of public funds (the so-called Bulogate affair), parliamentary investigative committees claimed for themselves a right of impeachment that the Constitution had not specifically granted them. By voting in favour of the president's removal from office, by an overwhelming majority, the deputies in effect put an end to an erratic regime built on a mystical, ultra-presidential vision of the exercise of state power.[30] But by creating, on

---

28 On Wahid's presidency, see the memoirs of his press secretary, the journalist Wimar Witoelar (2002), and Barton (2002). Witoelar's account is openly hagiographic, while Barton attempts to maintain a certain distance, even if his biography comes close to being an apologia.

29 For a remarkable study of the internal dissensions within the Nahdlatul Ulama in regard to Gus Dur's manner of exercising power, see Feillard (2002).

30 On this 'mystical' vision of power that underlay much of contemporary élite and popular political behaviour in Java, see Bonneff (2002) and Bertrand (2002), in particular pp. 120–6 on Gus Dur's arcane mystical counsellors and on the importance of 'secret meet-

the basis of an MPR decree, a procedure that would allow impeachment of the president, they above all undermined both institutional hierarchy and the balance of power between government branches. In the workings of the Indonesian constitutional system the 1945 Constitution (UUD 45) indeed takes full precedence over parliamentary decrees adopted in plenary session (Tetapkan MPR: TAP MPR), which in turn take precedence over DPR laws (Undang-Undang DPR: UU DPR), themselves usually considered as being on the same level as presidential instructions and decrees (Keputusan Presiden: Kepres).[31] This overlapping of executive and legislative powers raised a host of problems. The limits of each institution's sphere of action and the overarching hierarchy of prerogatives remained problematic given the absence of a constitutional council, one made up of judges independent of both the parliament and the Ministry of Justice. The forced ouster of Gus Dur set off an intense crisis in the ranks of Indonesian public-law jurists, but has not yet resulted in the adoption of measures that will definitely eliminate the many uncertainties concerning institutional operating procedures.

The new electoral provisions and the question of the Constitutional Court

In preparation for the 2004 elections a new set of legislative measures spelled out in greater detail the process by which the participating parties were to be selected. Article 3 of Law 31/2002 stipulates that to be authorised to compete parties must have permanent branches in at least 50 per cent of the provinces of the archipelago, as well as in at least 50 per cent of the regencies (Kabupaten) and/or municipalities of these provinces, and that in these regencies and municipalities branches must be located in at least 50 per cent of the districts (Kecamatan).[32] These technical prescriptions, intended to put politics firmly on a national basis and to get rid of bogus parties, are accompanied by a series of ideological strictures, the rejection of which can be punished by fines or imprisonment. For example, it is forbidden to violate the 1945 Constitution or the Pancasila (article 5.2) and parties are obliged to 'protect and defend the integrity of the Republic of Indonesia as a unitarian state' (Article 9). The law also provides for strict control of party financing. Parties are not to accept donations by foreign entities (Article 19.3) and individual campaign gifts must not exceed 200 million rupees (roughly £150) or 800 million rupees for firms (roughly $6,000) per fiscal year (Article 18). However, the state does provide parties with financial aid, calculated according to

---

ings' (*rapat gelap*) in his mode of governance.

31   For a useful introduction to the Indonesian legal system, see Lev (1972).

32   The texts of these laws are accessible on the KPU website, www.kpu.or.id, and on the presidential secretariat's website, www.ri.go.id.

the size of the party's representation in parliament. In addition, parties are required to present their campaign accounts to the KPU no later than one year after the elections (Article 9). The designation of party leaders, on both the national and the local level, must be decided by 'democratic consultation' (Article 13.2). Moreover Law 12/2003 provides the legal framework for the holding of elections. During this period, which lasts for three months and comes to a close three days before election day, 'incitation to violence' and defamation of an opponent on the basis of 'race, ethnic origins or religion' are treated as criminal offences punishable by law (Article 74).

The media are required to provide equal air time for all political parties and to broadcast all communiqués received from the KPU. In order to avoid overpolitisation of the National Elections Commission (which in 1999 had resulted in a deadlock, making it impossible to announce the election results on time), Law 4/2000 drastically redefines its make-up. The KPU is to be composed of eleven 'non-partisan' members. At present it is headed by the Aceh academic Nazaruddin Sjamsuddin, Professor of Sociology at the University of Indonesia, and is composed for the most part of jurists. The number of new parties, which had declined following the 1999 elections, rose dramatically in 2002 (five in 2000, fifteen in 2001 and sixty-nine in 2002). But only twenty-four parties were allowed to join the election race following a process of 'screening' led by the KPU.[33] This judicial revamping of the electoral system embodied the lessons learnt from the May-June 1999 campaign, marked by some clashes between party militants and above all by systematic recourse to slanderous attacks by the candidates. Some Islamic parties had then attempted to disqualify Megawati Sukarnoputri by describing her, in pamphlets widely distributed after Friday prayers, as an atheist enemy of Islam. Yet these new legislative measures, while they furnished the state with the legal means to better control the conduct of politics, did nothing to clarify the ambiguities of the texts fixing the areas of competence of the various institutions and the relations between them.

After laborious deliberations a Constitutional Court composed of nine judges, of whom three were named by the president, three by the parliament and three by the court itself, finally saw the light of day.[34]

---

[33] *Pidato Ketua KPU menjelang Pendaftaran Pemilihan dan Pendataan Penduduk Berkelanjutan (P4B)* [Address Delivered by the President of the KPU Concerning the Registration of Voters and the Completion of the Electoral Census], 7 April 2003.

[34] The selection process yielded the following results: the Constitutional Court will be presided over by Jimly Asshiddique, law professor at the University of Indonesia, and the Supreme Court justice Laica Marzuki will serve as vice-president; the remaining seven judges, most of whom have been Supreme Court justices, are Achmad Syarifuddin, Mukti Fadjar, Haryono, Achmad Rustandi, I Dewa Palguna, Sudarsono and Muarar Siahaan. The judges' term of office is for five years (non-renewable). For a detailed historical study of the Supreme Court, see Pompe (1996).

According to the law adopted by the DPR on 15 August 2003, the Constitutional Court has a duty to 'resolve electoral disputes and conflicts between institutions', to monitor conformity of laws with the Constitution, and is empowered to 'dissolve' those political parties that do not respect the provisions of the electoral laws. But because this jurisdiction was set up a mere eight months before the opening of the elections and the definition of its sphere of competence was still vague, it was hardly an effective instrument for regulating the interrelationship of the various institutions.[35] This is all the more true as party allegiances tarnished the magistrates' reputation for impartiality even before they took office. Haryono and Palguna are actually PDI-P deputies, Rustandi was said to be a choice 'dictated' by the PPP and Jimly Asshiddique, the law professor chosen to be the Court's president, was rumoured to be 'closely associated' with Golkar, which actively supported his candidacy.[36] Moreover legal experts have called attention to the lack of coercive means available to the Court to bring to trial and punish party campaigners involved in vote-buying.[37] Despite its lack of legitimacy, the Court managed to fulfil part of its role following the 2004 General Elections. It handed down rulings in 273 electoral disputes and thirty-eight of its decisions affected the number of seats held by political parties in the DPR, as well as a number of seats in the provincial and regency legislatures.[38] But since most of these electoral disputes were brought to its attention by vindictive party leaders, the whole procedure was instantly deemed by many observers a mere political instrumentalisation of law.

Yet the stakes are high. The election of the president of the republic by universal direct suffrage, presented by those who favour this option as the only effective means to attain stable governmental majorities, raises prickly questions concerning parliamentary prerogatives. Will the future

---

[35] See the criticisms expressed by members of the National Consortium for Law Reform (KHRN) in 'Legal Activist Slams Constitutional Bill', *Jakarta Post*, 12 July 2003.

[36] See 'Law Professor to Chair Constitutional Court', *Jakarta Post*, 20 August 2003, and 'RI Establishes Constitutional Court', *Jakarta Post*, 17 August 2003. The three judges designated by the assembly (Asshiddique, Rustandi and Palguna) were chosen by vote from a list of twelve candidates. The vote was ratified by the DPR Second Commission which also announced the results.

[37] See 'Campaign Law Full of Loopholes', *Jakarta Post*, 26 June 2004.

[38] See 'Court Completes Hearings in Electoral Disputes', *Jakarta Post*, 22 June 2004. Owing to the Court's rulings, the Prosperous Peace Party (PDS) took an additional seat in the West Papua Barat constituency after winning its dispute with the Democratic Party. The United Democratic Nationhood Party (PPDK) lost one seat in the house to the Pioneer Party, while in West Kalimantan the Reform Star Party (PBR) took one seat from the Freedom Bull National Party (PNBK). The National Mandate Party (PAN), which hoped to take an additional twenty seats in the House by filing complaints with the court, only won one seat in Central Sulawesi—at the expense of the Democratic Party. The Court also ruled that twenty-nine disputed seats at regency or municipal council level should be distributed among eleven political parties.

president not be tempted to exploit to the hilt his/her status as the people's directly chosen representative to cut back on parliament's power of impeachment? The political scientist Rizal Mallarangeng remarked, with a touch of wry irony, 'no one understands the true implications of these new measures, not even the élite that enacted them.'[39] Many critics of the presidential election law, which was adopted by the parliament in October 2000, point out that the larger political parties were unfairly advantaged. Only those groups having won at least 5 per cent of the DPR seats or 2 per cent of the votes cast will be authorised to propose a candidate (who cannot in any case be a former member of the Communist Party).[40] The risk of ending up with a one-headed executive is all the greater in that Megawati Sukarnoputri's ideological alliance with the military and her quasi-monarchical style of governing have reinforced the powers of the president in an evolution that began as soon as she became head of state in July 2001. Istana Merdeka, the presidential palace, has once again become the hub of the decision-making process. By way of proof, the decision to proclaim martial law in Aceh was taken in a meeting of the president's inner council and only afterwards were adequate appropriations voted by the assembly. The office of the presidential secretary-general, Bambang Kesowo, has rapidly been turned into the antechamber ('isolation chamber' according to some) of the executive.

Parliament's continuing fragility

The working conditions under which parliament operates are such that the power of the two houses is considerably weakened. First, the texts that define the relationship between the DPR and the 'senate' do not provide a clear definition of the 'shuttle' between the two houses by which legislative bills' proposals have to pass. Nothing is said, for instance, regarding how long the upper house can 'sit' on the preliminary draft of a bill that has been presented for consideration before giving a reply. The result is a lengthening of the legislative process, which may discredit parliament in the eyes of the electorate. Secondly, the new members of parliament, elected thanks to the *reformasi*, lack personal experience in the area of judicial expertise. Few of the representatives of the people have studied public law and fewer still have any knowledge of the internal functioning of the assembly (which enacts its own inner rules for its proceedings).[41] Thus it is tempting for them to vote 'blindfolded' for legislative bills,

---

39 Statement by Rizal Mallarangeng quoted in US-INDO (2003).
40 For a summary of criticisms, see 'Presidential Elections Bill May Produce Poor Candidates, Experts Say', *Jakarta Post*, 18 February 2003.
41 These remarks on the conditions in which parliament operates are taken from my current work on the new political élites of the *reformasi*, work initiated in March–April 2002 by a series of interviews with MPs from the various parties and presidents of parliamentary commissions.

and give as an excuse the obligation to obey party instructions.[42] Acute tensions arise because of the inexperience of the newly elected MPs and the questionable status in legal terms of certain emergency procedures, such as those of the select investigative commissions (the Pansus), often exploited for political purposes. Ade Komaruddin Mochammad, rising star of Golkar who claims to represent the 'young generation of rationally-minded' delegates, put it this way:

There is an attempt today to have the DPR commissions judge all the scandals: the Trisakti affair, the Pertamina affair and Bulog II [which involved accusations against Akbar Tanjung, leader of the Golkar] etc.[43] You can't turn around without running into an investigative commission. But these affairs have already been settled in political terms, since they all date from B.J. Habibie's presidency, and Habibie's record was condemned by parliament in August of 1999 and he has already been fined for that (*sudah divonis*). And Suharto has already been judged in political terms since the president has pardoned him and he is out of the picture! What's left of these affairs are criminal law cases (*hukum pidana*) that should be decided by civil courts, not by the parliament. Even the Trisakti case belongs to the past, since it no longer has anything to do with the DPR. But the problem is that most MPs haven't a clue; a lot of them have only just come out of the bush. Today the most important thing is political stability. Politics should be rational, not emotional. The deputies are still living in the Middle Ages, they spend their time running after status symbols when they ought to live like everyone else and remain close to the people. Take the case of Gus Dur: he's someone who comes from a well-known family of *kyai* [Islamic scholars]. He's from Purwakerta; he comes from a place where, in the *pesantren* [boarding houses for students of the Koran], the *murid* [students] think that if they drink water out of the basin in which their *guru* [master] washes his feet, they'll be even more intelligent! With politicians like that, rational politics are still a long way off.[44]

This continuing institutional instability is also both the cause and the consequence of the violent crisis that has shaken the major parties, all of which have been seriously weakened by internal dissension. Golkar almost split in two after Akbar Tandjung was indicted for embezzlement: the 'young Turks' of the party, who would like nothing better than to get rid of an embarrassing former New Order notable as quickly as possible, are in open revolt against old regime bigwigs. The PAN fell prey to a long-lasting quarrel between competing leaders of its local branches and the PPP had to accommodate dissonant voices in its executive committee in order to avoid a schism. Meanwhile the PDI-P was on the point of

---

42 See the scathing critique of the 'no-voting method' by Soedjati Djiwandono, 'Tyranny by the Majority: Current Decision-Making', *Jakarta Post*, 26 June 2003.

43 The Pertamina affair concerned misappropriation of funds of which the National Petroleum Company was victim, and the Trisakti affair concerned the responsibility of the police and the army in the shooting to death of three students on the campus of Trisakti University in Jakarta in 1998.

44 Interview, Jakarta, April 2002.

implosion on account of the all-out war waged in 2002 between Arifin Panigoro, the officially appointed leader of the party's parliamentary delegation, and Taufik Kiemas, the President's husband, reputed to be a shady businessman.[45]

The PDI-P, moreover, was greatly discredited by Megawati's quite unexpected decision to support Sutiyoso's campaign for re-election as governor of Jakarta (Steijlen, 2002). Sutiyoso, former deputy commander-in-chief of army special forces (Kopassus), is one of the figures most detested by the 'street people'.[46] Champion of authoritarian municipal policies, he constantly cracked down on street peddlers, *becak*-drivers and the Ciliwung slum-dwellers in order to curry favour with the middle classes, terrified by the supposed rise in delinquency. He even bulldozed the shantytowns that lined the *jalan tol* (the toll motorway taken by tourists and diplomats from Sukarno-Hatta airport to the centre of town) because they disfigured the landscape. Accused by NGOs of complicity in real estate scandals—such as the purchase for next to nothing of land in the red-light district of Kramat Tunggak shortly after the hundreds brothels that crowded the area were closed on his instructions—Sutiyoso is considered by many to be the 'number one enemy' of the capital's poorer neighbourhoods. And it was precisely these neighbourhoods that had, in the 7 June 1999 elections, provided one of the principal reservoirs of votes for the PDI-P. The President's public support for Sutiyoso shocked the municipal councillors of her own party and alienated a significant section of her popular electorate. Rumour had it in Jakarta that Megawati's move in favour of Sutiyoso was meant to pay back his under-the-table contribution to the PDI-P campaign funds—a deal that was said to have been struck by Taufik Kiemas. Whatever the reasons, the party scored very badly in the 2004 General Elections (19.5 per cent of the votes cast). The issue of 'money politics' (*politik uang*) now figures prominently in all leading newsmagazines and the disclosure of corruption scandals involving well-known party notables has become a routine part of the new media economy. A number of Jakarta-based NGOs, like Indonesia Corruption Watch,[47] publish detailed reports about the extravagant way of life of politicians. To answer growing criticism of its *laissez-faire* policy in that domain, the government set up an anti-corruption body in late 2003: the Corruption Eradication Commission

---

[45] For biographical information on Taufik Kiemas, see McIntyre (2000) and *Times Asia*, 160, 1 (15 July 2002).

[46] These remarks on Sutiyoso's authoritarian municipal policies are taken from an unpublished paper given at the colloquium 'Globalisation and the Urban Community', organised in late 2001 by the International Network on Globalisation at the Rikkyo University of Tokyo.

[47] The ICW was set up in June 1998. For more information, see the ICW website: www.antikorupsi.org.

(KPK), which has so far trained some sixty full-time 'anti-graft' senior prosecutors. However, this long-awaited initiative has yet to convince sceptical citizens and disillusioned country rating agencies.[48]

The rising menace of political militia

In addition it is important to take into account the degree to which the pursuit of political objectives outside the parliamentary framework threatens public life. Now that the anti-riot police have taken charge of big cities, violent mass demonstrations are mostly a thing of the past. But an extremely disquieting phenomenon is on the rise, indicating just how limited the power of the state is, and in consequence how little faith ordinary citizens are willing to put in the security forces and the judicial institutions. The lynchings of petty criminals, supposedly the work of 'crowds run wild' (*massa diamuk*),[49] are referred to in the national press in a way that reveals their underlying political significance: 'to take justice into one's own hands' (*main hakim sendiri*), in other words to take over the prerogatives of the state and thus break the monopoly of violence on which its authority rests. Although there are no reliable statistics documenting their rise in number, cases of lynching appear to be so commonplace in the villages and *kampung* (city neighbourhoods) that the police often refuse to open criminal investigations. The victims of these collective acts of aggression are usually *preman*, petty delinquents who 'stake out' bus terminals and markets where they extort 'protection money' from bus conductors and shopkeepers. When caught by a residents' night patrol (*ronda malam*), any 'stranger' found loitering in a village also risks a severe beating if he can't explain, in a sentence or two, who he is and why he is there.

This violent behaviour does not stem from a pathological urge unique to the Malay psyche (what colonial novelists referred to as 'running amok').[50] Each case of *main hakim sendiri* can in fact be taken as an indication of a loss of confidence in the state, henceforth as a means of reaffirming a local community identity—even if this reaffirmation takes a tragic form.[51] Lynchings are not, in Java in any case, infrapolitical acts.

---

48 See 'Anticorruption Body Urged to Solve Easy Cases to Begin With', *Jakarta Post*, 2 January 2004, and 'Megawati Approves Establishments of KPK, KPI', *Jakarta Post*, 27 December 2003. The degree of corruption of the new national and local political élite became a burning issue during the 2004 electoral campaign. A month before the campaign started a coalition of thirty-nine NGOs calling itself GerAK (Anti-Corruption Movement) publicly disclosed lists of candidates suspected of bribery. GerAK also accused the KPK of being supposedly absolutely inefficient.

49 On these lynchings, see Colombijn (2002).

50 The story of this colonial myth is told in Spores (1988).

51 For a critique of culturalist and economicist approaches to social violence in Indonesia, see Sidel (2001). For an astute political critique of the remanent idea of a 'culture of violence' peculiar to Java, see Fuller Collins (2002).

On the contrary, they reveal the existence, at a time when the central government's legitimacy is seriously challenged on the fringes of the country, of a deep longing for a kind of idealised political autarky, that is, a form of community-based 'self-government' (Bertrand, 2002: 85–101). The drastic increase in the cost of water and electricity, the catastrophic management of energy and transport infrastructures, the deterioration in public services and the ingrown corruption of the judicial system all militate against the state's claim to remain the sole focal point of citizens' allegiance. The alarmingly high number of instances of fiscal illegality and fraud, which take a heavy toll on tax revenue, is another symptom of breach of the contract binding citizens to the state.[52] The result may well be that 'too much politics kills politics', in the sense that the popular desire for change could in the end submerge the legal structures of the political system and erupt into its violent rejection.

The role of militia organisations must also be taken into account. Militia and paramilitary groups have long been a part of Indonesian political life.[53] In the years 1870 to 1920 the Dutch colonial state used professionals of violence as a means of indirectly maintaining control over the indigenous population (Schulte-Nordholt, 2002). The swaggering bullies, the *jago*, whose speciality was cattle stealing, also served as police informers (Schulte-Nordholt, 1991; Schulte-Nordholt and Van Till, 1999). This branching out of the state into criminal activities was accentuated during the struggle for independence (the period from 1945 to 1949, known as the 'Physical Revolution'). A number of republican Javanese guerrilla groups, from which the national army of the 1950s was to emerge, served as intermediaries for collusion between state authorities and the smuggling, gambling and prostitution syndicates. The New Order regime institutionalised these ties between crime bosses and security forces by creating in the 1980s the 'System for the security of the environment' (*Sistem keamanan lingkungan*, usually known by the acronym Siskamling). The regime's tacticians were concerned lest the criminal gangs from the red-light districts, which were called upon during election periods to provide muscle, take advantage of their privileged status to become too independent or join forces with the opposition. A decision was therefore taken to grant legal standing to members of the urban gangs: the *preman* (hoodlums) belonging to the Prems or to Massa 33 became civilian security agents (the *satpam* and the *hansip*), trained by the police and the army but paid by their private employers (Barker, 1999). And the Siskamling still exists. A look at the figures is enough to

---

[52] One can get an idea of the scale of this financial crisis by consulting the figures on the collection of corporate taxes and indirect taxes as given by Bertrand (2001b).
[53] This section of the article retraces some conclusions reached in an earlier publication (Bertrand, 2003b). The question of 'Islamic militias' such as the Laskar Jihad or the Front Pembela Islam will not be taken up here.

realise why it is still a burning issue: in 2001 the total number of *satpam* in Indonesia was revealed to be close to 200,000 (of which 90,000 were in Java) and the total number of *hansip* close to five million (International Crisis Group, 2001: 8). Compared to the size of the army (350,000 soldiers in uniform) and the police (250,000 men), the number of militiamen appears disproportionate. The creator of the Siskamling, former Chief of Police Awaloedin Djamin, is the first to admit that leaving law enforcement in the hands of the *hansip* and the *satpam* was a last resort, and one fraught with danger. But according to him, it is now too late to get rid of them, for they could never find other jobs and would inevitably end up swelling the ranks of the unemployed drifters.[54]

The objective assigned to the Siskamling was not only to reinforce political surveillance at the local level but also to rationalise the competition between the state security forces and the crime lords who controlled illegal markets in prostitution, drug trafficking, extortion and gambling. The idea was to create an operational structure—combining the army, the police and the criminal elements—that would manage lower city affairs jointly, from behind the scenes, by assigning separate areas for extortion rackets to each. But by authorising this partnership the system did not reduce rivalry between them. On the contrary, the result was, paradoxically, to aggravate competition, since it was publicly admitted that all three were engaged in the same types of activity and drew their power from the same kind of deadly violence (Siegel, 1998). This militia-like organisation of the state security forces had dramatic consequences. First, it accelerated the criminalisation of the state by encouraging adoption of criminal types of behaviour within the public institutions themselves. To judge the extent of this phenomenon one has only to turn to the increasingly frequent cases of lethal clashes between soldiers and policemen. Regular army squadrons and police units tend increasingly to act like gangs. They treat the areas under their authority as hunting grounds; they attempt to control, directly or indirectly, the illegal trafficking market; and they end up attacking each other armed with knives or sub-machine guns. On 29–30 September 2002 in Binjai near Medan (Sumatra) soldiers from an airborne unit (the Linud 100, dependent on Kodam 1), armed with rifles and grenade launchers, mounted an assault on a police station, killing seven policemen and three civilians. According to on-the-spot investigations, the attack was launched after the police had refused to free a drug dealer who had just been taken prisoner but was under armed forces protection (in return for a percentage of his sales) (Roosa, 2003). On 4 March 2003 members of an air force unit sta-

---

54 Awaloedin Djamin, *Menuju POLRI Mandiri yang Profesional* [Towards an Independent National Police that is Professional], Jakarta, Yayasan Tenaga Kerja Indonesia, 1999, p. 235, quoted in Barker (1999).

tioned east of Jakarta set fire to a police station and killed the officer on duty as reprisal for the humiliation of one of the airmen: the motorbike taxi belonging to a member of his family had been 'confiscated' (i.e. stolen) by the policemen.[55] The fact that the state security forces adopt the violent tactics characteristic of criminal gangs is without doubt one of the perverse consequences of the policy of negotiating with the criminal world—a policy fully institutionalised by the Siskamling.

The second dramatic consequence of the adoption of a militia style of organisation and its institutionalisation within the state administration is the criminalisation of the political domain. In one of the few existing regional studies of the election campaign in May-June 1999—that of the Province of East Java where a ferocious battle between the PKB, the PDI-P and the PAN took place—Arief Djati cautioned repeatedly against the danger of the rising spread of political militias (Djati, 1999). Today every political party has its own security force, organised as a full-fledged paramilitary corps. These security agents, known simply as *satgas*, wear army-style uniforms (combat jackets, berets, ranger outfits, badges, rank insignia) and are trained like soldiers. Despite (or perhaps because of) their reputation for violence, hundreds of members of Banser, the security contingent belonging to the youth movement of the Nahdlatul Ulama (the leading traditionalist Muslim organisation in Indonesia) were enrolled in the National Awakening Party security organisation.[56] Banser claims a membership of 425,000, but the true number is no doubt closer to 100,000.[57] The movement's publications always emphasise the Banser's contributions to community work, such as providing aid in case of a natural disaster or participating in the rebuilding of community structures in poor sections of town. They are thus portrayed in laudatory terms as 'warriors for mankind', devoted to serving the nation and the underprivileged.[58] However, when questioned individually Banser members make no effort to hide their passion for aggressive combat exercises, practiced under the close supervision of renowned mystical religious leaders such as Gus Munif or Kiai Maksum Jauhari.[59] True, Banser has never been

---

55 'Airforce to Discharge Members Involved in an Attack', *Jakarta Post*, 6 March 2003.
56 Interview with M.H. Rofiq, former ANSOR chief for East Java, Paris, February 2003. For an introduction to the Banser mythology, see the booklet *Gerakan Pemuda Ansor. Persaudaraan untuk Indonesia* [The Ansor Youth Movement: Fraternity for Indonesia], Jakarta: ANSOR, April 2001.
57 Banser is an acronym for 'Badan ANSOR serba guna', the 'catch-all service' of ANSOR.
58 See the pamphlet *Riyanto, Pahlawan Kemanusiaan. Profil pengabdian Banser* [Riyanto, a Hero of Mankind: Portrait of a Faithful Banser], PW GP Ansor Jawa Timur, 2002. The pamphlet is dedicated to the memory of a Banser member who died in the explosion of a bomb in a church in Mojokerto (East Java) while 'fulfilling his security duties on New Year's Eve'. Riyanto is depicted as a martyr and a model 'warrior for mankind'.
59 Interviews with Surabaya Banser members, September 2000.

involved in criminal activities, but it has initiated several violent campaigns, in particular when President Wahid was accused by the media of
adultery and corruption (Banser members laid waste to the offices of the
Surabaya-based newspaper *Jawa Pos*).

As for the 30,000 'security agents' of the PDI-P, their reputation for
brutality has been an established fact ever since they displayed their
strong-arm tactics in the 1999 elections during which, truncheons in
hand, they 'made safe' meeting areas (King, 2003). As these examples
show, the main threats to the peaceful unfolding of the *reformasi* process
came not only from *ancien régime* thugs but also from within the state
security apparatus and from within the new political parties. Almost all
of these parties, at first emphatically described by most foreign democracy-building agencies as the 'white doves' of democratisation, quickly
became nests of vested interests and began cultivating openly non-democratic ways of playing politics. By focusing too much on the D-Day of
the poll casting, many engineers of democracy may have forgotten to
take a closer look at what was going on at the very heart of the new
political field.

By focusing too much attention on statements issued by prominent public figures and on their political manoeuvring, without inquiring into the
system of stakes and rules that determine the stands they take, or by
featuring violent scenarios rather than recording the progressive steps towards furnishing a legal framework for political liberalisation, the critical observer can all too readily give the impression that the *reformasi* has
plunged the country into chaos. Yet what emerges as most striking about
the past six years of political vicissitudes is the slow but sure elaboration
of a set of rules governing the political system—rules enacted and implemented by still fragile but already assertive institutions such as the KPU
and the Constitutional Court. These rules are sometimes transgressed
and often ignored, but they nonetheless serve to mould (and moderate)
the way political actors behave. Certainly the relations between the parliament and the presidency, between the army and the new political élite,
between voters and deputies, between villagers and state authorities are
fraught with suspicion. While there is still little risk of territorial break-
up, the danger of political implosion remains.

Yet compromises have been found, a code of duties and sanctions
decreed, that could serve as a springboard for a new citizenship contract,
provided that types of political action which are outside the law—whether the work of the militias or the masses—are rapidly cut back. The role
played by the 'engineers of democracy' in this evolution has actually
been marginal. They neither hastened the coming of the *reformasi* nor
slowed its development. But by casting the broad issues of institutional

change within the confines of electoral fetishism they most certainly prescribed a very limited interpretation of Indonesian politics. Thus, whatever their intentions, they encouraged an élitist approach to the 'transition to democracy' that left aside essential questions such as the degree of representivity of parliament, and, a closely related question, the existence of forms of political activity lying outside the framework of the law.

(Translated by John Atherton and revised by the author)

Antlöv, Hans, 2004, 'National Elections, Local Issues: The 1997 and 1999 National Elections in a Village on Java' in Hans Antlöv (ed.), *Elections in Indonesia: The New Order and Beyond*, London: Routledge Curzon, pp. 111–37.

Barker, Joshua, 1999, 'Surveillance and Territoriality in Bandung' in Vicente Rafael (ed.), *Figures of Criminality in Indonesia, the Philippines and Colonial Vietnam*, Ithaca, NY: Cornell University Press, pp. 95–127.

Barton, Greg, 2002, *Abdurrahman Wahid. Muslim Democrat, Indonesian President: A View from the Inside*, Honolulu, HI: University of Hawaii Press.

Bertrand, Romain, 2001a, 'La démocratie à l'indonésienne. Bilan critique d'une transition qui n'en finit pas de commencer', *Revue internationale de politique comparée*, vol. 8, no. 3, pp. 435–59.

——, 2001b, 'Crise politique et société incivile en Indonésie', *Critique internationale*, no. 13 (October), pp. 42–51.

——, 2002, *Indonésie, la démocratie invisible. Violence, magie et politique à Java*, Paris: Karthala.

——, 2003a, 'Les *pemuda* en politique. Les répertoires d'action des marches protestataires des étudiants en Indonésie (1998)', *Le mouvement social*, no. 202, January–March, pp. 43–51.

——, 2003b, 'Les virtuoses de la violence. Remarques sur la privatisation du maintien de l'ordre en Indonésie contemporaine', *Tiers-Monde*, no. 174, June, pp. 83–104.

Bonneff, Marcel, 2002, 'Semar révélé. La crise indonésienne et l'imaginaire politique javanais', *Archipel*, no. 64, pp. 3–37.

Bourchier, David, 2000, 'Habibie's Interregnum: *Reformasi*, Elections, Regionalism and the Struggle for Power' in Chris Manning and Peter Van Diermen (eds), *Indonesia in Transition: Social Aspects of Reformasi and Crisis*, Singapore: Institute of Southeast Asian Studies, pp. 15–37.

Breman, Jan and Gunawan Wiradi, 2002, *Good Times and Bad Times in Rural Java: Case-Study of Socio-Economic Dynamics in Two Villages towards the End of the Twentieth Century*, Singapore: Institute of Southeast Asian Studies.

Briquet, Jean-Louis and Philippe Garraud (eds), 2002, *Juger la politique. Entreprises et entrepreneurs critiques de la politique*, Presses Universitaires de Rennes.

Colombijn, Freek, 2002, 'Maling, Maling! The Lynching of Petty Criminals' in Freek Colombijn and Thomas Lindblad (eds), *Roots of Violence in Indonesia: Contemporary Violence in Historical Perspective*, Singapore: Institute of Southeast Asian Studies, pp. 299–329.

Djati, Arief, 1999, *Mapping East Java's Transition: The Reformasi and the 1999 General Election*, Jakarta: IDEA.

Election Facilitation Center, 2 June 1999, *International Observers to the June 7, 1999 Elections*, Jakarta: United Nations Development Programme.

Elson, Robert, 2002, *Suharto: A Political Biography*, Cambridge University Press.

European Union Election Observation Mission, 5 April 2004, *Long Term Observer Working Booklet*, Jakarta.

Feillard, Andrée, 2002, 'Indonesian Traditionalist Islam's Troubled Experience with Democracy', *Archipel*, no. 64, pp. 117–44.

Fuller Collins, Elizabeth, 2002, 'Indonesia, A Violent Culture?', *Asian Survey*, vol. 42, no. 4 (July–August), pp. 582–604.

Garrigou, Alain, 1992, *Le vote et la vertu. Comment les Français sont devenus électeurs*, Paris: Presses de la FNSP.

Hermet, Guy, 1996, *Le passage à la démocratie*, Paris: Presses de la FNSP.

HONEST, Rectors' Forum Indonesia, May 1999, *Monitoring Form: Vote Casting and Counting Process, 1999 General Election Election Monitor*, Jakarta.

International Crisis Group, 20 February 2001, *Indonesia: National Police Reform*, Jakarta.

International Republican Institute, May 1999, *Buku Panduan Saksi Partai Pemilu 1999* [Handbook for Party Observers, 1999 General Elections], Jakarta.

King, Phil, 2003, 'Putting the (Para)military back into Politics', *Inside Indonesia*, no. 73 (January–March), pp. 19–20.

Lev, Daniel, 1972, 'Judicial Institutions and Legal Culture in Indonesia' in Claire Holt (ed.), *Culture and Politics in Indonesia*, Ithaca, NY: Cornell University Press, pp. 246–318.

McIntyre, Angus, 2000, 'Megawati Sukarnoputri: From President's Daughter to Vice-president', *Bulletin of Concerned Asian Scholars*, vol. 32, no. 1–2 (January–June).

National Elections Commission (KPU), May 1999, *Election Day Instructions for KPPS Members*, Jakarta.

——, 1999, *Collection of Election Laws*, Jakarta.

Pemberton, John, 1986, 'Notes on the 1982 General Election in Solo', *Indonesia*, no. 41, pp. 1–22.

Pompe, Sebastiaan, 1996, *Fifty Years of Judicial Development*, Leiden University Faculty of Law.

Reeve, David, 1985, *Golkar of Indonesia: An Alternative to the Party System*, Oxford University Press.

Roosa, John, 2003, 'Brawling, Bombing and Backing', *Inside Indonesia*, no. 73 (January–March), pp. 10–11.

Schulte-Nordholt, Henk, 1991, 'The *Jago* in the Shadow: Crime and Order in the Colonial State of Java', *Review of Indonesian and Malaysian Affairs*, vol. 25 (winter), pp. 74–91.

——, 2002, 'A Genealogy of Violence' in Freek Colombijn and Thomas Lindblad (eds), *Roots of Violence in Indonesia: Contemporary Violence in Historical Perspective*, Singapore: Institute of Southeast Asian Studies, pp. 33–61.

—— and Margreet Van Till, 1999, 'Colonial Criminals in Java, 1870–1910' in Vicente Rafael (ed.), *Figures of Criminality in Indonesia, the Philippines and Colonial Vietnam*, Ithaca, NY: Cornell University Press, pp. 47–69.

Sidel, John, 2001, 'Riots, Church Burning, Conspiracies: The Moral Economy of the Indonesian Crowd in the Late Twentieth Century' in Ingrid Wessel and G. Wimhöfer (eds), *Violence in Indonesia*, Hamburg: Abera Verlag, pp. 47–63.

Siegel, James, 1998, *A New Criminal Type in Jakarta: Counter-Revolution Today*, Durham, NC: Duke University Press.

Solidarity Center (ACILS), May 1999, *Summary of Election Monitoring Reports: Ujung Pandang Monitoring Team (March–first week of May 1999)*, Jakarta.

Spores, John C., 1988, *Running Amok: An Historical Inquiry*, Athens, OH: Ohio University, Center for International Studies.

Steijlen, Fridus, 2002, 'Sutiyoso's Reelection as Governor of Jakarta', *Bijdragen tot de Taal-, Land- en Volkenkunde*, vol. 158, no. 3, pp. 513–27.

Sulistyo, Hermawan and A. Kadar (eds), 2000, *Uang dan Kekuasaan dalam Pemilu 1999* [Money and Force/Power during the 1999 General Elections], Jakarta: KIPP Indonesia.

Sulistyo, Hermawan *et al.*, 2000, *Kekerasan Politik dalam Pemilu 99 (Laporan dari Lima Daerah)* [Political Violence during the 1999 General Elections. Report from Five Regions], Jakarta: PPW-LIPI.

Tornquist, Olle (ed.), 2002, *Political Violence: Indonesia and India in Comparative Perspective*, University of Oslo, Centre for Development and the Environment (SUM), SUM Reports 9-00.

UNDP-Jakarta, 7 June 1999, *Election Update: Official Newsletter of UNDP Indonesia's Electoral Assistance Programme*, vol. 1, no. 9.

US-INDO, 20 March 2003, *Political Succession and the 2004 Elections: Report of a Conference at the United States-Indonesia Society*, Washington, DC.

Wajah Dewan Perwakilan Rakyat Republik Indonesia. Pemilihan Umum 1999 [Profile of the DPR. 1999 General Elections], July 2000, Jakarta: Penerbit Harian Kompas.

Witoelar, Wimar, 2002, *No Regrets: Reflections of a Presidential Spokesman*, Jakarta and Singapore: Equinox Publishing.

POLITICS IN THE VILLAGE

VOTING AND ELECTORAL MOBILISATION IN RURAL CORSICA

Jean-Louis Briquet

In some regions in France local politics, and even more so rural politics, are conducted in an environment that sets them apart considerably from national politics. The act of voting in this case has nothing to do with the ideological conflicts that divide political parties. Instead it is limited to locally-circumscribed issues, takes place in a context of mutual acquaintanceship, and is frequently shaped by personal and family relationships. Hence, it is more easily expressed in terms of individual relationships (of friendship, trust, gratitude) than in abstract terms of political conviction. It can even be the compensation for (or anticipation of) material advantages that the elected official has granted (or promised) to some of his voters ('favours' of a clientelistic nature). In short, it meets criteria that diverge from the ideal of civic-minded citizenship that has taken hold as elective democracies have been shaped, an ideal that believes voting should be the manifestation of a specifically political opinion independent of the voter's private relations and interests (Garrigou, 2002; Romanelli, 1998).

Discredited as a parody of 'real' politics, or presented as a remnant of 'outmoded' traditional behaviour, local politics nevertheless have their own specific features and their own rationality. The practices they generate cannot be regarded solely from the standpoint of their distance from the 'dominant symbolism', in other words as the product of voters' political incompetence and their inability to act in accordance with the official norms of political legitimacy;[1] on the contrary, they bring to light the existence of various means actively employed by voters to assimilate the mechanisms of electoral representation according to their own interests and values. This chapter analyses some of the particular expressions of this phenomenon in the case of rural Corsica.[2]

1 This hypothesis was developed with respect to 'popular culture' by Grignon and Passeron: 'Any "dominated culture" functions like a culture, in other words as the symbolic control of a social condition despite the unequal relationships it has with other cultures' (1989: 79).
2 The analyses that follow have been drawn from research on political practices and clientelism in rural Corsica, the results of which were published in Briquet (1997).

AN ELECTION MEETING

In Venzolasca, a little village in northern Corsica, an election meeting was organised in preparation for the September 1988 departmental elections. Figures from right-wing Corsican parties came from the region's major city of Bastia to accompany one of the candidates on the campaign trail. By their arrival people had already gathered on the village square. Most of them were men, talking in small groups. Among them, as one of the participants divulged, were many of the 'heads of the most important families in the canton', which was a good sign, because they brought with them 'a bunch of votes' (those of most of their kin). Among the highly animated groups that had formed, the main topic of discussion was the odds on the candidate's victory. His supporters informed the candidate of the 'counts' they had made (the number of 'sure' votes in the village) and reminded him of the 'visits' he needed to make to the homes of certain voters to 'request their vote', to assure them that he was indeed taking care of what they had asked for (a job for a family member, an administrative issue to resolve, a 'recommendation' for a promotion or a transfer in the civil service etc.) or simply out of courtesy to those who had long backed him and expected him to show an explicit sign of familiarity. They also pointed out as yet undecided families that could possibly be 'brought around'.

The point was to 'turn out in numbers', to 'show the opponent we exist' and demonstrate to all present the support the candidate enjoyed among the personalities accompanying him. One of them was a deputy to the regional assembly, an influential surgeon in the hospital in Bastia and one of the city's right-wing leaders. People knew he had 'done a lot of favours' and that he was likely to do more. As one of the meeting's participants explained:

'With all the people here that owe him something, when he comes with him [the candidate] and shows that he's behind him, it's important ... People take that into account. Especially because he certainly has done a lot of favours: everyone has a relative that he treated at the hospital one day or another. Since he's such a helpful person, plenty of people have a sense of gratitude towards him. And then there are the jobs he's acquired for some people, especially at the hospital ... not to mention that now that he's at the Region [the Regional Assembly] he can do even more than before ...'

The meeting continued in the neighbourhood bar run by one of the candidate's sympathisers. On a sign from the proprietor everyone flocked to the counter and nearby tables to partake of the group *apéritif* paid for by the candidate. The politician gave only a very brief speech thanking those who had come to support him and wish him success. He then gave the floor to the regional deputy, who simply recalled the candidate's qualities: a 'devoted' man who 'had done and will do a lot for the canton'.

The main thing is not what is said in such speeches, but rather what the ritual indicates about the relationships that bind the candidate and his sympathisers. Friendship, sympathy and mutual aid are mentioned explicitly, but they are mainly displayed through the various 'tie-signs' between protagonists (Goffman, 1971): hugs, use of the familiar *'tu'* form of address, asides, cheerful greetings and joking are all signs of closeness and the personal nature of the political relationship. Personalisation is also manifested in the 'wings', where transactions that must be at least formally concealed from the public eye take place. And once the *apéritif* is finished the groups reform and the candidate mingles among them. He sometimes calls to one of his supporters, introduces him to the regional deputy, who moves aside with him to speak in a low voice. Nothing of what is said in these private discussions is revealed, but they are signs of intimacy often interpreted as requests for favours. Before leaving someone will ask the regional deputy to 'remember what he promised'. Later, in the car bringing us back to Bastia, the mayor of a neighbouring town who had come along with the candidate said:

'One thing that's important if you want to do well in an election is to trade favours …. The right favour at the right time for the right family is something that can tip the scale …. If it works, electorally speaking, it's sure to count.'

POLITICAL TIES AND 'AUTHENTICITY'

The preceding account clearly illustrates the basic differences between forms of electoral mobilisation in rural Corsica and those that prevail at the central level of the political field.[3] The political ritual is only rarely codified according to specific procedures that distinguish it from other types of social ritual. It reproduces modes of sociability that have been constituted outside the realm of politics, such as the *apéritif* (one of the principal rites of male sociability that regularly brings men together at the bar of one of the village cafés) or the 'visit' (a mandatory form of village sociability, particularly for women, which is expected at deaths, births and celebrations or as a simple sign of courtesy). It brings into play the general repertory of social relations, such as friendship, sympathy, mutual aid and gratitude. It manifests the existence of interpersonal ties, the political relationship seeming somehow to be their 'natural' extension. Few things about it are reminiscent of the official codes of an election rally as it has formed as a specific political ritual: there are no differences between, for instance, the people who speak from the podium and those in the audience. Nor are there signs of party affiliation (posters, party

---

3 Numerous researches on local politics in France indicate that this difference is not specific to Corsica but is also found in several other areas (see, for instance, Abélès [1989] and, for the 1960s and 1970s, Kesselman [1967] and Tarrow [1977]).

logos, distribution of tracts) or references to national political issues, or even to regional issues, except in a very allusive manner.

The local actors are totally aware of the illegitimate nature of these ways of doing politics , by the yardstick of the dominant beliefs. They know the risks of seeing some of their practices stigmatised, justifying them to the interviewer by explaining that they are consonant with behavioural norms that are only valid locally: 'You know, here, it's not like on the mainland: we vote for men, not ideas'; 'People, when they see how politics is done in Corsica, they say it's clanism ....[4] But there's something noble about clanism: a network of solidarity, trust and direct friendship with people that you can't find in the city or on the mainland any more.' The justification is made in the name of a certain 'domestic nature': the political choices and preferences are the result of an 'emotional' tie to the individual to whom one is personally bound by friendship or neighbourliness or because he has done favours.

Political commitments made in the name of the 'civic nature'[5] of politics are, moreover, liable to be suspected of lacking authenticity. 'Voting for ideas' often appears as an illusion that conceals the voters' true motives; 'ideologies' are considered irrelevant to political choices that are motivated primarily by the qualities of the people running and by 'human' relationships. 'The ideas of left and right may have their importance on the mainland, but here they're not essential, far from it', commented a local politician during an interview. 'What counts is the man, the relationship one has with him, the relationship he has had with your family .... Here politics is a matter of man to man much more than of ideology.'

The political tie is thus perceived and presented as a personal and affective tie, as opposed to the neutral and anonymous relationship promoted by the ideal of civic-minded citizenship. Hence the act of voting in Corsican villages often has an ostentatiously manifested public nature. Contrary to the official legal definition, ballots are only rarely cast in secret, but instead in such a way that everyone can clearly display his political commitments. Until recently the use of the voting booth was unusual, although legally mandatory, because it exposes the person who uses it to the risk of being suspected of duplicity ('he has something to hide'). Electoral choices are openly expressed: on election day only one ballot paper is selected; it is shown clearly to those in the room before it is inserted into the ballot box; voters go to the town hall in groups of

---

[4] The term 'clan' or 'clanism' is often used to describe (and usually to denounce) political groupings dominated in Corsica by the big regional notables (*capipartiti*, i.e. 'party leaders'), linked to local elected officials and networks of voters (often family networks) by clientelistic exchanges and interpersonal solidarities.
[5] Regarding 'domestic nature' and 'civic nature', as well as the conflicts between the two 'natures', see Boltanski and Thévenot (1987).

'like-minded' people to wait for the results; they will celebrate victory together (or console one another over defeat) at the 'party' café.[6]

However, sometimes the vote cannot be exhibited publicly, but it remains the sign of a personal tie, as this anecdote, related by a regional deputy, illustrates:

'I was running for the first time in a canton where there was a family that was very close to me. I'd helped out one of their sons by getting him a job in the departmental administration. Besides, these people had been very close to my father, they were friends of the family. But in this canton my opponent was their cousin and they had always voted for him. So the mother comes to see me and says: "You know full well we can't vote for you, but we'll give you some votes anyway." What she meant was that, out of the five or six votes the family had, they'd give me two or three. And that's what they did. It was complicated, actually, because they couldn't say they were voting for me. It was simply impossible with respect to their cousin and the rest of their family; it would've caused too many problems. So what they did, they went through the voting booth, taking only the ballot papers printed with their cousin's name. But I had given them ballot papers with my name, which they'd kept in their pockets. So that way they could vote for me without anyone knowing.'

The vote is therefore inseparable from the person who casts it, in keeping with a rationale that Marcel Mauss described with regard to gift-giving when he pointed out that the 'thing given' creates a bond between the two individuals that is a bond of the soul. In the same way that a gift converts a material relationship into a 'spiritual relationship' (Mauss, 1950: 160), the vote in this case displays an 'authentic' bond between people.

THE RECIPROCITY OF FAVOURS

However, this authentic bond is not entirely unambiguous: on the one hand it is stated in terms of moral obligation (the duty of friendship); on the other it is sustained by pragmatic exchanges ('favours'). Voting in fact provides access, through clientelistic exchanges, to resources that local politicians can distribute (jobs, social benefits, public works contracts etc.). Even if the voter's private interests are not immediately satisfied, this aim remains latent in a relationship perceived as a long-term commitment that creates mutual obligations. These obligations include, for the elected official, 'doing favours' and interceding on behalf of his voters; and, for the voter, responding to this favour with political loyalty,

---

6 The term 'party' (*partitu*) here refers to local political groupings that claim allegiance to the same partisan label, the opposing groups being described as 'counter-party' (*contrapartitu*). This denotes a fairly cohesive network of sociability that is both social and political (each 'party' for instance has its favourite bar; the members of a 'party' often share the same recreational activities, hunting in particular) and a common identity space ('being of the same party' is an attribute often used to describe relations between people).

especially at election time. As a retired civil servant living in a small rural town explained:

'Imagine someone gave my son or my daughter a job. I admit that it binds us [with the politician who gave the job] .... Suppose someone does someone else a favour: his son was incapable of finding work, but someone found him a job. Well, you're not going to spit in the face of someone who helped you: I think that's normal. I must say, in all honesty, that for me to get appointed in Corsica, a Corsican deputy [I knew] had to intervene and he earned my gratitude .... When the favour is a big one, you can't refuse to vote for the person, it bonds us and I don't want anyone calling me an ingrate.'

Refusing to vote for someone who has done a favour for oneself or a member of one's family is seen as a 'betrayal' or a breach of the legitimate rules of conduct within the local group. This type of behaviour is often punished by a loss of reputation ('you can't count on him'; 'he's ungrateful') or by exclusion from networks of sociability around which the village 'party' is organised.

On the other hand an elected official's refusal (or inability) to fulfil his voters' demands for favours usually results in defection. A promise not kept or a job not given can lead to withdrawal of voter support, as a village mayor explains while recounting the difficulties he faces due to increasing requests from his voters:

'It's true that we have to do favours, but you have to be careful with favours, because they're like dynamite. You can gain twenty votes on one side if you find someone a job, but you can also lose forty on the other .... You make some people unhappy and they come and say to you: "What! We voted you in and you won't give us anything." ... Favours can turn against you, and the guy that you placed, even if he voted for you, can make you lose votes.'

Along similar lines, another rural mayor complained during an interview of his fellow citizens' attitude, saying they always demanded more 'favours' and 'promises' than he could possibly deliver. He explained that in the village where he was elected, '[his] party is losing more and more votes.' 'When you've been mayor for twenty years, there's always something that's not right, favours that haven't been granted, work that hasn't been done .... So people go across the street [and support the mayor's opponent].'

The ambiguity of this type of political relationship is reminiscent of what Julian Pitt-Rivers (1961) highlighted with respect to the 'paradox of friendship': although the friendly relationship should be sustained by an exchange of favours, it is still formally disinterested. So 'while a friend is entitled to expect a return of his feelings and favour, he is not entitled to bestow them in that expectation' (Pitt-Rivers, 1961: 139). The same can be said of the electoral exchange in Corsica: although it can provide access to material resources and personal advantages, it should not be presented as merely a 'trade', but as the consequence of a moral relationship between people. The distinction between 'emotional friendship' and 'instrumental friendship', often used to differentiate between affective friendly relations and those that have an immediate practical aim (Wolf, 1966), vanishes here: with regard to local beliefs about what constitutes legitimate conduct, voting can both express an individual's authentic commitment (based on loyalty) and satisfy pragmatic interests. The political exchange is thus transformed into a moral obligation of reciprocity. The act of voting, like that of doing a favour, is more significant in the intentions it reveals (the sign of a bond) than in the results it produces (the personal favour for the voter or the election support for the politician). A former national deputy elected in the 1970s in a northern Corsican voting district explained during an interview:

'In Corsica you may be exploited to the hilt, but on the other hand a whole family will be devoted to you. I've had entire families vote for me and I'm sure they've remained loyal to me ... An elected official is constantly called on to do favours, and if he doesn't, he'll definitely lose votes. I used to work in a ministry in Paris, and I spent all my time finding a job for somebody or subsidised housing for someone else. I also had to intervene to get civil servants transferred when they wanted to come back to Corsica .... But I never had a complaint about any of the people I helped: they were all loyal voters.'

The material dimension of the political exchange is not concealed (a vote is in response to 'appeals' and 'favours'), but it only surfaces as the consequence of feelings that go beyond it ('loyalty' and 'devotion') and are its condition of possibility.

CLIENTELISM AND POLITICS

The political ties just described are akin to those analysed in the social sciences through the notion of clientelism. Although they emphasise the material aspects of the clientelistic relationship, these analyses have all explored its 'moral' dimension. Doubtless clientelism is first of all 'characterised by a simultaneous exchange of different types of resources—above all, instrumental and economic as well as political ones (supports, loyalty, votes, protection)'; but 'a strong element of interpersonal obligation is prevalent in these relations, an element often couched in terms of personal loyalty of reciprocity and attachment between patrons and clients' (Eisenstadt and Roniger, 1984: 48–9). Jeremy Boissevain (1974) has underlined the role of the values of friendship in groups in which relations are both instrumental and highly personalised ('cliques', clientelistic networks). Most social anthropology research devoted to rural communities in the Mediterranean world—which in the 1960s and 1970s most systematically tackled the question of clientelism—have also highlighted the importance of cultural codes of friendship and interpersonal loyalty in systems of 'patronage' (Davis, 1977: chapter 3; Albera *et al.*, 2001: 275 ff.).

In the framework of these highly inegalitarian communities, where material and symbolic resources have been monopolised by a small group of 'patrons' or 'notables', reciprocity helps to legitimate their power and maintain their authority. In order to be accepted, social and economic domination in fact implies an array of ideological justifications, one being that it is rooted in an 'exchange of mutual benefits' (Lemarchand, 1981: 10). Reciprocity is thus a way of converting subjection into 'moral agreement' (Davis, 1977: 132), which can take the form—with the institution of voting as the means of selecting political office holders—of voter loyalty. Gratitude and giving, devotion and loyalty, thus perform the transformation of 'economic capital and symbolic capital, which produces economically-based dependencies that are veiled as moral relations' that Pierre Bourdieu speaks of in his analysis of the foundations of political authority in societies with weak institutions (1980: 210).

The dominance of the notables in nineteenth-century Corsica obeys this logic, as the account (reported in 1887 by a Paris journalist) given by a 'party leader' in the north-western region of Saint-Florent shows:

You see our house: of the four brothers, only one is married. In that way we avoided fragmenting our holdings and scattering our influence. One of my brothers manages our properties. I, because I'm the eldest, handle the political side. I give my life and I'd almost say my fortune to our clients and our clients give us their votes; that's our secret .... Our property is rented out to some fifty households of settlers according to fairly easy terms and we do not always require that they be fulfilled to the letter. It's been nearly two hundred years already .... In some villages our parcels are so mixed up with other inhabitants' land that if we were to ban herds from grazing on them, no one would be able to put their animals to pasture .... We leave grazing open. Our woods are left open as well; any of our friends can go and gather what they like. This indulgence, which is indispensable to their type of existence, gets us another three hundred voters .... Added to that are families who, due to a bond of kinship or out of tradition, are used to following ours ... (Bourde, 1887: 11–12)

The notables' power in this case derives from their ability to redistribute some of their wealth in exchange for recognition of the status they lay claim to—a status that is ratified by the vote. To achieve this, they not only need to possess resources that are rare, but also to adopt 'conducts of life (*lebensführung*) that bring them prestige ... and predestine them for domination': gifts (entailing a moral debt), benevolence (which is at the root of the 'social esteem' granted to the notables) and 'conducts of honour' consonant with their position of excellence (Weber, 1964 [1922], vol. 2: 698).

Among these resources, those that the notables dispensed using their own goods (land, personal assistance, gifts, but also bribes or threats to withdraw their protection) were prevalent in Corsica until the late nineteenth century. From that time on the importance of pasture and farming activities declined somewhat in village community economies, emigration—to towns on the mainland or to the colonies—increased considerably and incomes grew more and more dependent on jobs and public transfers. Under these conditions the notables, if they wanted to keep their clienteles, came to distribute new types of goods (public subsidies and aid, civil service jobs, 'recommendations', preferential treatment etc.). Some heirs of large families of Corsican notables were able to adapt to these new constraints: they strengthened their positions within local administrations; they increased their influence in national government (by acceding to ministerial positions or the senior civil service); they used their networks of alliances (among their kin, in the circles of sociability they belonged to, or with municipal elected officials associated with them) to form the backbone of organised regional political groupings with ties to the national parties. In this way they were able to maintain their authority, by using resources made available through new forms of state intervention (regional public policies, social policies of the welfare state etc.) to their advantage.

Paths to notability were nevertheless open to new political entrepreneurs belonging to the local middle class (lawyers, doctors, civil servants, teachers). Access to elected office, even—for those in the highest standing—to central governmental institutions, senior civil service careers or leadership roles in political parties, allowed them too to take part in controlling channels of public resource allocation. With the spread of public education they were able to earn prestigious social titles (university degrees, senior professional positions), allowing them to compete with the former notables in the field of 'social esteem' and individual prestige. They consequently adopted some of the notables' methods, such as providing assistance and charity, socialising with voters or forming political loyalty through clientelistic exchanges. This phenomenon, which can be observed in several other regions in France (Garrigou, 1998: 67 ff.), was all the more blatant in Corsica since the people were very dependent, in their daily lives or their strategies of social climbing, on support from politicians (access to jobs and public assistance, support for emigration, job 'recommendations'). The lack of industrialisation, the importance of emigration, the strength of acquaintanceship ties over a small area that long remained fairly undeveloped and sparsely populated[7] have, moreo-

---

7 Corsica today has slightly over 250,000 inhabitants, of whom nearly half live in the two major urban areas (Ajaccio and Bastia). Urban dwellers have maintained close contacts with their native villages: many have a house there where they go at weekends or on holiday; some continue to vote there. Emigration began in the late nineteenth century and took on massive proportions from the early 1920s to the late 1950s, resulting in a decrease in population to slightly less than 300,000 at the beginning of the twentieth century and to

ver, prevented social groups from mobilising on 'ideological' grounds that might compete with the power of the notables—as is often the case in urban environments or among blue-collar workers' groups.

The power of the notable thus persisted in Corsica even as political activities were undergoing a profound transformation. The establishment of political parties, increased state intervention, bureaucratisation—all processes with which 'political modernisation' is currently identified—fed various forms of the political tie that remain alive even today. The regional development policies conducted after the Second World War, for instance, gave local politicians new means, which were often distributed through the channel of clientelistic networks. In Corsica and elsewhere the, moreover, organisation of local political-administrative power in post-war France reinforced the notables' influence by raising their status to that of mediator between the central authority and peripheral societies (Grémion, 1976) and ensuring them control over resources which, in some cases, helped maintain their clienteles (Médard, 1981). This is how political modernity has concretely taken shape in Corsica, through practices considered to be 'traditional': the intermediation of notables and clientelistic reciprocity have played an active part in establishing and effectively operating modern political institutions—voting, political parties, government agencies or local authorities.[8]

USES OF POLITICS

In such a context political relationships continue to be perceived as personal relationships, which implies assistance and protection on the part of politicians and gratitude and loyalty on the part of voters. These relationships have of course evolved to some extent. Some voters have gained in autonomy as their living conditions have become less and less dependent on decisions made by their 'protectors'—when they have a steady income, for instance (civil or military pension, retirement, civil service salary), or if they have entered the job market more easily (through emigration, an expanded job market due to national economic growth, or the democratisation of public education). Also electoral transactions have sometimes given rise to more direct and more explicit deals—the 'moral' dimension of the political tie disappears in relations openly guided by ulterior motives and interests (vote-buying, corruption). Moreover, new political groups have appeared that have criticised the power of the notables and sought to promote alternative modes of

---

190,000 in 1962, at which time the trend reversed owing to the arrival of new population flows in Corsica (repatriates from Algeria when it was decolonised, young people wanting to return to their 'native land') and a relative economic boom due mainly to tourism.
[8] These processes, simply mentioned here in passing, are analysed in greater detail in Briquet (1997).

public action—rooted, in particular, in the nationalist protest movement beginning in the mid-1970s.[9]

But these phenomena have not radically transformed the predominant forms of the political tie in Corsica. Intercession by local elected officials remains essential to many individuals, whether they need to find a job (particularly in sectors where political 'recommendations' are still effective, such as certain local branches of the civil service) or enter local power networks—where decisions to allocate subsidies or public works contracts are made, administrative permits are granted etc. Family ties, the duties of friendship and ties of solidarity remain openly asserted motives for voter choices, even among people who have long since broken free from the dependence on notables as far as their living conditions are concerned. For instance, one woman of Corsican family living in Paris, where she completed her university education and now works as a senior manager in a computer firm, but who returns to her family village for vacation, explained in these terms why she continued to cast her vote there:

'To me, I couldn't care less about voting in Paris ... I don't even know who my district mayor is, and I don't want to know. Here I know who I'm voting for, I have my family, I have a lot of friends. When I vote, I know what it means, I vote for someone I've known forever, who I can go see when I want to ... I give my vote to X [the village mayor], because he was my father's best friend, as well as his closest political ally in the canton [her father, deceased at the time of the interview, had been a regional deputy]. My whole family does the same thing; and I'm not afraid to say I vote out of family loyalty.'

Here the act of voting shows her attachment to her home community and kin, but it is also a reward given to a political ally who acted in favour of a family member. It retains a 'moral' dimension, involving people who are united by loyalty, friendship and gratitude. In Corsican villages this dimension is still heavily present: voting expresses individuals' grounding in a community, their membership in groups that are at the same time 'marks of identity' and networks of solidarity within which favours can be exchanged and the pragmatic transactions of everyday life can occur. And for these reasons voting and the expression of political identity have to be public.

Specific expressions of the political tie thus do exist in Corsica, but they differ enormously from those that have come to be seen as legiti-

---

9 After the Communist Party in the years following the Second World War, regionalist and nationalist movements calling for greater regional autonomy and Corsica's independence, sometimes with recourse to violence, have been the main actors in the criticism of notables and 'clans'. These movements have, however, generally been excluded from local power structures and, when they have been included in them, often have not managed to avoid reproducing internally the same practices they criticised. On the regionalist and nationalist movements in Corsica, see Crettiez (1999).

mate in the building of elective democracies. The social sciences have often analysed this difference through the lens of opposition between 'traditional' societies and 'modern' societies. Clientelistic exchanges, the personalisation of political relations, the low ideological content of voter choices, all appear to be signs of a 'traditional' culture set apart from the categories of 'modern' politics, in terms of both the state's bureaucratic rationale and civic-minded citizenship. Even more, they are allegedly an 'obstacle to the institutionalisation of authority' and a long-term legitimation of institutions (Graziano, 1980) or the reason for these institutions' lack of efficiency due to the absence of a 'civic culture' able to stimulate trust and cooperation among people and thereby encourage the development of democracy (Putnam, 1993). In this case there is a great risk of presenting certain types of political behaviour as a set 'culture' or of only considering them insofar as they deviate from the established norm of democratic legitimacy (as an indication of a dearth of civic culture, a political 'pathology' or a 'failure' of democratisation).

Certainly these types of behaviour do not conform to the norm. But this fact in no way drains them of meaning. They are less a sign of the voters' political 'incompetence' than a result of the way they come to terms with representative democratic institutions, according to values and motivations that differ from those proclaimed in official institutions. Voting in fact brings into play personal investments that are mainly practical in nature: by voting, individuals gain access to rare resources (mainly those distributed by the state via the notables) that they can, at least in part, turn to their advantage; their vote gives them power—also partial and limited, but real nonetheless—over their 'protectors', who are then committed to 'doing favours' and responding to their demands.[10] It is thus through non-institutional channels (local solidarity networks, clientelistic groups) that the state's outside contributions (public policies, 'modernisation' projects, dissemination of voting procedures) have been integrated, reinterpreted and adapted by the local society.[11] To make them their own and to keep control over them, local actors bring into play specific cultural codes (the duties of friendship, loyalty and reciprocity).

In this regard Corsican society is not as 'exotic' as it seems. Certain recent events (for instance, corruption scandals that have erupted in 'developed' democracies) demonstrate that interpersonal obligations,

[10] All other things being equal, these phenomena are akin to those analysed by Jean-François Bayart (1993) with respect to African societies, when he shows that 'the principle of reciprocity, whether symbolic or concrete, institutionalised by the personalisation of social and political relations' is as much an instrument of power for the dominators as it is a means to compel them to redistribute to those indebted to them the 'sinecures and other benefits of power' (Bayart, 1993: 231–3).

[11] By a process that is found in other social contexts, for instance in southern Italy, as Gabriella Gribaudi has well described (1990).

informal relations and pragmatic exchanges have a central role in many social activities—and particularly in political activities. There is indeed a wide gap between the official models societies and institutions produce of themselves and the actual practices that take place. This discrepancy is hardly characteristic only of societies, such as Corsica, that are perceived at first glance as 'traditional'.

(Translated by Cynthia Schoch)

Abélès, Marc, 1989, *Jours tranquilles en 89. Ethnologie politique d'un département français*, Paris: Odile Jacob.

Albera, Dionigi, Anton Blok and Christian Bromberger (eds), 2001, *Anthropology of the Mediterranean*, Paris: Maisonneuve et Larose.

Bayart, Jean-François, 1993 [1989], *The State in Africa: The Politics of the Belly*, New York and London: Longman.

Boissevain, Jeremy, 1974, *Friends of Friends: Networks, Manipulation and Coalition*, Oxford: Blackwell.

Boltanski, Luc and Laurent Thévenot, 1987, *Les économies de la grandeur*, Paris: Presses universitaires de France.

Bourde, Paul, 1887, *En Corse. L'esprit de clan, les mœurs politiques, les vendettas, le banditisme*, Paris: Calmann-Lévy.

Bourdieu, Pierre, 1980, *Le sens pratique*, Paris: Minuit.

Briquet, Jean-Louis, 1997, *La tradition en mouvement. Clientélisme et politique en Corse*, Paris: Belin.

Crettiez, Xavier, 1999, *La question corse*, Brussels: Editions complexes.

Davis, John, 1977, *People of the Mediterranean*, London: Routledge.

Eisenstadt, Shmuel and Luis Roniger, 1984, *Patrons, Clients and Friends*, Cambridge University Press.

Garrigou, Alain, 1998, 'Clientélisme et vote sous la IIIe République' in Jean-Louis Briquet and Frédéric Sawicki (eds), *Le clientélisme politique dans les sociétés contemporaines*, Paris: Presses universitaires de France, pp. 39–74.

——, 2002, *Histoire du suffrage universel en France 1848–2000*, Paris: Seuil.

Goffman, Erving, 1971, *Relations in Public*, New York: Doubleday.

Graziano, Luigi, 1980, *Clientelismo e sistema politico. Il caso dell'Italia*, Milan: Franco Angeli.

Grémion, Pierre, 1976, *Le pouvoir périphérique. Bureaucrates et notables dans le système politique français*, Paris: Seuil.

Gribaudi, Gabriella, 1990, *A Eboli. Il mondo meridionale in cent'anni di trasformazione*, Venice: Marsilio.

Grignon, Claude and Jean-Claude Passeron, 1989, *Le savant et le populaire*, Paris: Seuil/Editions de l'Ecole des Hautes Etudes en Sciences Sociales.

Kesselman, Mark, 1967, *The Ambiguous Consensus: A Study of Local Government in France*, New York: Alfred A. Knopf.

Lemarchand, René, 1981, 'Comparative Political Clientelism: Structure, Process and Optic' in Shmuel Eisenstadt and René Lemarchand (eds), *Political Clientelism, Patronage and Development*, Beverly Hills, CA and London: Sage, pp. 7–32.

Mauss, Marcel, 1950 [1923–4] 'Essai sur le don' in *Sociologie et anthropologie*, Paris: Presses universitaires de France.

Médard, Jean-François, 1981, 'Political Clientelism in France: The Center-Periphery Nexus Reexamined' in Shmuel Eisenstadt and René Lemarchand (eds), *Political Clientelism, Patronage and Development*, Beverly Hills, CA and London: Sage, pp. 125–71.

Pitt-Rivers, Julian, 1961 [1954], *The People of the Sierra*, University of Chicago Press.

Putnam, Robert D., 1993, *Making Democracy Work: Civic Traditions in Modern Italy*, Princeton University Press.

Romanelli, Raffaele (ed.), 1998, *How Did They Become Voters? The History of Franchise in Modern European Representation*, The Hague and London: Kluwer Law International.

Tarrow, Sydney, 1977, *Between Center and Periphery: Grassroots Politicians in Italy and France*, New Haven, CT and London: Yale University Press.

Weber, Max, 1964 [1922], *Wirtschaft und Gesellschaft*, Berlin: Kiepenheuer & Witsch.

Wolf, Eric R., 1966, 'Kinship, Friendship and Patron-Client Relations in Complex Societies' in Michael Banton (ed.), *The Social Anthropology of Complex Societies*, London: Tavistock, pp. 1–22.

FROM ACCLAMATION TO SECRET BALLOT

THE HYBRIDISATION OF VOTING PROCEDURES IN
MEXICAN-INDIAN COMMUNITIES

David Recondo

In 1995, at the very moment when Mexico put into effect its first 'free and fair' elections under the auspices of the newly constituted Federal Electoral Institute,[1] the state of Oaxaca, in the south of the country, officially recognised the 'habits and customs' (*usos y costumbres*) by which rural communities designated municipal authorities. The State Legislature, after a long period of negotiations, had approved a reform of the electoral code designed to legalise the traditional procedures that the government and the 'official' party—the PRI[2]—had used for decades as a means of maintaining their hegemony over the Indian municipalities (*municipios*). Henceforth the authorities designated by the communities would be accredited without reference to political parties, and the State electoral authority,[3] as well as the State Legislature, would have no choice but

---

[1] Instituto Federal Electoral (Federal Electoral Institute). Created in 1990, the IFE is a public independent institution in charge of the organisation and administration of federal elections. It is meant to be independent of the government and political parties. Its steering body is the General Council, formed by members who have the right both to speak and to vote (a President Councillor and eight Electoral Councillors) and by members who have the right to speak but not to vote (including one representative for each political party legally registered in the State). The President Councillor and the Electoral Councillors are elected by a two-thirds vote in the Chamber of Deputies.

[2] Partido Revolucionario Institucional (Institutional Revolutionary Party). Founded in 1929 as the Partido Nacional Revolucionario (National Revolutionary Party) by President Plutarco Elías Calles. In 1938 it became the Partido de la Revolución Mexicana (Party of the Mexican Revolution), and it adopted its present name in 1946. PRI leaders controlled the federal government without interruption from the date of the party's creation through to 2000.

[3] Each State of the Mexican Federation has a public institution in charge of the organisation and administration of the election of the governor, the members of the State Legislature and the Municipal Councils. In Oaxaca this authority is called the Instituto Estatal Electoral (State Electoral Institute) (IEE) and was created in 1992. It has practically the same structure as its federal counterpart: the General Council is headed by a President Councillor and six Electoral Councillors that have the right to speak and to vote. The other members have the right to speak but not to vote (including each representative of the political parties legally registered in the state). The President Councillor and the Electoral Councillors are elected by a two-thirds vote in the State Congress.

to validate the elections organised by the village assemblies.[4] This reform was one of a series taken by many Latin American countries in the course of the 1990s to recognise cultural diversity in legal terms. Other countries, such as Colombia and Ecuador, have likewise passed special legislation concerning the autonomy of indigenous communities and the question of their access to political representation.[5] But the novelty of the reform adopted in Oaxaca lies in the fact that it sanctioned electoral procedures which, in several respects, went contrary to the principles and practices of universal secret suffrage on which elections above those at the municipal level were based. Thus the local electoral law legitimised two different voting procedures: voting according to tradition (with procedures that could vary from one municipality to the next) and universal suffrage by individual and secret ballot (akin to that in Europe).[6]

Even if these two types of suffrage are employed at different political levels (that of the municipalities for traditional voting procedures and the state and federal level for universal suffrage), their coexistence within the same country affects the way elections take place. Certain phenomena, such as the ban on setting up ballot boxes decreed by municipal authorities, the violation of secrecy when it comes to filling out the ballots, or even the record absenteeism for elections above the municipal level, have given rise to a variety of explanations. For some observers, the irregularities that have come to light point to a profound contradiction between two political cultures: universal suffrage by individual and secret ballot is seen as totally incompatible with communitarian customs.[7] For others, on the contrary, these incidents only reflect the manipulation of communitarian leaders intent on keeping control of local power. Those

---

[4] The election of the municipal councillors, the state deputies and the governor has to be validated both by the IEE and the State Legislature.

[5] For a comparative study of multicultural policies in Latin America, see Van Cott (2000).

[6] The electoral code approved in 1995 by the Legislature of Oaxaca allows the citizens in more than 70 per cent of the municipalities (418 out of 570) to elect their municipal councillors according to local traditions (most of the time by a public ballot). Nevertheless, the State governor, the State deputies, the president of the Republic, the federal deputies and the senators are elected by universal, individual and secret ballot all over the country. This means that the citizens who live in a traditional municipality (*municipio de usos y costumbres*) practise both kinds of voting procedures at different times (local, state and federal elections are staggered: the president of the Republic, the senators and the governors are elected every six years; the local and federal deputies are elected every three years; municipal elections are held every three years in non-traditional municipalities, elsewhere they can take place at different times in between the three-year official term).

[7] Those who support this argument are divided between those who see secret ballot as the epitome of democracy in action and therefore believe that the assimilation of this procedure at the local level is the required condition for opening the road to further political development (Trejo and Aguilar, 2002); and those who see universal suffrage as a Western form which, if imposed on Indian communities, will necessarily lead to conflict and hamper their development (Bellinghausen, 1997).

who share this view believe that universal suffrage by individual and secret ballot is a neutral political technique that can work in any cultural context (Viqueira, 2000: 217–44). Nevertheless, both approaches fail to capture the complexity of the relationship between voting procedures and culture.

This chapter explores the interactions between the two ways of voting that coexist in Oaxaca and the uses local actors make of this institutional duality. To begin with it describes the extent to which the material realities of voting are expressions of widely different cultural presuppositions, a fact that is in contradiction with the supposed neutrality of electoral procedures. A brief description of the procedures used by the communities to choose municipal authorities will highlight what differentiates them from the mechanisms of electoral democracy. Subsequently it shows to what extent local voting cultures are not hermetic systems, but on the contrary are characterised by innovative hybridisation and constant evolution. It analyses how the very mode of suffrage adopted becomes itself a strategic issue for local political actors, and how disputes over the legitimacy of electoral procedures contribute to produce—by hybridisation—innovative institutional configurations.

COMMUNITY VOTING AND UNIVERSAL SUFFRAGE: FUNCTIONAL DIFFERENCES

The electoral code of the State of Oaxaca, amended once in 1995 and again in 1997, distinguishes between two kinds of municipalities: on the one hand the traditional municipalities (*municipios de usos y costumbres*), where the election of municipal authorities is held according to each municipality's traditions—most of the time by a public vote, without formal participation of political parties—and on the other hand the 'party-based' municipalities (*municipios de partidos políticos*), where the voters elect the municipal authorities from party lists by universal, individual and secret ballot. The first type is largely in the majority, constituting 418 of the 570 municipalities in Oaxaca. These communities have preserved a local government system inherited from the colonial era. The system is based on what anthropologists have called the civil and religious hierarchy or *sistema de cargos* (system of duties or offices) (Carrasco, 1961: 483–97). Community members are required to participate in activities undertaken for the common good. Every member is obliged, throughout his lifetime, to take on specific duties (*cargos*) without being paid. As a rule the level of responsibility and the prestige associated with these duties increase over time. The hierarchy includes religious duties (organisation of patronal celebrations, upkeep of church buildings etc.), administrative duties (the various offices of the municipal council—the *ayuntamiento*) and duties in agricultural affairs (*comisariado de bienes comunales* or *comisariado de bienes ejidales*).[8] Other tasks having to do with public works, with the upkeep of schools or the administration of government welfare programmes are also included in the community organisation chart.

The administration of the municipality is thus considered a compulsory service. Terms of office run from one to three years depending on the level within the hierarchy. In most cases the members of the *ayuntamiento* change every year and not every three years as in the rest of the municipalities. Each term of service is followed by a rest period that can vary in length. But services rendered to the community are not limited to carrying out the *cargos*. Community members must also participate on a regular basis in unpaid public works (the construction of public buildings, the building or maintenance of roads etc.). Those who refuse to collaborate in community undertakings are subject to penalties ranging from fines to imprisonment or expulsion. Everyone is thus obliged to fulfil a minimum number of community duties, but only a minority accumulate enough influence and prestige to take their place among the elders.[9] Alongside the council of elders and the municipal council (*cabildo*), the village assembly plays a vital role in the decision-making process. According to rules that vary greatly from one municipality to the next, adults and married members regardless of age meet at regular intervals to deal with matters of general interest or to designate municipal authorities. The traditional procedures for designating these officials, commonly known as *usos y costumbres* (uses and customs), probably constitute one of the most original aspects of this form of local government. Like the institutions described above, these procedures vary greatly from one municipality to the next. However, a recent survey of more than 400 municipalities established that a certain number of characteristics were common to all (Velásquez Cepeda and Méndez Lugo, 1997).

In the great majority of cases those chosen for municipal duties are designated by the citizens of the community meeting in general assembly. Citizenship is only rarely granted to all members of the commu-

---

8 Community Agrarian Boards. These commissions were created after the 1910 revolution to handle land reform programmes and administer the communal lands and *ejidos*. Communal lands (*bienes comunales*) are the lands that were traditionally held in common by the indigenous villagers since the colonial era. The *ejido* is a collective form of land tenure established after the revolution in order to distribute the land made available by the breaking up of the *haciendas* (large landholdings). It was intended to function as a cooperative, similar to the Soviet *kolkhoz*.

9 The elders, *principales* or *tatamandones*—their name varies depending on the region— are those who have climbed to the top of the community hierarchy. They possess a moral authority that makes them the functional equivalent of municipal councillors. Until the 1960s and 1970s they still had the power to influence decisions in all areas of community life, including the appointment of members of the *ayuntamiento*.

nity; it is attributed on the basis of participation in community tasks. Regardless of age, those who have founded a family and own a parcel of community land are obliged to work for the community; in so doing they acquire the right to participate in collective decisions. Women do not always participate in the assembly, although the survey found that in 70 per cent of municipalities they did so (Velásquez Cepeda, 2000: 225). The role of the elders can vary greatly; ethnographic studies have underscored the extent of their influence, but today they are no longer the only deciders. Sometimes they confer with outgoing officials in order to establish a preliminary list of those whose turn it is to serve as local officers or who possess the necessary qualifications. The final decision, however, is always put to the general assembly.

Criteria for eligibility are, as a general rule, also linked to community service. Selection is based on the person's record in terms of community tasks accomplished. The elders, together with outgoing officials and village inhabitants, pass judgement on the merits of each candidate, including behaviour in public, the degree to which the candidate has indicated respect for community norms and values etc. In addition to moral criteria there are others that, when it comes to the higher ranks such as mayor (*presidente municipal*), have to do with intellectual or technical skills: knowing how to read, write and speak Spanish and so on. Those chosen must also possess the economic capital required to support their families during the term of service. Although the performance of public duties is the basic factor in determining membership in the group and hence citizenship, in most cases those selected must also be native born. However, someone from outside the community who has married a native must also take part and can therefore rise up the community hierarchy.

Voting by tradition, voting as consecration: the community ethos materialised

This distinctive way of conceiving the exercise of power determines the way elections are held. Votes are almost never cast in secret. Voting is above all a means of ratifying a decision issuing from previous debate. The village inhabitants, meeting in assembly, exchange opinions as to the qualifications of the candidates until a consensus is reached. The discussion can go on for hours, sometimes even for days. The act of voting serves, in a more or less formalised manner, to express agreements reached in common, rather than to decide by vote tallying who is to exercise a public office. However, there are a multitude of differences between the various procedures adopted, differences that reflect the extremely hybrid nature of traditional voting. In a good number of municipalities members of the local élite concerned about issues of legality— for the most part school teachers—have applied procedures used in trade union or school meetings to the village assemblies: verification of the quorum, designation of a moderator and a team of assessors whose job it is to organise debate, tally of the votes etc. In this case formal listings are drawn up of candidates for each post to be filled (mayor, municipal councillor, policeman, judge etc.). Candidacies are then submitted to the assembly to be voted on. The assessors then usually proceed to count the votes and the post is awarded to the candidate with the greatest number. Candidates 'eliminated' along the way are, as a general rule, put up for the next highest position in the hierarchy of officers, so that ultimately all those designated by the assembly end up, without exception, as members of the municipal council.

However, this broad description does not take into account the great diversity of voting procedures. In more than half the traditional municipalities voting is by a show of hands. Elsewhere each voter records his vote on a blackboard, deposits it in a ballot box or communicates it in secret to an assessor. In cases where the proceedings are less formal, voting can also be by acclamation or applause. And in isolated cases voters line up behind the candidate of their choice (see Table 1).

Table 1. TRADITIONAL VOTING PROCEDURES

Voting procedure	*Number of municipalities*
Show of hands	209
Marking a cross on a blackboard	79
Ballots and ballot boxes	40
Show of hands or some other procedure	34
Acclamation	10
Ballots	9
Applause	3
Election lists	3
Orally	2
Lining up behind the candidate	1
Communicated in secret to an assessor	1
Outgoing officers designate their successors	1
No reply	20
Total	412

Source: *Catálago municipal de usos y costumbres*, CIESAS-IEE, 1997. Certain municipalities reported that several procedures were in use, but that the show of hands was the most frequent.

Note: The survey, conducted in 1996, covered 412 municipalities classified as traditional in 1995. Six other municipalities were added to the list for the 1998 elections, bringing the total to 418 traditional municipalities as against 152 party-based ones.

These voting procedures indicate to what extent the principle of majority decision and that of consensus are closely connected. Even if—as competition for the control of local government becomes keener—reliance on majority voting tends to replace recourse to consensus, legitimisation and ratification still fulfil an essential function alongside that of the election in strict terms. Elections are above all ritual acts, the essence of which is symbolic: the purpose is to reassert the unity of the community by publicly expressing one's consent. If the election is secret, it is no longer certain that it will perform the function of unifying the community and providing consensus. Secret elections weaken the process by which those in the opposing minority, or those who are undecided, come to accept majority decision. The explanation given by a San Agustín Chayuco *tatamandón*[10] illustrates perfectly this way of thinking:

'[With the secret vote] people say one thing, but then they fill out the ballot another way ... They turn it into a farce. It's better when the vote is on the blackboard, then you can really know how each person is voting. ... That way people who don't know whom to vote for add their crosses where there are the most crosses. Even if they don't agree.'[11]

Yet the anthropological interpretation should not blind us to another, far more prosaic explanation: refusal to introduce the secret ballot when voting on collective decisions comes also from community leaders and from the *caciques*[12] anxious to limit dissent. The cohesion of the community implies as well the stability of the power structure, a fragile equilibrium that traditional rituals serve to preserve and legitimise. Local authorities are particularly keen to see that voting is kept public, by a show of hands for example, because they want to ensure that the people for whom they have done 'favours' will vote for the right candidate.

The vicissitudes of secret balloting in traditional municipalities: tales of a misunderstanding

Alongside the municipalities where the sense of community is strong and the exercise of power is considered a duty that brings prestige with it, there exist municipalities, for the most part larger and more politicised, where interest groups are structured so as to facilitate alliances with political parties. Competition for power is more out in the open, partly because those in power have had access, since the 1980s, to substantial

---

10 Mixtec word for elder.
11 Interview with Pedro Nicolás Alavez, a *tatamandón* and President of the PRI municipal Committee in *San Augustín Chayuco*, 20 November 1999.
12 A term derived from *Kassequa*, the name of the Indian chiefs of the Caribbean. The Spanish used it to refer to the native lords of New Spain. In twentieth-century usage it refers to political leaders in rural or urban post-revolutionary Mexico, in particular those issued from the ranks of the people.

financial means. Certainly the line between the two kinds of municipalities is hard to draw: all of the Oaxaca municipalities are characterised by a certain degree of hybridisation, a subtle and unstable balance between communalisation—where the collective rationale takes precedence over the individual—and sociation—where increasing individualism, due in part to modernisation and the urbanisation that goes with it, prevails over traditional methods of social control.[13]

By constituting two distinct categories of municipality (one traditional, the other based on party politics), the law inevitably establishes an institutional duality. This duality gives rise to conflict when it comes to municipal elections, as we shall see below; but it also creates problems when it is a question of elections above the municipal level. In all the municipalities of Mexico, whether in Oaxaca or elsewhere, state and federal representatives, governors, senators and the president of the republic are elected by universal suffrage both individual and secret. Candidates must be accredited by an officially recognised party. Elections patterned on the most classic of democratic models are thus held alongside elections for municipal officers that often contradict the very principles on which the democratic model is based. The coexistence of the two procedures inevitably creates problems. Some analysts, such as José Antonio Aguilar and Guillermo Trejo, have shown that the organisation and holding of federal elections are more conflictual in municipalities where traditional procedures are the rule for local elections (Trejo and Aguilar, 2002). The conflicts arise not only on election day but also during the process of selecting and training those to be in charge of the polling places.

Clashes tend to occur when the municipal authorities or the elders decide to replace the women and younger members of the election committee—who have been chosen by lot to organise the polling stations—with people who rank higher in the community hierarchy. According to the criticisms voiced in one of the Mixtec municipalities, the older generation does not tolerate young people being in charge of polling places 'because they have not yet served as *mayordomos*'.[14] In many instances husbands replace wives or simply keep them from attending the training sessions that the IFE[15] organises for those who will be setting up the polling stations. The same thing holds true for religious dissidents: municipal authorities frown on these 'black sheep' exercising 'official'

---

13 We refer to Max Weber's classic distinction between two ideal-types of social relation: communalisation (*Vergemeinschaftung*) when relations are based on tradition and on a strong feeling of belonging to a specific group, and sociation (*Vergesellschaftung*) when relations are based on mutual interest and individual rationality (Weber, 1995 [1922]: 78–9).

14 A traditional function of a religious nature. The *mayordomo* himself pays for the feast held in honour of the patron saint of the village.

15 Instituto Federal Electoral (Federal Electoral Institute). See note 1.

duties during the elections. Also, frequently a husband will vote in the name of his wife or of those of his children who have reached voting age but are still not independent. Family heads arrive at the polling stations with the election cards of all the members of the household and fill out the equivalent number of ballots. This manner of proceeding appears so normal that the polling station assessors do not always refuse. The holder of the voting cards has only to hold out his thumb for the assessor to stamp with indelible ink as stipulated by the law. These 'anomalies' are indicative of a quite special way of conceiving and practising citizenship. For the elections above the level of the municipality suffrage is 'universal, secret, direct and individual', but for traditional elections suffrage is neither universal, nor secret, nor individual.

In many municipalities only men are allowed to attend assembly meetings. And here again, not every man, since, as mentioned earlier, the right to vote and to be elected depends on other factors, usually having to do with community service. Once married and head of a household, all men, even those under eighteen years of age, must take part in the *tequios*[16] and fulfil public duties. However, in certain communities bachelors are assigned to perform civil and religious duties—of a menial nature—and thus can acquire the right to speak in assemblies. Here again the criteria vary from one community to the next. In addition to the women and the young, those who are not born in the municipality in question or who live in outlying communities are often barred from becoming members of the assembly that elects municipal officials, unless they have assumed some of the duties assigned by the main village[17]—and in some cases they are not granted permission to do so. Maintenance of these traditions means that by and large suffrage is not universal but qualified, although the qualification required here is not the payment of a tax but participation in common tasks. Moreover voting is not necessarily personal or individual, since the head of the household can vote in the name of his wife and children. It is not direct either, since in certain regions it is an official from the *agencias* who comes to the main village assembly and takes part in the election of the *ayuntamiento* as a representative of his community. For many years this form of collective, indirect voting characterised the elections above the municipal level as well: local authorities would fill out all the ballots themselves, acting in the name of their communities. From the 1990s on this practice was no longer possible except in local elections. The new election regulations and the rallying of opposition parties meant that real polling stations were established and

16 A term that comes from a Nahuatl expression referring to community work. Adults are obliged to participate without pay.
17 Most Mexican municipalities are subdivided into several hamlets, gathered around a main village; the outlying hamlets, categorised as *agencias*, are dependent administratively on the chief village and the officials that head them have very few prerogatives.

that only those with an election card could vote. Still, however, even at the state and federal level, decisions as to whom to elect can sometimes be taken collectively; once in the polling booth the voters simply ratify individually the decision taken in assembly.

Boycotting the election and abstaining: when one voting method excludes another

In Oaxaca the contradictions between the two legally recognised and institutionalised procedures are intensified by the fact that the electoral law forbids the participation of political parties in more than 70 per cent of the municipalities. Even though the traditional way of voting is limited to local elections, the fact that it has been legalised has given rise to abuses that have discouraged the consolidation of political parties.[18] Local authorities, who see political parties as a threat to community unity, often revert to rabid anti-electoralism. In the 1997 and 2000 Federal Elections and the 1998 elections in the State of Oaxaca for deputies and governor, the local authorities went so far as to forbid the candidates from campaigning within the limits of their municipalities. Certain municipalities even blocked the holding of elections. In 1997 the municipalities of San Pedro y San Pablo Ayutla, Mazatlán Villa de Flores and Eloxochitlán de Flores Magón took measures of this kind. In 1998 San Juan Quiahije followed suit. In 2000 it was the turn of Santiago Zacatepec, San Juan Cotzocón and Estancia de Morelos—an *agencia* of Santiago Atitlán—to block the setting up of ballot boxes, as did San Juan Quiahije.[19] In each of these municipalities justifications given for the decision to forbid campaigning or installing ballot boxes varied, but some common characteristics emerge. In almost every case decisions of this nature were taken when there was an internal conflict between two factions, one of which was supported by the PRI. In order to block its rivals, the faction lacking government support took a stand in favour of local autonomy and local custom, objecting to recourse to party politics considered as less favourable to its cause.

The boycotting of elections has other causes as well, causes closely tied to those given above, which strikingly reveal the lack of legitimacy of the electoral system and provide insight into the political culture of the indigenous élite in regions far from the centres of power. Local authorities attempt to pressure the government into providing solutions to longstanding demands concerning, for instance, such issues as additional financial support, the settlement of legal disputes (often concerned with land holdings) or the opening of a secondary school. In this connection

---

18 At the federal level all candidates have to be accredited by a political party. The law forbids running as an independent.

19 In 2000 Ayutla, Mazatlán and Eloxochitlán accepted taking part in federal elections.

the authorities consider the elections as 'government business': something that is official but cannot serve as a means for citizens to influence the orientation of public policy. They are probably partly right to treat the elections simply as a means for the government to acquire legitimisation, as a show painstakingly staged by the PRI in order to reinforce its hegemony. Under the monolithic regime of the PRI elections were, until the 1990s, simply a ritual designed to legitimise candidates of the 'official' party.

A boycott of elections is a sign, as well, of a new political trend that has taken shape following the emergence of the neo-Zapatist guerrilla movement in the state of Chiapas. Centred around a demand for autonomy, this movement has challenged a regime it does not believe represents interests of indigenous people. Here again the battle is fundamentally anti-PRIist, even though the political party system as a whole is dismissed as deficient. Organisations such as the OIDHO,[20] the United Front of Mayors of the Mazatec[21] Region and SER, A.C.[22] share this viewpoint. Their aim is to consolidate areas where a degree of autonomous political power exists and control by the corrupt PRI machine can be resisted. They demand as well that a new system of political representation should be set up, independent of political parties, a system that would recreate, at the level of the region, an expanded version of the traditional system: indigenous candidates would be selected by the regional assemblies, taking into account their record in community and municipal affairs (Regino, 1998: 17).

Although this movement holds promise of political change in the future, in the context of the elections of 1997, 1998 and 2000 it only served to encourage abstention—which was particularly profitable for the PRI. Experience has shown that as a general rule the percentage of abstention is higher in the traditional municipalities than in party-based municipalities. On 2 August 1998 the average abstention in the traditional municipalities reached 53.8 per cent, whereas in the party-based municipalities it was 48.8 per cent: a difference of 5 per cent between the two types of municipalities. The difference was even greater in the Federal Elections of 2000: in party-based municipalities the average rate of abstention was

20 Organizaciones Indígenas para la Defensa de los Derechos Humanos de Oaxaca (Oaxaca Native Organisations for the Defence of Human Rights): non-governmental organisation founded in 1993 by young indigenous lawyers and dedicated to the defence of the civil and political rights of the indigenous people of Oaxaca.
21 Frente Único de Presidentes Municipales de la Sierra Mazateca: association of mayors of the Mazatec region, in the north-west of the State of Oaxaca, dedicated to promotion of the economic and political autonomy of local governments.
22 Servicios del Pueblo Mixe, Asociación Civil (Services of the Mixe people Civil Association): NGO founded in 1988 by young educated leaders of the Mixe ethnic group, based in the north-east of the State of Oaxaca and dedicated to the defence of social, civil and political rights of their people.

Table 2. LEGISLATIVE ELECTIONS, 2 AUGUST 1998,
STATE OF OAXACA

Abstention (%)	Traditional municipalities	Party-based municipalities
50–60	116	41
61–70	74	12
71–80	28	2
81–90	7	0
91–100	3	0
Total	228	55

Source: State Electoral Institute of Oaxaca.

38.6 per cent, whereas in the traditional municipalities it reached 48.9 per cent. Abstention had come down by 4 per cent compared to 1998, but the disparity between the two types of municipalities had doubled. If one distinguishes between municipalities on the basis of the level of abstention, the contrast is even more striking: in 1998 in 228 traditional municipalities (55 per cent) abstention exceeded 50 per cent for the legislative elections, whereas only fifty-five party-based municipalities (36 per cent) reached such a high level. Indeed the highest rates of abstention are to be found in traditional municipalities: thirty-eight municipalities registered over 71 per cent abstention whereas only two party-based municipalities reached the same level (see Table 2).[23]

The contrast became more marked for the Federal Elections of 2 July 2000: in 171 traditional municipalities (40 per cent) abstention exceeded 50 per cent, whereas only in eleven party-based municipalities (7 per cent) the abstention rate went as high as 50 to 60 per cent. Again the highest rates of abstention were to be found in the traditional municipalities: no party-based municipalities registered an abstention rate of 60 per cent or above, yet fourteen traditional municipalities had between 71 and 90 per cent (see Table 3).[24]

It is tempting to assume a direct connection between customary electoral practices (now legitimised by the law), abstention percentages and the level of the PRI vote. As political parties are forbidden to take part in municipal elections, it is difficult for them to distribute their programmes and support their candidates, who hence often encounter serious prob-

[23] The three municipalities with 100 per cent abstention were those where the local authorities refused to set up ballot boxes: Mazatlán Villa de Flores, Eloxochitlán de Flores Magón and San Juan Quiahije.
[24] Among the three municipalities that registered over 80 per cent abstention were Santiago Atitlán (89 per cent) where one of the *agencias* (Estancia de Morelos) decided to invalidate all the ballots, and San Juan Quiahije (85 per cent), where two of the three polling stations—those located in the main village—were not even installed.

Table 3. FEDERAL ELECTIONS, 2 JULY 2000

Abstention (%)	Traditional municipalities	Party-based municipalities
50–60	121	11
61–70	36	0
71–80	11	0
81–90	3	0
91–100	0	0
Total	171	11

Source: State Electoral Institute of Oaxaca.

lems when they attempt to campaign in traditional municipalities. The authorities, in the name of respect for tradition and community unity, will frequently prevent them from holding public meetings or distributing campaign material. Certain municipalities, such as Ayutla or Tlahuitoltepec, in the Mixe region, even went as far as to forbid the display of election posters or the painting of party slogans on the walls of the village. In most cases those penalised by these measures are the opposition candidates. In the 1997 Federal Elections, for example, Aristarco Aquino, the PRD[25] candidate in the fourth district,[26] complained of having encountered serious difficulties in his electoral campaign. In several municipalities local authorities prevented him from distributing leaflets or from engaging in door-to-door campaigning.[27] PRI candidates were often treated far more favourably. In most municipalities they continue to be seen as the 'official' candidates that must be humoured as a condition for the continuation of government aid. Sometimes PRI candidates pressure the municipalities' authorities into summoning a meeting of village inhabitants and the representatives of the *agencias* in support of the party. In other cases, however, the local authorities enforce the same rules on all the candidates, but even then the PRI candidates are at an advantage since their party is the only one the electors know. Even if their campaign has not provoked much interest, they know that when it comes time to fill in the ballot the voters will be quick to recognise the PRI logo decked out in the colours of the national flag. In the remote regions the governing party controls a hard core of followers through patronage. Opposition candidates have far more limited means at their disposal and have to deal with the reticence, or on occasion outright hostility, of community and local authorities, whether the latter are pro-PRI or not.

25 Partido de la Revolucíon Democrática (Democratic Revolutionary Party), founded in 1989 by PRI dissidents and former members of the 1968 student movement.
26 Electoral district 4 is located in the Mixe region; here most of the population is native and all the municipalities are in the traditional category.
27 Interview with Aristarco Aquino, Oaxaca, 2 August 1997.

Nonetheless it would be premature to jump to the conclusion that refusals to vote in secret and the particularly high levels of abstention merely indicate cultural incompatibility. An essentialist approach to culture would have us believe that electoral democracy is a transplant imported from the West that conflicts with community forms of social organisation. This is what the Indian-centred, anthropological discourse suggests when it underlines the split between the community model of democracy based on consensus and the Western model of democracy based fundamentally on majority rule. In the case of the former, consensus is seen to be the result of a lengthy process of deliberation; no significant decision can be taken outside the framework of the community assembly, or without unanimous consent. This mode of decision-making is then seen as being in total contradiction with the rule of the majority that prevails in Western democracy. The latter involves a choice between several options that are distinct, and most often irreconcilable, and it requires that there should be a vote. The final decision represents the choice of the majority, which the minority is forced to accept. The consensual model, on the other hand, emphasises unity and complementarity, and does not require taking of a formal vote. The terms that appear in a document put together by the members of SER, A.C. are particularly revealing in this regard:

Suffrage entails the use of the vote. Voting assumes that there exists a majority and a minority. In our indigenous communities the designation of public officials is based on the concept of complementarity. Consensus is thus the ideal way for us to designate public officers. (Quoted in Bellinghausen, 1997)

SER, A.C. leaders distinguish in these terms between consensus and 'universal, free and direct suffrage by secret ballot' that lawmakers intend to implement in all the Oaxaca municipalities. They believe all decisions concerning the community should be taken collectively and in public, so as to *produce* consensus. Voting is seen as a 'debasement' of the traditional procedures of decision-making, an 'importation' introduced by school teachers seeking to apply in the assemblies the rules learned in the school context: speaking in turn, raising one's hand to request the floor, not making too much noise etc. The result would be the banning of the 'murmur' (*cuchicheo*) of the assembly and consensus, in favour of voting by a show of hands and majority rule, 'Western' procedures that distort indigenous practices (Díaz Gómez, mimeo). What we have here is an idealised version of the way community assemblies function. It is based on an essentialist concept of a culture that forms a closed, coherent whole, impervious to outside influence. The introduction of a new procedure, such as the secret ballot and the use of ballot boxes, is then seen as likely to violate the traditional ways of deliberating. This approach appears to us to be misguided, as misguided in its way as the approach that assumes the secret ballot to be neutral in cultural terms, comparable, for example, to the introduction of the motor car: a tool that indigenous people can make use of without being obliged to break with their traditional patterns of sociability and collective organisation.[28]

TRADITIONS AND ELECTORAL DEMOCRACY: A QUESTION OF 'ELECTIVE AFFINITIES'

In accentuating the distinctive characteristics of the traditional electoral regime, one ends up forgetting that it shares one crucial aspect with electoral democracy: the vote. Voting may, as pointed out, function differently in terms of form and significance, but it is nonetheless an integral part of Indian culture. Far from being incompatible, traditional procedures and those of electoral democracy have certain 'elective affinities'[29] rooted in the past history of Mexican municipalities. The idea of elections belongs to this tradition. They are neither a recent importation nor a form of acculturation. When the *pueblos de indios* were first established during the colonial period the Spanish introduced the custom of rotating public duties. This represented a radical break with pre-Hispanic forms of social organisation that historians have shown to be hereditary (Romero Frizzi, 1996: 45–73). In the course of the sixteenth century the Spanish established Indian republics (*repúblicas de indios*) with *cabildos* subject to election. Certainly exceptions were frequent in the early years of a colony, and the purchase of public offices or rotation among a select few (the *principales*) were common expedients in many *repúblicas* in Oaxaca and elsewhere. Nonetheless the basic principle of designating local authorities by a process of election became an integral part of municipal organisation. From that time on the *caciques*, whose hereditary powers were recognised by the Spanish, had to share power with elected officials.

Procedures for the election of *alcaldes* and *regidores*[30] underwent change throughout the colonial period. José Miranda, author of a history of the ideas and institutions of *Nueva España*, classified the various procedures for the election of municipal officers under two general headings: on the one hand the *repúblicas* in which suffrage was limited to a

---

28 The historian Juan Pedro Viqueira, among others, considers electoral democracy to be an 'efficacious political instrument' that can be embedded in differing cultural contexts and that is 'in no way tied to that region of the world where it was invented and put into practice for the first time' (Viqueira, 2000: 217–44).

29 Term used by Max Weber in his study of the Protestant Ethic and the spirit of capitalism. We have adopted the definition given by Michael Löwy: 'A process by which two cultural forms—religious, literary, political, or economic—enter, on the basis of certain structural analogies, into a process of exchange which entails community of choice, convergence, symbiosis and, in certain cases, fusion' (Löwy, 1999: 42–50).

30 Municipal councillors.

select group consisting of nobles (the *principales*), officeholders (both past and present), elders and a few *macehuales* (commoners); on the other the *repúblicas* in which suffrage was extended to all the inhabitants of the *pueblo de indios* in question (Miranda, 1978: 133). Between these two extremes a whole range of cases existed in which suffrage was more or less restricted. Nonetheless the principle of election of public officials gradually replaced that of heredity. From the end of the eighteenth century onward the *caciques* and other *nobles* were supplanted by a class of *principales* who occupied the various civil positions and controlled the paying of tribute and commercial exchanges with colonial authorities (*alcaldes mayores*). Certain scholars refer also to a gradual *macehualisation* of the administration of the *repúblicas* as the nobility gradually lost its prerogatives and legitimacy and an increasing number of commoners gained access to public office. Indian society remained stratified, but it underwent profound transformations; wealth tended to replace nobility as the basic criterion of distinction.

Municipal institutions went through major changes in the period after independence, but the Indian communities of Oaxaca preserved many of the elements characteristic of the colonial *repúblicas*. The *ayuntamiento* replaced the *cabildo*, bringing with it new official positions such as *presidente municipal* or *síndico*,[31] which came into existence as early as the second half of the nineteenth century, along with those of *alcalde*[32] and *regidor*. These public positions were still assigned by annual rotation and officeholders were still elected by the village inhabitants (*vecinos*). In keeping with the laws of the Republic, suffrage was limited to males. Yet the communities continued to set their own criteria of citizenship and eligibility in conjunction with the establishment of new state institutions. One of the major factors acting to change community and municipal organisation stemmed from the measures taken by the central government to end all forms of corporatism. These measures provided for individual financing of the Catholic Church (*mayordomías*) instead of collective financing (*cajas de comunidad*). Historians trace to this era the codification of the hierarchy of civil and religious duties, a feature still found today in the municipalities of Oaxaca (Chance and Taylor, 1985: 1–26). Beginning in this period access to civil positions was predicated—at least in part—on the prestige acquired by those who could afford to spend lavishly on religious feasts.

The Revolution introduced the *municipio libre* and universal suffrage, yet local communities continued with their own electoral procedures. Suffrage remained more or less restricted and the *principales*, along with the new class of *caciques* issuing from the land reforms of the 1930s and

---

31 Corresponds to a municipal prosecutor.
32 Corresponds to a municipal justice of the peace.

1940s, often played a determining role in the designation of municipal officers. In general outline, however, the description that José Miranda has provided of electoral procedures in the colonial era would appear to hold true for the post-revolutionary period as well. There existed a seemingly infinite variety of situations which could evolve significantly over time, but which could be defined in terms of two opposite poles: on the one hand suffrage restricted to a limited number of *principales* and local officials, and on the other a greater degree of participation by the citizens. However, in all cases the procedures for designating public officers were founded on the legitimacy of 'popular' suffrage: no decision was taken without being ratified at some juncture by a body, more or less large, representing the members of the community (Velásquez Cepeda, 2000: 115–25).

Even if voting according to traditional procedures does not fulfil the same functions as voting in an electoral democracy, it serves nonetheless as a 'traditional matrix' out of which the modern forms of election, competitive and individual-centred, can be interpreted and even appropriated by indigenous citizens. And this is all the more true in that traditional procedures were characterised by an initial hybridisation, as we have seen above. They do not constitute a form of democracy that differs in essence from those invented by Western societies; on the contrary, from the start they were grounded in a logic that was itself hybrid if not self-contradictory. This is particularly evident in the decision-making procedures where consensus was combined with majority rule. Anthropologists are no doubt correct to point out that decisions in indigenous communities were not taken on the basis of an individual canvassing, and that voting 'by a show of hands' was a procedure imported by teachers motivated by an ideal of modernisation and acculturation. More than likely the 'vote' recorded in the colonial archives or the more recent municipal archives refers in reality to modes of decision-making close to the 'palaver' described by African scholars. The anthropologist Aguirre Beltrán gives the following description of the 'indigenous vote' during the colonial era:

The voters talked on in a general clamour, interrupting each other continually as they discussed the competence of the candidates and their standing. From time to time, one of the voters, whose job it was, summed up the discussion; and then it continued until unanimity was attained. (Aguirre Beltrán, 1991: 40–1)

Nonetheless the idea of majority rule seems gradually to have taken root within tradition. Even if consensual deliberation is still the rule for the day-to-day affairs of the community (allocation of the budget, decisions on community work projects etc.), majority rule and individual voting are more frequent when it comes to designating public office holders. According to the 1997 survey cited above, only some fifteen municipalities still elected local officials by acclamation. Elsewhere, at one point or another in the process, a genuine election was held in which a relative majority (half the voters plus one) served to decide between the candidates that had been pre-selected by the elders, previous office holders and/or the municipal assembly itself. Juan Pedro Viqueira has shown this to be the case for the indigenous municipalities of the Altos region in Chiapas: for many years the elections were rituals of consecration that served only to confirm decisions already taken by the *caciques* or the leaders of the 'official' party (Viqueira, 2000: 225–8). But Viqueira goes on to show that this custom also served to establish a form of legitimacy based on the approval of the majority. Even if the vote was often no more than pretence, since the outcome had been determined beforehand, it still became a key element of political legitimacy. When, from the 1960s on, quarrels broke out between local factions, voting ceased to be a ritual and served to decide between candidates. Acclamation or plebiscite had given way to individual balloting and the counting of votes.

This evolution of voting procedures in the indigenous municipalities prompts us to tone down the differences between community practices and those of electoral democracy. There existed a native tradition of individual voting based on majority rule. To presuppose a basic incompatibility between community practices and those of electoral democracy is thus an exaggeration. Furthermore forces that are not only cultural but specifically political in nature have recently accentuated the hybrid character of traditional voting: once the law has sanctioned several modes of voting, the choice between them becomes a strategic issue in the battles waged for control of local power.

VOTING PROCEDURES: AN ISSUE AND A TOOL IN POLITICAL STRATEGIES

The legalisation of traditional procedures opened up new areas of dispute in the 1998 Municipal Elections. The decisions as to what electoral regime (traditional or party-based) was to be adopted and what specific voting procedures were to be used were strategic issues to be argued and negotiated between the various political forces, both local and regional. Several months prior to the 'official' municipal elections[33] the political parties and outgoing public officials—or in some cases groups within the municipal hierarchy—demanded that the local election system be changed. Opposition parties proposed that forty-three municipalities, classified as 'traditional' in 1995, should be subject to the political party system in the 1998 elections. The PRI proposed only two. On the other hand the PRI came out in favour of nine requests for change in the op-

---

[33] The elections were held 4 October 1998 in the party-based municipalities.

posite direction: reversion to traditional procedures for municipalities in
which political parties had been active in 1995. Five other municipalities shortly followed suit. Lengthy negotiations held in the offices of the
IEE[34] led to six municipalities joining the ranks of the traditional. The
other municipalities kept the same regime as in 1995. These demands for
change were an integral part of the political strategy pursued by groups
bent on using the new regulations either to gain local power or to maintain their control over it. Most requests for a 'reversion' to traditional
procedures came from outgoing officeholders finishing up their terms,
all of them PRI members.[35] Conflicts arose when opposition groups
chose to contest such decisions.

One of the most striking examples is that of San Agustín Chayuco in
the Santiago Jamiltepec region on the Pacific shore. San Agustín Chayuco is a small municipality with a majority Mixtec population.[36] In 1998
the outgoing mayor, Máximo Flores Alavez, elected on the PRI ticket
in 1995, asked of the IEE that elections should be held in assembly and
voting should be by a show of hands without the participation of political parties. The purpose, he explained, was to put an end to the split in
the community to which the PRD-PRI rivalry had led and to recover the
sense of unity of former years. He had the support of the village elders—
the *tatamandones*—and the regional leaders of the PRI. In fact what the
outgoing mayor wanted was to find a way to exclude his PRD 'enemies',
who had lost the previous election by only sixty-four votes and who
were proclaimed winners in 1998. 1995 was in fact the first time a PRD
slate had competed against the PRI list adopted by the village assembly.
The recently recruited *perredistas*[37] were drawn from the poorest section
of Chayuco. Most of them were small-scale producers who had missed
out on the government subsidies for production and sale of coffee. Their
rival, M. Flores Alavez, was one of the principal community leaders. A
charismatic figure, well versed in the art of exploiting the patronage of
PRI regional leaders, he had consolidated his power, starting in the late
1980s, on the basis of his handling of INI[38] aid programmes for coffee
production, fruit growing and cattle breeding. Pushing aside the elderly
caciques, he had established himself as the perfect intermediary in cultural, political and economic affairs.[39]

---

34 Instituto Estatal Electoral (State Electoral Institute). See note 3.

35 Opposition groups formulated this demand in only four municipalities. Most of them
were PRI dissidents who disagreed with their party's choice of candidates.

36 4,594 inhabitants according to the last official census (INEGI, XII Censo General de
Población y Vivienda, 2000).

37 PRD militants and their supporters.

38 Instituto Nacional Indigenista (National Institute for Attention to Indigenous People).
Created in 1948, the INI is the federal public institution in charge of social programmes
established for the benefit of the indigenous people of Mexico.

39 He founded and managed several regional associations of *ejidos* that were organised to

PRI leaders, in search of a new set of leaders capable of confronting the mounting power of the PRD, had supported his candidacy in the 1995 elections. In 1998, however, the proposal to revert to the traditional system of election was M. Flores Alavez's own idea, conceived as a means of maintaining his local power base and keeping control of local affairs after his departure from office. By acting to defend traditional ways he won the support of the *tatamandones*, whose influence and prestige had been in decline throughout the previous decades, owing in part to the economic and cultural transformations through which the community had gone. His initiative, which enhanced the prestige of tradition, was no doubt linked to the fact that he himself was slated to become a *tatamandón* after his term as mayor, once he had served as *mayordomo* for the traditional village feast. By reinstating the elders at the centre of the local power hierarchy he guaranteed that he would be in a position himself to continue influencing the decisions of future municipal authorities. The case of Chayuco demonstrates to what extent the new community leaders, allied to the PRI, can make use of the recently legalised 'recipes' for traditional procedures to exclude their rivals. At stake in these conflicts is primarily the control of financial resources that grew exponentially in the context of the decentralisation process undertaken by President Ernesto Zedillo (1994–2000). Opposition parties demanded fairer representation within the *ayuntamiento*, but the PRI refused to share power. For the outgoing mayor and the candidates he supported in the 1998 elections, the traditional system was a way of limiting the part played by the opposition, both in the elections and in the formation of the *ayuntamiento*—for posts within the municipal council are not assigned according to a system of proportional representation.[40] The opposition continued to call for elections 'in due and proper form' in order to prevent manipulation of the assembly and guarantee that it was represented within the *ayuntamiento*. In 1998 it finally succeeded in establishing a hybrid procedure with ballot boxes, and with ballots on which photos of the chief candidates figured but without party logos. Only those in possession of an election card were allowed to vote.

The very form the vote takes (secret or not, by a show of hands or with ballots and ballot boxes) is a crucial issue in negotiations, since it determines whether or not certain sectors of the community will take part. Local factions will argue for a public vote or a secret vote according to their standing in the community and their financial resources. As a general

---

receive and distribute the INI subsidies for coffee production and cattle breeding. But he also practised traditional medicine, which contributed to his prestige and gave him considerable influence in the communities of the region.

[40] In the case of party-based municipalities, the electoral law states that, for the municipal council, a limited number of seats must be attributed in proportion to the number of votes each of the opposing slates has received.

rule outgoing officials and groups that control the economic resources of
the village are zealous partisans of public voting. This tradition, which
they advocate as a key element in the constitution of community identity,
furnishes them with the means by which to control patronage networks.
In such conditions the opposition is expected to call for secret elections
with lists of candidates drawn up beforehand, so as to avoid placing the
nomination and election of candidates in the hands of an assembly that
can easily be manipulated. More significant still are the disputes that
break out, once a secret voting procedure has been adopted, over the
format of the election ballots: PRI supporters insist that the party logo
appear on the bulletin; dissidents argue for lists of candidates without
any identifying labels. Thus it was that in 1995 in Mazatlán Villa de
Flores, in the Mazatec region, the PRI wanted at all costs to make use of
the party logo; it knew how much more eloquent the symbol was for voters than just a plain photograph of the chief candidate, as requested by its
adversaries. The party logo can mobilise the traditional electorate of the
'official' party even if the candidate himself is relatively unknown.

Here again, though, we must avoid reducing the issue to a clear-cut
conflict between modernists, favourable to secret voting, and traditional-
ists who accept only elections by assembly. The emergence of hybrid
voting procedures proves to what extent the dialectic between modernity
and tradition is more complex and ambivalent than a polar opposition
would suggest. We have dwelt on cases in which the forms and procedures of voting have been subject to open dispute and negotiation. Elsewhere, in many municipalities, accommodations were reached within
village assemblies without giving rise to open conflict. And sometimes
inhabitants of a town decide unanimously—without any prompting on
the part of the federal authorities—to replace elections by a show of
hands with elections with ballots and ballot boxes. Thus in 1998 and in
2001 some twenty municipalities opted for a hybrid procedure combining debate in assembly and secret vote. The purpose, as announced, was
to preserve 'the social peace' and political stability. While purists were
quick to detect the dangers of acculturation, others considered that, on
the contrary, such solutions were the only way to avoid bloody battles.
Generally, secret voting, when adopted in such circumstances, proved
to possess the qualities ascribed to it by the official election authorities:
it provided a means of avoiding retaliation and the pressuring of voters, and ensured that each citizen could freely express their choice. The
transformation has been striking: the ties that bound the individual voter
to his or her community and to its patronage network are being severed.
Citizens are now called upon to formulate an opinion that, in arithmetical
combination with the opinions of others, will decide between competing
candidates. We have here all the advantages of secret balloting as codified in the West in the course of the eighteenth and nineteenth centuries:

the creation of a closed and protected area, designed to ensure the privacy essential to the exercise of personal choice (Ihl, 2000: 88–9). A far cry from the hubbub of the assemblies in the course of which small groups dispersed in clusters gather to discuss specific problems, each member giving vent to his opinion privately or for the benefit of the assembly as a whole, the final decision being the product of a collective rumination.

The adoption of the secret ballot in elections held at a predetermined time in a closed-off area necessarily involves a redefinition of the criteria for citizenship and eligibility. Women—and even children and adolescents—can no longer take part in decisions in a more or less informal manner; who can or cannot vote has to be clearly determined (men and women who have come of age, those who have founded a family regardless of age, permanent residents etc.). The fact that the vote is confidential and takes the form of an electoral ballot necessarily implies that the 'electoral body' has to be defined and a list of the eligible must be drawn up by municipal authorities. The make-up of the electoral body is also affected by the vote being in written form: illiteracy, widespread in the indigenous regions, makes it difficult to vote in an 'autonomous' manner and recourse to assessors, appointed by the assembly, or to family members to assist in the process means that voters might easily be considered 'under influence', with all that can imply. Rumours of fraud inevitably circulate: advice given by third parties is immediately considered suspect in a context in which the voter is being called upon to act as a rational individual capable of reaching his own opinion in full awareness.

The material characteristics of the voting process are in themselves sufficient to transform the way in which power is understood and exercised. The possibility of fraud necessarily implies competition (between individuals and between groups) for the control of power, which in turn presupposes the structuring of interest groups and the emergence of the municipality as the locus of access to precious resources. Municipal offices cease then to be treated as non-paying duties rewarded by prestige alone. From the 1980s onward the decentralisation of the federal budget has served to hasten this evolution, and the municipality has become a seat of power instead of serving as a mere framework for the organisation of 'collective work'. Last but not least, when suffrage takes the form of secret ballots the process of individualisation, already at work in the traditional context, is accelerated. Access to public offices is decided by tallying the precise number of votes cast and the individual emerges as the basic unit of decision-making.

Yet even here the differences between secret elections and traditional voting procedures have not prevented the emergence of the most unexpected combinations. The municipalities that have adopted the secret vote do not always exclude collective consultation. On the contrary, such consultations are often the high points in a process of decision-making that merges collective deliberation and individual resolution in an indissoluble whole. Often villagers, meeting in assembly, go over in detail the relative merits of those considered apt to exercise public office. Secret, individual voting then provides the means of deciding between alternative lists that have already been clearly defined or distributing the various municipal offices among pre-selected candidates. In any case, while it is true that individual suffrage (whether it be secret or public, universal or limited) is by no means value-free—either in cultural terms or in strictly political terms—its implementation does not necessarily exclude modes of decision-making that manifestly belong to other cultural registers.

The state of Oaxaca provides a remarkable laboratory for the study of material voting cultures. The coexistence of two distinct electoral regimes allows us to come to grips with factors that are less discernible elsewhere: voting procedures and their material features both reflect the legitimate representations of power and shape social and political relations. The constant exchange between traditional voting—in which consecration takes precedence over selection—and universal suffrage, secret and individual, proves to what extent election modes are neither instrumental techniques devoid of inherent values, nor the product of an ontological otherness that would make it impossible to embed them in differing cultural contexts. From this vantage point the deviations that experts in electoral democracy deplore, when studying secret ballot elections as they are held in the indigenous regions of Mexico, reflect the appropriation of a new political technique rather than its categorical rejection due to supposed cultural incompatibility. Grafting democratic procedures necessarily entails shifts in significance, which make it possible for the same voting process to be interpreted and employed in markedly different ways in differing social and cultural contexts.[41]

(Translated by John Atherton and Cynthia Schoch)

Aguirre Beltrán, Gonzalo, 1991, *Formas de gobierno indígena*, Mexico City: Fondo de Cultura Económica.

Banégas, Richard, 1998, ' "Bouffer l'argent". Politique du ventre, démocratie et clientélisme au Bénin' in Jean-Louis Briquet and Frédéric Sawicki (eds), *Le clientélisme politique dans les sociétés contemporaines*, Paris: Presses universitaires de France, pp. 75–109.

41 Several authors have shown that electoral misdemeanours on the part of citizens and political actors (fraud, vote buying etc.) have always played a key role in the learning process that made it possible for democracy to take root in Western as well as non-Western societies (Garrigou, 2002: 242–3; Banégas, 1998: 83–4).

Bellinghausen, Hermann, 1997, *La Jornada*, 22 February.

Carrasco, Pedro, 1961, 'The Civil-Religious Hierarchy in Mesoamerican Communities: Pre-Spanish Background and Colonial Development', *American Anthropologist*, no. 63.

Chance, John K. and William B. Taylor, 1985, 'Cofradías and Cargos: An Historical Perspective on the Mesoamerican Civil-Religious Hierarchy', *American Ethnologist*, no. 12.

Díaz Gómez, Floriberto, 'Comunidad y comunalidad', mimeo.

Garrigou, Alain, 2002, *Histoire sociale du suffrage universel en France (1848–2000)*, Paris: Seuil.

Ihl, Olivier, 2000, *Le vote*, Paris: Montchrestien.

Löwy, Michael, 1999, 'Le concept d'affinité élective en sciences sociales', *Critique internationale*, no. 2 (winter).

Miranda, José, 1978, *Las ideas y las instituciones políticas mexicanas, primera parte, 1521–1820*, Mexico City: Universidad Nacional Autónoma de México.

Recondo, David, 1999, 'Usos y costumbres y elecciones en Oaxaca. Los dilemas de la democracia representativa en una sociedad multicultural', *TRACE (Travaux et Recherches sur les Amériques du Centre)*, no. 36 (December), pp. 85–101.

Regino Montes, Adelfo, 1998, 'La elección por partidos ¿único camino?', *En Marcha. Realidad Municipal de Oaxaca*, no. 6 (August).

Romero Frizzi, María de los Angeles, 1996, *El sol y la cruz. Los pueblos indios de Oaxaca colonial*, Mexico City: CIESAS-INI.

Trejo, Guillermo and José-Antonio Aguilar, 2002, 'Etnicidad y consolidación democrática. La organizacíon de las elecciones en las regiones indígenas de México' in David Recondo *et al.*, *Dilemas de la democracia en México: los actores sociales ante la representación política*, Mexico City: CEMCA-IFE.

Van Cott, Dona Lee, 2000, *The Friendly Liquidation of the Past: The Politics of Diversity in Latin America*, University of Pittsburgh Press.

Velásquez Cepeda, María Cristina, 2000, *El nombramiento. Las elecciones por usos y costumbres en Oaxaca*, Oaxaca: IEE.

—— and Luis Adolfo Méndez Lugo, 1997, *Fronteras de gobernabilidad municipal en Oaxaca: ¿qué son los usos y costumbres en la renovación de los ayuntamientos?*, Oaxaca: CIESAS-IEE.

Viqueira, Juan Pedro, 2000, 'Los indígenas y la democracia: virtudes y límites del sistema electoral y partidista en Los Altos de Chiapas' in Juan Pedro Viqueira *et al.* (eds), *Democracia en tierras indígenas. Las elecciones en Los Altos de Chiapas (1991–1998)*, Mexico City: CIESAS-COLMEX-IFE, pp. 217–44.

Weber, Max, 2003 [1904], *The Protestant Ethic and the Spirit of Capitalism*, London.

——, 1995 [1922], *Economie et société*, Paris: Plon.

COMMODIFICATION OF THE VOTE AND POLITICAL SUBJECTIVITY IN AFRICA

REFLECTIONS BASED ON THE CASE OF BENIN

Richard Banégas

The hope for democracy kindled at the beginning of the 1990s in sub-Saharan Africa by a wave of national conferences and the first multiparty elections seems now to have been totally shattered as events unfold: the derailing of the multiparty system and reforms, a proliferation of putsches, neo-authoritarian regimes, state criminalisation and increasingly frequent recourse to war as a means of gaining power. In all but a few isolated cases transition processes have either failed or not led to the changes expected: élite renewal did not really take place and political practices have gone on virtually unaltered. In many cases former autocrats have managed to hold on to power or return to office through elections or by force. And when new groups have taken control, they have all too often resumed the predatory practices employed by former governments, leaving the impression that 'democratisation' has amounted to only 'cosmetic' changes, masking the continuity of postcolonial 'politics of the belly' (Bayart, 1993)—a popular adage that denotes a process of clientelism, patrimonialism and straddling.

Many commentators consider that introducing pluralist elections in particular, far from helping to interiorise mechanisms for pre-empting violence, has on the contrary raised the level of violence overall. And yet on closer inspection it seems that beneath the apparent stability of hegemonic structures in Africa the whole configuration of the public sphere has been deeply disrupted by the institutionalisation of universal suffrage, and that closely connected with these changes, significant shifts have occurred within the moral economy of power and political *imaginaires*. These shifts can be detected, notably, in the very act of voting and the beliefs associated with it, which testify to a significant evolution in the very foundations of governmentality (Banégas, 2003). This chapter focuses on these sea changes as it unravels two processes in operation: appropriation of the vote and the learning curve undertaken by the 'ordinary' citizen of southern Benin in the face of political pluralism in a country regarded as a laboratory for democracy in Africa. In so doing it attempts to reveal the underlying mechanics and ambivalences of the process of political subjectivisation of the 'citizen-individual'—meaning here a dual process, of the voter being enrolled as a citizen and the voter becoming an autonomous individual as a political subject: or, in the Foucauldian sense, a double process of 'subjectivisation'.[1]

Four complementary hypotheses will be put forward. First, to show that while the implementation of competitive voting has failed to fundamentally transform the structures of power, it has nevertheless brought about tangible changes within what Lonsdale calls 'the interior architecture of civic virtue' (Lonsdale, 1992: 330). These changes have found expression in increasing obedience to the rules of electoral 'civility' (Deloye and Ihl, 1993). But given that this subjectivisation of Beninese citizens through the institution of voting remains a highly ambivalent and paradoxical process, as will be shown, it will be proposed that it is partly in the melting pot of electoral clientelism that people learn how to vote and 'civic virtues' assert themselves. Nevertheless, for a fuller understanding, a third hypothesis must be considered: that the way human behaviour and political *imaginaires* associated with the act of voting evolve is closely related to the material nature of election transactions in their most concrete aspect; in other words, that the domestication of an 'imported' political modernity is inextricably linked to the globalisation of goods and objects belonging to the 'material civilisation of success' (Warnier, 1993). To explore the process of political subjectivisation through voting, these material transactions must be taken into account. But is that enough? As a final point it is suggested that the analysis of material voting cultures should be integrated within a wider approach to 'lifestyles' which correlates the social dynamics of individuation with the political rationales of electoral subjection.

THE POLITICAL SUBJECTIVISATION OF THE 'CITIZEN-INDIVIDUAL'

Studies of the politicisation of the French working classes at the time of the Third Republic have shown that the introduction of universal suffrage and its exploitation for political ends profoundly reshaped the electorate, making public opinion gradually a more private affair and leading to an increasingly 'disciplined' electorate. As they domesticated voting techniques, citizens were themselves being domesticated by this 'political technology of virtue', and gradually subjected to the standards imposed by 'civilised' electoral practices. Garrigou reminds us that 'mindful of the way the electorate "makes" the election, we tend to forget that the election first "made" the electorate, that is, bestowed on it a social role defined in terms of a series of responsibilities and behavioural norms ....

[1] That is, 'constituting them as "subjects" in both senses of the term' (Foucault, 1976: 81).

By participating in electoral politics and adopting the more urgent im-
peratives of conviction and party discipline, the electorate was gradually
enrolled .... The freedom of the vote was ordained and materialised in
legislative procedures [which] succeeded in freezing the individualisation of the elector's role in the objectivity of the act of voting' (Garrigou,
1992: 9ff).

How has the situation in Benin evolved since 1990, the year when the
process of democratisation was implemented? Has the introduction of
new rules of the political game resulted in tangible changes to individual
behaviour patterns in the public sphere? Within a much shorter time
scale than it took to establish universal suffrage in France, Beninese citizens have experienced this electoral enrolment, and voters clearly now
take their role 'seriously', although in very different ways. Interviews
show that mastering the institution of voting has produced noticeable
changes in political conduct: altered attitudes finding expression notably
in a gradual evolution of an 'economy of patience' (Hirschman) keeping
pace with the temporalities of electoral democracy; acceptance of rules
and procedures of a constitutional state; progressive incorporation of the
disciplines of voting; integration of measures for violence prevention;
and the emergence of new attitudes 'exteriorised by codes and interior-
ised by behaviour' (Garrigou, 1992: 19).

Listening to interviewees has shown in the first place a significant
development in the correlated perceptions of the vote and elected representatives' political accountability. With each successive election—and
many elections have taken place since 1990—Beninese voters have come
to understand the meaning and usefulness of voting; they have become
acquainted with the rules and procedures of a pluralistic democracy. This
means the vote is now viewed less as a hard-won right and more as
a civic duty, the exercise of which endows political subjectivity with
added value. A few of those interviewed, it is true, considered the selection of competing candidates to be first and foremost 'a choice made by
God', the vote cast merely giving expression to the Lord's 'mysterious
ways'.[2] In practice, also, electoral choices broadly following the dictates
of collective and clientelist rationales,[3] which are theoretically antithetical to the free expression of individual opinions, can be seen. Yet what
emerged from the surveys conducted was that the vote is more and more
frequently considered a private affair, an individual choice, which goes
hand in hand with a process of 'personalisation of opinions'. While the

2 In a way, an inversion of the traditional phrase *vox populi, vox Dei*: 'I would say that
God knows who is right for the Benin', a Ouidah shopkeeper explained to us. 'God already
knows and has already named the one who is going to lead our country to its destination.
We only have to pray to God that He will send him to us.'
3 This is demonstrated by the surveys conducted by Wantchekon (2003) during the 2001
elections.

civic duty of the Beninese voter, under the single party regime, arose out of mass mobilisation typical of 'elections without choice' (Hermet, Linz and Rouquié, 1978), the reintroduction of pluralism turned the ballot paper into a vehicle of political subjectivisation. It is interesting to note in passing that of the lexical innovations born out of the new democratic system, the Fon language (*fongbe*) terms associated with electoral procedures, such as 'vote' or 'voter', are formed around the stem *mé*, which denotes a person.[4] Respondents indicate more or less confusedly that what is at stake in the expression of suffrage is as much the choice of leaders as the assertion of the citizen-individual within the new pluralist public arena. Especially where young people are concerned, obtaining the right to vote is a way of 'standing up for oneself' closely linked to the 'developing subject' Mbembé talks about (Diouf, Memêl Fotê, Mbembé, 1997). This is a major feature of political subjectivisation.

The citizen's subjectivity and individual dignity given by voting can be clearly seen in voters' beliefs about elected officials' accountability to their voters, many of whom today claim to consider themselves the real wielders of power. 'You are not God', remarked Charlemagne (a young baker from Ouidah), defiantly challenging an imaginary delegate.

'If we elect you as our leader, what power can you have without your subjects, and what force? It is we who have the power. What if you ask me a favour and I refuse? You ask someone else who also turns you down. Are you still our leader then? It is our duty to respect and obey that grants you power. But without us and without our backing, you have no power at all. ... When you become president, don't go thinking that it's just you who hold power. There are young people there, too, who have granted you power, and you have to work with them...'

'We are the ones who vote, and it is we also who reject', confirmed Assiba and Sophie, vegetable sellers on the Dantokpa market in Cotonou.

'If Kérékou [head of state] lasts another five years and he's good, we'll see. If he doesn't produce results, he'll have to stand down and someone else will take over .... If you are elected and you act wrongly, we'll speak out and start asking questions. Under the old Kérékou regime we couldn't say anything. But now we can say without fear: "You, our elected representative, have acted wrongly. Look, we are of the same blood, what you have done is not right." ...'

With each successive interview it was noticeable that these opinions were not only those of the young men who could now 'stand up and be counted as men', asserting their political subjectivity through the freedom of suffrage. The same sentiment is found among the older generation who sometimes affirm, without a hint of bitterness, that 'nowadays people say what they think. They criticise those in power without fear. Now we have elections. If the person elected does not do what he said he'd

---

4 See Centre national de linguistique appliquée (1995: 53).

do, the electoral process ensures he'll be sidelined' (Daah Agblonon, a retired teacher, lineage chief in Abomey). These reflections are just some of the indicators of the domestication of democratic procedures. They testify to the enrolment of Beninese citizens in their function as voters and to their mastery of the pluralist vote. But there is more to this than first meets the eye. Though rather a long way from the electoral realities of the Democratic Revival, these images of citizen-individuals capable of calling their elected members to account in turn nurture a growing sensation of self-esteem, which is of considerable interest in the context of a study of how practices and *imaginaires* related to political responsibility evolve.

Voting became progressively, with each successive election, a favoured instrument by which to sanction authority, with the individual's vote in this regard acquiring a greater value than any collective protest action—which was certainly not the case under the single party system. Elections have become well and truly the first principle of legitimacy. The testimonies collected on this theme show that the Beninese élite are not the only people to see representative democracy as the 'only game in town' (Linz, 1990: 158), the only possible way of coming to power: enlightened by a series of elections leading to two peaceful transfers of power, in 1991 and 1996, most ordinary people when asked also appeared to be convinced that voting is the best option. Enmeshed in democratic 'rules of the game', they themselves will now quite regularly offer procedural views of politics that testify both to the spreading of civic virtue and to the 'disciplining' of the electorate through the institution of voting. In the words of Cosme, a young Bopa garage mechanic:

'At meetings we tell the leader involved that it is we who have voted him in: "If you don't take any notice of what we are asking you to do, you risk losing our support." .... We can't be too hard-line, because when we ask him to do something, he in turn has to go to his superiors. And then if we don't support him, he can't meet our demands either .... We can't get too upset with him. If a leader doesn't do a good job, we will use the proper procedure to get him dismissed from his function.'

Some people view this respect for democratic procedures as a necessary condition for citizen 'confidence', but also, very significantly, as a condition for divine absolution:

'When I hear Kérékou talking about God in his speeches I say it is a good thing. But what shocks me a little is that it is not enough to go on about the "Bible", about "God" or "Jesus Christ". It's what happens in practice that counts. You have to practise what you preach. Happily he has done nothing so far that goes against the Constitution. Because the Constitution is what the president and the politicians have to respect. If they go on about God and then don't respect the

Constitution, then God won't answer their prayers.' (Gualbert, tyre retailer, Ak-pakpa district, Cotonou)

Finally our survey reveals not just indications of familiarisation with voting procedures in a pluralist system but also assimilation of the time frames peculiar to representative democracy. The elector's 'disciplin-ing' by the electoral machine finds expression in the development of an 'economy of patience', a kind of overlay to the election agenda, as elections are increasingly considered by the people interviewed to be the 'proper time' to air grievances and call the representatives to account. This integration of time constraints governing electoral democracy manifests itself quite often in refusal to judge the elected representative before the end of his term, and by insistence on adherence to election calendars, which more and more 'stake out time limits for political ac-tion' (Santiso, 1994: 1083).

'We have to let the election winner lead the country. When his term is over, if he is doing badly, the people will throw him out. If you keep on at him, telling him over and over again that what he is doing is no good, you will destroy the country. You have to wait until his term is over before letting the people assess his track record. If they are happy, he [the elected representative] will be able to carry on; otherwise the people will decide on someone else.' (Assiatou, a woman elder and Bopa district chief)

'Just because we are part of a democracy, we can't say any old thing ... It is not right to insult and demolish someone. The leader is the leader even if he's no good. If he's a bad leader, we still have to respect him until it's time to elect someone else.' (Adrienne, a Banté shopkeeper)

The second change in leadership in 1996 surely reinforced the Beninese citizens' induction into the practice in electoral democracy of the 'wait-ing game'. By proving that it was possible for their leaders to return to power peacefully, this changeover probably helped convince them to forego the notion of an instant power conquest in exchange for a promise of future access to this power, and to realise that it was not necessarily dangerous to subject their interests to the 'institutionalised uncertainty' (Przeworski, 1991) of pluralist democracy.

  This line of inquiry could be pursued to identify other indications that the rules and procedures of pluralism have been learned—for example, by observing how they have permeated many different social domains—and show in this way that since the process of democratisation began Benin has been going through a chequered but very real metamorphosis leading to the emergence of a 'civic culture' characterised by the voters' enrolment and 'discipline', by their appropriation of the vote and their espousal of the electoral temporalities of democracy, and above all by the value attached to of the notion of political accountability, which in itself indicates measurable progress in beliefs about the relation between governors and governed. But this would be going too far. To render more faithfully the concrete manifestations of domestication of the pluralist vote we have to insist on the ambivalence of these budding 'civic virtues'. To this end, the following section will seek to show how these new beliefs about power are adapted—in a complex and sometimes paradoxical way—to a moral economy structured by values and discourses which, *a priori*, have little elective affinity with democracy: in particular that of 'politics of the belly'. We will see in this way that the political subjectivisation of the 'citizen-individual' more readily follows the path of electoral clientelism than the directions explored in Almond and Verba's 'civic culture' (Almond and Verba, 1963), or the 'good governance' guidelines set out by international aid organisations.

ELECTORAL CLIENTELISM: A PARADOXICAL VEHICLE FOR CIVIC VIRTUE?

Since the National Conference in February 1990 the Beninese have frequently been summoned to the polls for local or national elections. With each consultation, and as the party system became stronger, clientelist politics played an ever-greater role in mobilising support, which led many observers to think the grafting of the pluralist vote was failing to take. However, our research indicates that the electorate were on many occasions able to turn the clientelist relationship to their advantage, and in the process maintain the widest possible margin for action with regard to political 'bosses'. In his description of the 1995 legislative campaign Jérôme Adjakou Badou provides us with a colourful example:

It is Sunday 19 March 1995 in a small village in the Zou province, southern Benin. The election campaign is in full swing. A crowd is waiting under a big mango tree. Suddenly a four-wheel drive pulls up, greeted by the villagers' applause, and in a stentorian voice someone starts singing the praises of their distinguished host. He is a good man from a good family, a worthy candidate to represent the region in the National Assembly. The man gets out of the car and dances a few steps. Cheering! Women rush up, some laying down their 'wrappers' [traditional garments] for him to walk on, and others wafting their 'wrappers' over him. 'The worthy deputy' takes out of his pocket a wad of notes. 500 CFA franc notes are rapidly stuck to the foreheads of some participants by way of greeting. The man is welcomed by the village chief who leads him off to a nearby hut before returning to sit down to rapturous applause. Clearly pleased, the chief announces to the crowd that their guest has just handed over 100,000 CFA francs plus enough to 'wet their whistle'. Hurrah! There follows much singing, drinking, proffering of thanks. Leaflets bearing the party logo are handed out to all those present who, in return, promise to vote for this deputy, worthy of their glorious ancestors. ... The same day, the village entertained five delegations from five different political parties. Four of them have been 'nice'. Hands on hearts, all the villagers promised to vote for each of the four parties. The fifth delegation was considered to have been rather sparing with his money. The candidate made a fifteen-minute speech in favour of national unity, regional integration, a better price on the international market for Beninese cotton ... Some listened to him, out of politeness, while others dozed. The speaker rounded off his speech with a scathing attack on those who want 'to try and corrupt our people'. 'I respect you too much to offer you money to engage your support', he concluded. The people looked incredulously at one another. A young man cleared his throat and asked: 'Could our guest tell us what he has brought with him?' General approval. The candidate explains that he has planned 'to pour water on the ground in honour of their ancestors'. A member of his entourage places a demijohn of *sodabi* [the local liquor] at the centre of the circle. 'What! He's brought us *sodabi*? He can't even rise to a sealed bottle with a lid [i.e. a bottle of imported liquor]!' Half-hearted promises of support are then offered. (Badou, 1995: 8)

Another observer completes the picture:

In the villages people have set up reception and handling committees to orchestrate these events. As soon as a candidate for the post of deputy or political party leader announces that he is planning to visit, his photographs and leaflets are stuck up everywhere. As soon as he arrives a crowd of 'militants' greets him. They sing and chant party slogans in support of the candidate. Following a honeyed speech, ... the candidate, pleased to have been so warmly welcomed by the crowd of militants, hands out bank notes to thank them. Only hours after he has left, another group, specialists in cleaning up in the wake of these gatherings, tears down the bills, photographs and leaflets of the generous donor and in a trice the same place is ready to receive another candidate. In these villages tomtoms, benches, chairs and other folk instruments are often left where they are in the assigned public area, because these visits are so frequent. (Zinsou, 1995: 6)

These descriptions, corroborated by other eyewitness accounts, indicate that the Beninese voters have succeeded in adapting to the new rules of the democratic system while profiting—literally—from the political competition they engender. Some have chosen to play the flattery game, but most have accepted, without scruple, money from each candidate while casting their vote freely on election day as a function of other criteria and interests.[5] In some instances farming communities or inhabitants of a particular district have mobilised as a 'reception committee' to maximise the profit extracted from the election campaign. Nevertheless, more often than not the path of personal gain has been followed, leading sometimes to a rapid increase in wealth. The introduction of pluralism has, in particular, reinforced the position of intermediaries: the village chief, for example, religious leaders, distinguished figures, or simply clever individuals who have managed to make themselves indispensable to the various candidates and their parties as meeting organisers. But these 'brokers' are not the only beneficiaries of the financial fall-out from elections. Contrary to what is suggested by the popular but false picture

---

5 Primarily regional and native land factors. See Gbégnonvi (1995).

that has built up, ordinary citizens are by no means falling prey to the 'halter vote'[6] as offered by these brokers. They haggle over their vote and take care, each at their own level, to exploit the electoral currency to the full, so giving rise to an undeniably instrumental rationale for the act of voting, comparable in every way to that of citizens in well-established democracies.[7] Such an electoral rationality expresses itself in the outcome—many of the 'big men' who conducted campaigns featuring generous handouts suffered bitter defeats—but is also evident in the surveys we have conducted on this subject. It reveals an undeniable ability to adapt to a multiparty system. Far from consecrating the electorate's subordination, as is often asserted by analysts of clientelism, the clientelist relationship as wielded by the lowest rung of society appears to be a major vehicle for initiating citizens into the new pluralist principles. This is of vital importance. In contrast to the naïve views of democratic socialisation, we must never forget that 'it is sometimes in this way that [voters] learn to attach a value to placing a vote in the ballot box' and that 'citizenship in its infancy in the first instance was referred to as "the bought vote"' (Badie and Hermet, 1990: 314). It is first of all through this function of utility that the pluralist vote acquires its meaning; it is in this way that the procedures and time-frames of representative democracy are assimilated.

However, the ordinary citizens have not just extracted an immediate, circumstantially available, profit from electoral clientelism; they have also made the clientelist relationship an instrument wielded to exact a historic revenge on the political 'big men'. The run-up to an election is indeed perceived by most citizens as the time when one can get back from politicians the money they have amassed since they came to power or, in an even broader sense, since independence itself. The following justification cropped up continually in the interviews recorded, with that self-righteous assurance characteristic of those convinced of their own moral superiority: 'We are recovering money stolen from us!' Elected representatives are considered beholden to their electorate by virtue of their privileged position, and will face a sudden increase in demands when they go back to their villages for the weekend during this pre-election period: medical prescriptions, participation in funerals, all kinds of grievances, the deputy becomes a kind of 'honoured guest provider' or 'fund-dispensing social worker', as former members of parliament who had been thus besieged by their electorates complained. This logic of reciprocity and redistribution subtending the moral matrices of power

---

6 To adapt a colloquial Brazilian expression ('*voto de cabresto*'), which refers to the electoral practices of 'brokerage'. These phenomena and their evolution are explored by Goirand (2001).

7 See Downs' classic work (1957) and also Birnbaum and Leca (1986), especially the chapter by Pizzorno (1986).

was certainly not born of the multiparty system. However, it has substantially proliferated as competitive politics have become institutionalised, and this in turn has made it increasingly necessary for political entrepreneurs to demonstrate their 'love of their village'.

On a symbolic level the pluralist vote introduced a significant break with the past. Pitting political offers one against the other made possible a symbolic reversal of dependency between ordinary citizens and the 'big men' who solicited their votes, and so a period of power-reversal between citizen and government ensued.[8] In fact, of course, the inequality of resources characterising any clientelist relationship, along with the social disparities on which it is based, remain undisturbed by the introduction of new political game rules. Nevertheless the Beninese voters became more conscious with each successive election that the candidates were at their mercy, and that their votes exacted a price from the candidate in payment for an age-old and longstanding relationship of subordination. This in itself is not inconsiderable. Clearly these 'popular modes of political action' manifested thenceforward in the deployment of the pluralistic vote are indisputable evidence of a process, though an ambivalent one, by which representative democracy is appropriated. But to understand the inner workings of this reappropriation of the vote 'from below' one has to go beyond the utilitarian approach to electoral transactions, to look at the social practices and moral matrices within which beliefs about power and money are embedded. This facilitates an understanding of why clientelist redistribution, while morally reprehensible, is still considered to be both an ethical and a civic virtue, and as such constitutes one of the major idioms of democratic accountability.

THE HYPOTHESIS OF THE COMMODIFICATION OF DEMOCRACY

We must not lose sight of the teachings of Polanyi and Weber: like economic transactions, electoral transactions are always 'embedded within social relationships' (Polanyi, 2002) and 'receive their nature from the meaning assigned to them by human activity' (Weber, 1971). In other words, the moral economy of clientelist democracy is an integral part of the material conditions of daily life. So to understand the 'moral alchemy' which serves to legitimise clientelism we need to find out in which of the current sociability practices the electoral exchange is implanted.

---

8 A tyre retailer in a working-class district of Cotonou, Gualbert, puts it this way: 'It is we who have the power. What if you ask me a favour and I refuse? You ask someone else who also turns you down. Are you still our leader then? It is our duty to respect and obey that grants you power. But without us and without our backing you have no power at all. ... It's funny: they [the deputies] only approach us at election time. So we're right there waiting for them. ... Since we're in a democracy, we wait for the right moment. We know that when the time comes, they'll need us. So we wait.'

In his study of the moral economy of corruption in Africa, based on
his experiences in Nigeria, Jean-Pierre Olivier de Sardan emphasised
the increasing monetarisation of social relationships on the continent,
which, according to him, had been a 'facilitating' factor for clientelism.
In Nigeria, as in Benin and elsewhere in Africa, it is indeed noticeable
that the majority of social events, and particularly family-oriented ceremonies such as weddings, baptisms and funerals, for which payment
had been made in kind in the past, had now assumed a financial character
and were subject to soaring inflation. He also stressed that 'even ordinary
interpersonal relationships constantly take on a monetary character as
well. Even though in Europe our daily consumption requires us to constantly reach into our pockets in order to pay, our daily social interactions
remain relatively free from money transactions. In Africa, on the other
hand, cash payment is often required: "taxi money" for your visitors;
coins for your friends' children; money to buy a new wrapper for your
cousin who is going to a school party; a bank note for your mother-in-
law you have run into in the street .... There is no area of life (not even
the marital domain) in which money is not constantly an issue' (Olivier
de Sardan, 1996: 110). Other anthropologists have also drawn attention
to this ongoing intrusion of cash into social relationships, especially in
kinship relations. Among the Maka people in Cameroon, for instance, a
young bride's father will conspicuously count the notes brought as bride
prize before loudly taking umbrage at its small amount. Similarly, it is
customary for a Beti bridegroom to pay a little supplement for his bride's
'plane ticket' so she will be able to 'take off' from her parents' home.
Often the suitor must also pay more because he has stolen an 'indecent
glance' into his future wife's cleavage![9] Even if not always ostentatious,
the circulation of money plays a part in all social relationships. It is part
of a moral economy of accumulation and reproduction that instructs private and public behaviour.

This tendency is very pronounced in the southern Benin area, which
had a lot of contact early on with international trade flows. In these urban and rural societies where trade represents the basis of the economy,
money is involved in all areas of everyday life, from major events such
as funerals and weddings to the most commonplace interchanges between friends or relatives, whether in the context of work or family relationships. The data collected during our surveys reveal the influence
of this 'monetarisation' of social relations on political *imaginaires*. The
recurring theme of money in power representations broadly suggests
how closely linked money as a medium, social relations and self-fulfil-
ment are. This is illustrated by the common gesture of placing a bank
note on someone's forehead by way of greeting, to pay them tribute or

[9] See Geschiere (1994).

to wish the person good fortune. It is within these social rituals and this monetary *imaginaire* that electoral transactions of clientelist democracy and their associated political subjectivisation processes are manifested. It is through the material vector of 500 CFA franc notes used in 'forehead greetings' that the benefits of democratic modernity assert themselves, and the civic virtues associated with them are articulated. In this regard it is interesting to note that on election day the Beninese now tend to stick their ballot papers to their foreheads to make their wishes for success come true: the interchangeability between bank notes and ballot papers being stuck on the forehead is in itself significant. It shows that money is both a preferred means of political subjectivisation (sticking a ballot paper to one's forehead is obviously *also* a way of broadcasting one's personal political views) and a means of incorporating the act of voting.

The key to understanding the Beninese voters' attitudes toward political power and elections resides in this monetarisation of the sociability of daily life. 'The purchase of consciences', and more generally the clientelist relationship, derive legitimacy from their own daily banality, as that relationship is integrated within a continuum of moneyed social transactions which gives it its 'moral' character. Nevertheless these monetary procedures of political subjectivisation are highly ambivalent. Like the 'bitter' or 'sick' money from the diamond mines spent lavishly by the *boumeurs* and *dijibundeurs* of Kikwit, the money from clientelist dealings has a pernicious or even dangerous quality (De Boeck, 2000). While it contributes to an uptake of civic virtues, 'it is also capable of ruining everything' (according to Assiatou, the elder woman Bopa district chief).

One could go on to question whether, over and above the straightforward monetarisation of electoral transactions, the permeation of the pluralist vote in popular *imaginaires* is not mediated by the very materiality of the bank notes themselves, and the distribution of imported merchandise which, more than all other types of merchandise, represents forms of 'knowledge distribution', as Appadurai (1986) would describe it. One could recall, for instance, the election campaign scene described by Jérôme Badou and the offended reaction of the inhabitants of a small Zou village when they were faced with a 'mean candidate' who placed on the ground a simple demijohn of *sodabi* to honour the memory of their ancestors. The indignation of the voters, who expected something more than just the traditional *sodabi* from the candidate, was not merely a sign of an acquired taste for imported alcohol. It was evidence of material processes of the 'domestication of modernity' as observed by Rowlands (1996) and Warnier (1993) in Cameroon. Over and above its banal and venal nature, it indicates that it is also via the 'sealed' bottle—a symbol of modern material culture—that the benefits of political competition and those of 'democratic graft' are put to the test.

Our hypothesis is that this experimentation with pluralism via the material vector of drink could not be dissociated from *local* usages of the 'sealed' and imported bottle. They only acquire meaning when we consider the symbolic and social significance of the 'sealed bottle'. Without going so far as to establish a 'cultural biography' of these objects of modernity, as Kopytoff and Appadurai suggested, we may content ourselves with the remark that in southern Benin the 'sealed bottle' (*ahan kpatré*) is at the heart of a constellation of symbols forming a kind of 'grammar' of social relationships, religious, trade-related or matrimonial. Each kind of imported drink corresponds to a specific usage and expresses a precise message: for instance, Dubonnet (fortified wine) is the proper beverage for marriage relationships. The suitor has to give a 'sealed' bottle of Dubonnet to his father-in-law if he wants to win his fiancée's hand. As indicated by its local name—*ase d'ekon*, i.e. 'what is held by the cat', implying 'cannot be taken by the mouse' (this name referring also to the logo on the bottle)—it is the drink of ownership, of appropriation. It is also a 'woman's drink', as opposed to whisky which denotes manliness. The gin bottle, especially the green one called *bécwé*, or the bottle of *Schnaps King stars*, is the essential ingredient of the ritual offering to *vodùn*. Together with bank notes, candles, cigarettes and, of course, the calabash full of leaves and food it mediates the relationship with the divine and with ancestors. The gin bottle is also indispensable in daily interactions as a mark of sociability when one goes, for example, to 'ask for news of a household', whether it be news of a relative or of a friend. And St Jacques rum—called *dobliba*—is also a 'sealed bottle' with a 'cultural biography' filled with social meanings: it symbolises justice and rigour and represents the yardstick by which saleswomen measure oil and paraffin for lamps. The St Jacques rum bottle is the '*litre par excellence*' and so is used as the basis for working out the right price. It is the common liquid measure now used by everyone: it cannot be replaced by another benchmark measure, such as a Martini bottle, which is specifically used by groundnut saleswomen, who have in turn pitched their price range with precision according to this kind of 'sealed bottle'.

What does all this have to do with the institution of voting and democracy in Africa? Not much, at first sight. And yet, in the perspective of a political anthropology of material cultures of modernity (Warnier, 1999) these fine distinctions in meaning turn out to be not insignificant. The hypothesis was put forward that in the framework of these local uses for imported objects of modernity exchanges in clientelist democracy and, ultimately, the forms of its domestication assume their full meaning. In other words, with respect to the imaginary concepts that relate to this materiality we can interpret the dynamics of cultural hybridisation to which democratic graft gives rise.

CONCLUSION: ANALYSE THE MATERIAL
CULTURES OF VOTING

Let us propose by way of conclusion, in a comparative perspective, a methodological avenue: namely, that in order to grasp the essence of the electoral act, it is important to analyse material cultures of voting and election transactions, even if these are clientelist in character. Furthermore, this analysis should be included as part of a wider approach to material cultures and 'lifestyles' (and especially to modes of consumption), which would allow us to study the evolution of political *imaginaires* and modes of subjectivisation at the interface between the global and the local. This would involve primarily incorporating the study of *political* subjectivisation processes born out of the act of voting within the framework of *social* dynamics of individuation being driven by these new 'glocalised' lifestyles. For instance, the way Senegalese citizens used ballot papers during the February 2000 election, which led to the historic defeat of the PS and the victory of Abdoulaye Wade's '*Sopi*' party (meaning 'change' in Wolof), attests to an undeniable process of voter autonomisation with respect to existing community structures and religious influence (the marabouts' familiar *ndigël*) that had hitherto dictated political conduct. This affirmation of an autonomous citizen, referred to by some as 'the transmutation ... of the *taalibe* into a citizen-individual',[10] is an integral part of the deeper trend towards social individuation that has been making its way across Senegal for a few years, as it has in other African societies (Marie, 1997), and which is visibly expressing itself in the spreading of new lifestyles characterised by an ethos of individual success.

Here, as elsewhere, new figures of social success are appearing in the public arena. They are conspicuously individualistic and they testify to a redistribution of moral reference points and, ultimately, to a major reshaping of modes of political subjectivisation (Banégas and Warnier, 2001). As, for instance, in the case of 'Tyson', the renowned Senegalese wrestling champion who suddenly found himself at the focus of the 2000 election campaign. His reputation and popularity—especially among the urban young of Dakar—were based upon his ability to succeed on his own by freeing himself from the fetters of traditional community rules. Draped in the American flag, but also infused with the local values of wrestling, he was able to prove through his work, especially through physical training, that victory is the fruit of individual and physical capability as well as self-sacrifice to hard work. In other words, the individual is no longer just a product of his social background but above all the product of his own actions. And in particular the product of his act of voting, the polling booth playing, as we know, a vital role in the social

---

10 Diop, Diouf and Diaw (2000: 170). In the Muridiyya (Mourides) brotherhood the *taalibe* is usually bound to absolute obedience to his sheikh or marabout.

and political subjectivisation process. To understand the voting behaviour of the young Senegalese who voted for '*Sopi*', we need to see them in relation to the social dynamics of individuation, as brought about by social movements such as *bul faalé*, or rap music, which engender new lifestyles strongly infused with the ethos of individual success (Havard, 2001: 63–77). The fact that certain political parties model themselves on this pattern (such as Talla Sylla's Jëf Jël party) and that some politicians take on Tyson's body postures all bear this attitude out.

Approaching the electoral act of vote-casting via material cultures such as Senegalese wrestling, bank note 'forehead greetings' or the 'sealed bottle' offered by a candidate campaigning in southern Benin probably is not the most direct analytical path to take in a study of electoral behaviour, which normally employs different methods. But if we start from the premise that the evolution of political *imaginaires* is inseparable from their relationship with materiality,[11] we need to take a serious look at those trivial events and little daily rituals showing, each in their own way, complex and ambivalent facets of citizen-individual 'subjectivation'—in the dual Foucauldian sense—to the virtues of electoral procedures.

(Translated by Philippa Bush and Cynthia Schoch)

Almond, Gabriel and Sydney Verba, 1963, *The Civic Culture*, Princeton University Press.

Appadurai, Arjun, 1986, *The Social Life of Things*, Cambridge University Press.

Badie, Bertrand and Guy Hermet, 1990, *Politique comparée*, Paris: Presses universitaires de France.

Badou, Jérôme A., 1995, 'La leçon des paysans béninois', *Le Matin*, 29 May.

Banégas, Richard, 2003, *La démocratie «à pas de caméléon». Transition et imaginaires politiques au Bénin*, Paris: Karthala.

—— and Jean-Pierre Warnier (eds), 2001, 'Figures de la réussite et imaginaires politiques', *Politique africaine*, special issue, no. 82 (June).

Bayart, Jean-François, 1993, *The State in Africa: Politics of the Belly*, London: Longman.

——, 2005, *The Illusion of Cultural Identity*, London: C. Hurst & Co.

Birnbaum, Pierre and Jean Leca (eds), 1986, *Sur l'individualisme*, Paris: Presses de la FNSP.

Braud, Philippe, 1991, *Le jardin des délices démocratiques*, Paris: Presses de la FNSP.

11 And conversely, materiality only materialises in *imaginaires*. See also Bayart (2005: 181ff.).

Centre national de linguistique appliquée, 1995, *Vocabulaire des élections. Français/Fon*, Cotonou: CNLA.

De Boeck, Filip, 2000, 'Domesticating Diamonds and Dollars: Identity, Expenditure and Sharing in South-western Zaïre' in Peter Geschiere and Birgit Meyer (eds), *Globalization and Identities*, Oxford: Blackwell, pp. 177–210.

Deloye, Yves and Olivier Ihl, 1993, 'La civilité électorale: vote et forclusion de la violence en France', *Cultures et conflits*, nos 9–10, pp. 75–96.

Diop, Momar Coumba, Mamadou Diouf and Aminata Diaw, 2000, 'Le baobab a été déraciné. L'alternance au Sénégal', *Politique africaine*, no. 78 (June), pp. 157–79.

Diouf, Mamadou, Harris Memêl Fotê and Achille Mbembé, 1997, 'L'Etat civil de l'Etat en Afrique' in GEMDEV, *Les avatars de l'Etat en Afrique*, Paris: Karthala.

Downs, Anthony, 1957, *An Economic Theory of Democracy*, New York: Harper.

Foucault, Michel, 1976, *Histoire de la sexualité. La Volonté de savoir*, vol. 1, Paris: Gallimard.

Garrigou, Alain, 1992, *Le Vote et la vertu. Comment les Français sont devenus électeurs*, Paris: Presses de la FNSP.

Gbégnonvi, Roger, 1995, 'Les législatives de mars 1995', *Politique africaine*, no. 59 (October), pp. 58–69.

Geschiere, Peter, 1994, 'Parenté et argent dans une société lignagère' in Jean-François Bayart (ed.), *La réinvention du capitalisme*, Paris: Karthala, pp. 87–113.

Goirand, Camille, 2001, *La politique des favelas*, Paris: Karthala.

Havard, Jean-François, 2001, 'Ethos *"bul faalé"* et nouvelles figures de la réussite au Sénégal', *Politique africaine*, no. 82 (June), pp. 63–77.

Hermet, Guy, Juan José Linz and Alain Rouquié (eds), 1978, *Elections without Choice*, London: Macmillan.

Huard, Raymond, 1989, 'Comment apprivoiser le suffrage universel?' in Daniel Gaxie (ed.), *Explication du vote*, Paris: Presses de la FNSP.

Linz, Juan J., 1990, 'Transition to Democracy', *The Washington Quarterly* (summer).

Lonsdale, John, 1992, 'The Moral Economy of Mau-Mau: Wealth, Poverty and Civic Virtue in Kikuyu Political Thought' in B. Berman and J. Lonsdale (eds), *Unhappy Valley: Conflict in Kenya and Africa*, London: James Currey.

Marie, Alain (ed.), 1997, *L'Afrique des individus*, Paris: Karthala.

Olivier de Sardan, Jean-Pierre, 1996, 'L'économie morale de la corruption en Afrique', *Politique africaine*, no. 63 (October), pp. 97–116.

Pizzorno, Alessandro, 1986, 'Sur la rationalité du choix démocratique' in Pierre Birnbaum and Jean Leca (eds), *Sur l'individualisme*, Paris: Presses de la FNSP, pp. 330–70.

Polanyi, Karl, 2002 [1944], *The Great Transformation: The Political and Economic Origins of our Time*, Boston, MA: Beacon Press.

Przeworski, Adam, 1991, *Democracy and the Market*, Cambridge University Press.

Rowlands, M.-J., 1996, 'The Consumption of an African Modernity' in M.J. Arnoldi *et al.* (eds), *African Material Culture*, Bloomington, IN: Indiana University Press, pp. 188–213.

Santiso, Javier, 1994, 'A la recherche des temporalités de la démocratisation', *Revue française de science politique*, vol. 44, no. 6.

Wantchekon, Léonard, 2003, 'Clientelism and Voting Behaviour: A Field Experiment', *Politique africaine*, no. 90 (June).

Warnier, Jean-Pierre, 1993, *L'esprit d'entreprise au Cameroun*, Paris: Karthala.

——, 1999, *Construire la culture matérielle*, Paris: Presses universitaires de France.

Weber, Max, 1971, *Economie et société*, Paris: Plon.

Zinsou, Isidore, 1995, 'Le poids de l'argent', *La Tribune*, 1 April.

RETURN OF THE REPRESSED

INDONESIA'S NEW ORDER ELECTIONS REVISITED[1]

John Pemberton

'Historical events often seem more important to their witnesses than they do to historians who judge them later. When this thesis was completed in September 1972 it still appeared to me that the election it describes was a major landmark in the consolidation of the Suharto government and I thought that the enormous social problems apparently ignored by Suharto would not prevent his administration from surviving for many years. Now as I write in the wake of the January 1974 demonstrations that rocked Djakarta, the solidity of the New Order appears to have been a very ephemeral thing indeed and divisions within the armed forces in particular have been laid bare. Few Indonesians would wager that another twenty years will be given to the New Order to carry out its programme of accelerated modernisation.' (Ward, 1974: vii)

The first signs in Solo's neighbourhoods of the 1982 Indonesian national election were the concentrated efforts of local teenage boys to remove motorcycle mufflers and the sudden appearance of hundreds of campaign posters. This was one morning in mid-March. Within hours the streets of the small but densely populated Central Javanese city of half a million people buzzed in anticipation of the April political campaigns leading up to election day, 4 May. Thus began the third in a series of general elections completed by Suharto's New Order government.

THE SETTING

Like the preceding elections of 1971 and 1977, the 1982 election was to focus on membership of the national parliament, although local provincial and municipal legislative bodies would be chosen at the same time. Three official choices were slated numerically: the PPP (Partai Persatuan Pembangunan), the Muslim 'United Development Party'; Golkar (Golongan Karya), the Suharto government's so-called 'Functional Group'; and the PDI (Partai Demokrasi Indonesia), the 'Indonesian Democratic

---

1 The original version of this essay appeared as 'Notes on the 1982 General Election in Solo', *Indonesia*, 41 (1986), 1–22. The journal *Indonesia* is published by Cornell University's Southeast Asia Program. The essay reappears here in an edited and updated form with a postscript that includes a critical re-evaluation of the original. I would like to thank Ben Anderson, Nancy Florida and Jim Siegel for their comments on drafts of this essay.

Party', a partial fusion of Sukarno revivalists and Christian politicians. There was absolutely no doubt that Golkar would win the election, just as it had in the past with 62.8 per cent of the national vote in 1971 and 62.1 per cent in 1977.[2] The immense Golkar had been engineered by the Suharto government for the 1971 General Election, the first election held under the New Order government, some sixteen years after the Sukarno government had held the first general election in Indonesian history in 1955. Describing the 1971 election, Masashi Nishihara noted the new feel of a New Order election:

A comparison of these elections with those of 1955, the only other national elections held in Indonesia, would not prove very meaningful, since the two elections were held under very different circumstances. The 1955 elections saw some forty political parties and groups freely campaigning for legislative seats, while in 1971 the participating groups were limited to ten parties including the government's Golkar. The Communist Party (PKI), generally regarded as the largest party by late 1957, has been banned since 1966. The youngest voter in 1955, who would then have been 18 years old, was 34 years old in 1971, and voters between 17 and 33 years old in 1971 cast ballots for the first time in their lives. Thus, in studying the 1971 elections, it is appropriate to emphasise the means by which the Suharto government tried to organise its electoral victory rather than the manner in which the Indonesian voter responded to the election campaign. (Nishihara, 1972: 3)

A key logic by which the Suharto regime organised its 1971 and subsequent victories is reflected in the politically ambivalent nature of the term 'Golkar'. Although designed to actively participate in and 'win' New Order elections, Golkar was not defined as a 'political party', but rather as a 'group' (*golongan*) of 'functional occupations' (*karya*). Under the long reach of its 'protective' banyan tree emblem Golkar encompassed a wide range of civil servants. Implicitly, however, Golkar commanded a large majority of New Order voter-subjects who felt obliged to identify with their local ruling administrators and hence with the Suharto government and in turn the Indonesian Armed Forces that supported it. At bottom a vote for Golkar appeared to be a vote for 'government' itself. In the 1971 election design nine officially designated 'political parties' (*partai politik*) were slated to run against Golkar. However, at that time the word '*politik*' was marked by a sinister and for many frightening tonality

---

2 The real weight of these wins becomes apparent in light of the make-up of the national parliament (DPR). Leo Suryadinata (1982: 7) notes: 'The grip on Indonesian politics by the military-dominated government can be seen in the composition of the DPR .... The national DPR consisted of 460 members, 360 of which were elected, while 100 were appointed (25 civilians and 75 military) by the government (President). The structure clearly favoured the government.' Thus of a total 460 (elected and appointed) seats, the military-government controlled 327 in 1971 and 332 in 1977. All voting tabulations in this paper are taken from Suryadinata.

acquired following the hundreds of thousands of 'political' killings—expressed in New Order terms as 'anti- or pro- PKI'—which accompanied Suharto's rise to power in 1965–6. Thus the 1971 'political parties' were suspects cast as potential threats to the new national stability. Promoted as a commanding alternative to party politics, Golkar emerged, by definition, as *the* apolitical choice.

The force of the New Order's 'apolitical' politics was expressed in a series of campaign regulations prepared for the 1971 election. Criticism of the government or its officials was banned. Moreover any 'discrediting' of organisations, including political groups, was strictly forbidden. Writing on the 1971 election in East Java, Ken Ward summed up the situation: 'The whole burden of these regulations was that the election and the campaign would be held in an absolutely security-guaranteed, indeed antiseptic atmosphere, devoid of political content, of political or ideological dispute, and even of social or political differences' (Ward, 1974: 14).[3] A correlative set of regulations fell directly on the candidates themselves. Thorough screening procedures administered both by local committees and by the Kopkamtib (Command of the Operation for the Restoration of Security and Order, a security body established by Suharto in 1965) determined a candidate's acceptability by disqualifying those deemed a threat to national security. Again Ward (1974: 84) summed up:

For hundreds and thousands of East Javanese ..., Golkar was almost the only organisation guaranteeing prestige in official society, the chance of a political career (albeit under military guidance in an avowedly apolitical atmosphere), and offered the prospect of remunerative employment. At best, joining Golkar could bring access to the sympathetic ear of the Kodim commander; at worst, remaining in a party, or joining one, brought official displeasure and suspicion.

By 1977 the political party structure had again been altered by the Suharto government, which consolidated the nine formal parties of 1971 and reduced them to two: the PPP, the new officially approved Muslim party, and the PDI, a potentially nostalgic, Sukarno-tinged party. Substantially domesticated by New Order political strategy, the two parties now functioned as a convenient reminder of all that New Order security was fabricated against: the state politics of 'Islam' on the one hand, and the rhetoric of 'Revolution' on the other. Positioned as choice Number Two on the ballots, Golkar appeared all the more a 'neutral' alternative to the 'extremist' tendencies of party politics. The successful staging of the 1977 election demonstrated that the Suharto government was anything but the 'ephemeral thing' that Ward and many other analysts had anticipated during the open protests of the mid-1970s. Rather than undermine

---

3 My summary of the 1971 election owes much to Ken Ward's perceptive analysis.

New Order solidity, the 1974 demonstrations provided yet another opportunity for the Suharto regime to display its commitment to security.
The 1977 election brought this home by presenting a nationwide public
event in which New Order security was, in effect, commemorated.

The 1982 General Election fell right on schedule, exactly five years
after the 1977 event was completed. The youngest voters of 1955 were
now approaching their fifties, while students of the activist '1966 Generation' were drifting into their forties. Considered alongside the noticeable youth of most campaigners, these updated calculations assumed a
new significance in 1982. For the majority of voters, the now familiar
Pemilu (from *Pemilihan Umum*, General Election) was customarily won
by Golkar and termed a *sukses* (literally, success). For many, Golkar's
sukses(es) formed the whole of their electoral memory, all the way back
to childhood. During the 1971 election the strategy behind the Suharto
regime's transformation of the *sukses* into the transitive verb *mensukseskan* ('to success') was still visible: the government's campaign command to *Mensukseskan Pemilu* meant to 'Golkar' the election. However,
by 1982 *sukses* had a history; victory was assumed. Now *Mensukseskan
Pemilu* meant, in a twisted sense, to 'secure' a victory already scored.[4]
If Golkar meant 'government', Golkar *sukses* meant 'election'. Government officials matter-of-factly noted that elections were held regularly
'in order that the requirements of "*demokrasi*" be fulfilled'.

Perhaps because of *Pemilu*'s almost ceremonial regularity, the
government felt moved to declare the 1982 General Election a *Pesta
Demokrasi*, a striking phrase translated by the foreign press as 'Festival
of Democracy'. Strange as this translation may sound, *Pesta Demokrasi*
is in fact an even stranger image for democratic elections. Rather than refer to 'festival' (which carries its own highly celebratory, at times carnivalesque, semantic force), the Indonesian—especially Central Javanese
Indonesian—term *pesta* usually refers to formal receptions regularly tied
to public ceremonies and domestic rituals. Thus the ideal 1982 election
scene envisioned by the New Order government was that of, say, a Java-
nese-Indonesian ceremonial wedding reception where guests are ushered
to socially pre-designated seats to act as entertained but quiet witnesses
for an event executed with close to perfect predictability—as well as,
perhaps, a hint of festivity. Nearly untranslatable, *Pesta Demokrasi*
sounds a little like a 'Formal Democracy Reception'. It was in this spirit
that President Suharto addressed the opening ceremonies of the National
Conference of Governors, District Chiefs and Mayors in February 1981
in preparation for *Pemilu* 1982: 'We must perceive the General Election as a grand *pesta demokrasi*, as a use of democratic rights which
is responsible and absolutely not turned into something that makes us

---

4 I am indebted to Ben Anderson for the 'secure' suggestion.

tense and holds us in its clutches' (Lembaga Pemilihan Umum, 1983: 39–40). By March 1982 the official formula—we must perceive the General Election as a *pesta demokrasi*—had been repeated religiously throughout the New Order bureaucracy, down to the lowest level. Central Javanese administrators felt it their duty to act as responsible local hosts for what came to be thought of as an *upacara nasional*, a national rite. One unusually enthusiastic low-ranking Solo official even beamed in anticipation of what he imagined would be an *'upacara kolosal'*.

From the very beginning of the 1982 campaigns in Solo Golkar's posters were virtually indistinguishable from government billboards calling on the public to *Mensukseskan Pemilu* 1982. Golkar handouts cautioned that the election was not a goal in itself but rather 'an education in national politics'. In front of all local administrative offices stood a Golkar placard which read:

The Victory of Golkar guarantees material and spiritual happiness. The Golkar family deeply respects Religion and a belief in God. The Golkar family is always disciplined, orderly, and polite. The Form that best fits workers, businessmen and people of culture is Golkar. Golkar honours the sacrifices of national Heroes.

With these five themes, its standard proclamations on the good of Development (*Pembangunan*) and the need for Security (*Keamanan*), its regal emblem of the protective banyan tree and its invitation to join in the *Pesta Demokrasi*, Golkar controlled most of Solo's visible space.

However, towards the end of March signs of the two 'political parties' began to emerge with new posters, many in Javanese rather than Indonesian. *Menyang Mekah Munggah Kaji, Nyoblos KA'BAH Tentreming Ati* ('Go to Mecca and Make the Haj. Vote KA'BAH [Mecca's shrine and the PPP's emblem] for Peace at Heart'); *Aku emoh dipekso* ('I ain't gonna be forced') captioned a comic book hero choosing the PDI. The language became more hard-hitting as 'anti-corruption' slogans attached to PPP and PDI posters implicitly stuck to Suharto with his Golkar. Soon poster politics gave way to graffiti warfare. 'Hotel Banteng'—the *bantèng* or wild bull was the PDI's emblem—appeared above one underpass used for shelter by homeless itinerants, 'Ka'bah Station' above another. Solo had become a rising sea of political script.

Because the campaign posters appeared around entrances to the hundreds of small roads and alleys which open into Solo's neighbourhoods, they seemed to identify each of those neighbourhoods as PDI, PPP or Golkar. However, this identification was actually superfluous. Most everyone already knew local voting histories: the few massive districts of the powerful mosques, old textile centres and 'Arab' quarters were PPP; the poorest neighbourhoods at the city's edge, particularly those near the bus terminal, garbage dump and river bank, as well as a few Christian blocks went PDI; and all the rest was Golkar. The place for campaign life, for real political movement, was not the neighbourhood, but the streets, especially Solo's long main street, Slamet Riyadi. Here campaign billboards competed with one another, alongside Indonesian ads and Kung Fu and Charles Bronson banners featuring films like *Love Massacre*, to form the graphic background for campaign action. By late March, on every afternoon well over a thousand demuffled 100 cc Yamahas and Suzukis screamed past neighbourhoods sometimes in tight formations of a dozen or so, sometimes alone dare-devilling in and out of traffic, occasionally *en masse*. All revved their engines in cadence, as if sounding the designated campaign numbers in composite sequence. All were headed for Slamet Riyadi to travel its legendary length, spin off at top speed through side streets towards the city's edge, and regroup to do it again. 'Ah, it's the campaign!' retorted an old man with a sort of bemused complacency. The sound alone signalled politics; something was in gear.

THE EVENTS

Sunday 4 April brought Solo its first full-scale political rally in a campaign schedule which allotted one Sunday to each of the parties during the first three weeks of the month. The final weekend was saved for three successive days of campaigning packed back-to-back just before the *Minggu Tenang* ('Week of Quiet') which directly preceded the 4 May election day. For the opening rally Slamet Riyadi was lined with parked *becak* ('pedicabs'), positioned as a temporary and overstuffed grandstand, with kids on shoulders straining to see what would happen, and with hawkers making a quick killing (before the rains set in) on soft drinks, mechanical toys and an arsenal of noisemakers. As the first group of this Sunday's Golkar motorcyclists raced past, standing and displaying two fingers for Number Two as well as for 'Victory', police pressed the spectators back. Then came large open trucks, normally used for transporting sugar cane, livestock or army troops, one after another hauling more Golkar supporters with banners and loudspeakers proclaiming, in so many words, 'Development'. Small army vans took position at each major intersection. The sheer noise and pressure of crowding recalled the annual *maleman* ('night fair') in Solo; however, this enormous 'night fair' was taking place in broad daylight, which gave it an uneasy feel, as did the overriding sense of anticipation.

Without warning PPP trucks appeared with the amplified call *Hidup Ka'bah* ('Long Live Ka'bah') and index fingers pointed skyward for Number One and His supremacy. A campaign scheduling mix-up had placed Golkar and the PPP face to face on Slamet Riyadi. As if summoned by the first drops of rain, army troops and police moved quickly towards the crowds of spectators, the great bulk of whom fled equally fast. Within minutes several truckloads of Golkar men emptied into the streets throwing threats, then rocks at the PPP marchers who, though clearly outnumbered, responded. However, when the brief clash was almost over a large group of PDI motorcyclists arrived to join the scattering PPP supporters. Now there were real blows, wounding some, several probably seriously. The remaining Golkar supporters ran to take refuge in the luxury-class Hotel Cakra. As an ambulance pulled up, PPP trucks and PDI motorcycles took off. Several hundred reassembled spectators, many of whom just moments ago had joined in on the PPP-PDI side, stood in the street staring at a pair of armed soldiers positioned on the corner nearest the hotel. One of the soldiers began fiddling with his rifle, then shouted hoarsely, almost as if threatened: 'What are you looking at? The street is for going somewhere. Go!' That was all it took; the crowd did not disobey.

By early the next morning most of Solo had heard of the *peristiwa* ('incident'), the 'Hotel Cakra Incident'. A Golkar motorcycle had been hit by a PPP motorcycle, and this had in turn triggered a clash that left three PDI followers dead, it was said, in front of the Hotel Cakra. Had it not rained, Solo would have ignited. This was the rumour that swept through the *warung*, the hundreds of tiny food stalls and gossip stands which appear, each with its own lamp-glow attraction, along the city streets and dim alleyways of Solo at night. Just as the normally insignificant motorcycle collision in front of the Hotel Cakra was said to have set off what followed, so the rumour triggered others. Thus it was added that on the night of 27 March PPP headquarters in nearby Yogya were attacked by a group of armed Golkar men. One of the five PPP officials inside could not escape and was said to have been chopped up—his nose and legs cut off and the remains thrown into a well. Police ordered that the body be buried immediately, to prevent stories. The next day memorial services had been held for the PPP victim at a local mosque in Yogya; that night PPP followers ripped down hundreds of Golkar campaign posters. This story of mass retaliation recalled, in turn, other stories, often including the well-known 18 March Lapangan Banteng Incident in Jakarta when an apparent conflict between PPP and Golkar campaigners at a central Golkar rally touched off an incident which destroyed cars, buses, shops and offices, and ended in over three hundred arrests. If this had occurred in Solo, it was figured, it would have spread 'like fire' all over Java.[5] From the *warung* stories there emerged one phrase, one Javanese word, which repeatedly recalled the sound of persons rushing forward, drawn into what might later become an incident: *grubyug*, or better yet, *gumrubyug*, that unmistakable thunder of crowds on the

---

[5] For *Tempo*'s version of the Yogya story, see *Tempo*, 3 April 1982, p. 14. For the Lapangan Banteng report, see *Tempo*, 27 March 1982, pp. 12–15; 3 April 1982, pp. 12–13; and 10 April 1982, pp. 12–13.

move, that uncertain point when the attractive everyday pleasure of *ikut-ikutan*, of 'just tagging along' on a Saturday night escapade, for instance, gathers an irreversible momentum and moves toward an obsession all its own. By the end of the first campaign week in April this haunting, audible sense of Javanese political movement was rumoured nightly in almost every street gossip spot in Solo.

The following Sunday, 11 April, was clearly the PDI's; there would be no campaign scheduling mix-up this time. At a central point on Slamet Riyadi, almost in front of the Hotel Cakra, a great reviewing stand was constructed for the day's visiting PDI national officials. The stand's rigid scaffolding structure, erected on a spot just a stone's throw from the previous Sunday's incident, appeared to counter *grubyug* politics. For above all else, the imposing stand did not move. As before, truckloads of campaigners flanked by loose squads of motorcycles roared past. But this Sunday there were no breaks in the noisy political trafficking on Slamet Riyadi. The army and police were outnumbered by PDI youth who joined in pushing back the enormous crowds of spectators pressed along the six-mile campaign route. After an hour an amplified and un-nervingly familiar sound emerged from the noise:

'It is written in the book Ramayana that in the country of Northern Kuru there was no heat which was too hot, no cold too cold, no sweetness too sweet, no bit-terness too bitter. Everything was calm, oh so calm. No hot, no cold, no darkness, no shining light. "Like unto the divine coolness and tranquillity that cometh from a blessed cycle of heavenly waters." In the book Ramayana it was thus stated.

Hmm... But a country like this cannot become a great country because there is no ... "UP and DOWN, UP and DOWN!" The struggle is not there. All is cool and calm. Enjoy but don't enjoy too much; and don't be too sad. That's it, calm, calm in Northern Kuru. Do you want to become a People like that? No! We don't want to become a People like that. We want to become One People, forged together by the conditions, every day. Forged, almost crushed to bits. Rise up again! Forged, almost crushed to bits. Rise up again!'

The voice, blasting from a slow-moving *becak* through a well-distorted loudspeaker—like those used for daily mobile film ads—was that of the late Sukarno. In this 1982 campaign parade, the old taped speech recalled the restless, spirited *zaman politik*, the so-called 'political era' when a plethora of political parties campaigned vigorously in 1955. Flanked by a large familiar portrait of Indonesia's first president, the speech also brought to mind 'the Struggle' and the hopeful '*zaman Revolusi*' when Indonesia's political independence was proclaimed in 1945. But indi-rectly the impassioned 'political' sound of the speech recalled the threat-ening sense that '*politik*' had acquired since 1965. '*Politik*' is something to be marked out and then observed, from a safe, well-defined distance. The reviewing-stand officials stood, applauded and waved three fingers for the PDI.

The long parade of PDI people moved slowly, taking three hours to pass. The marchers were predominately young and male, costumed in black T-shirts, jeans and red bandannas. But most also wore some reference to the '*zaman Revolusi*': smudged charcoal faces with casually dangling cigarettes and 'tough' glances; 'bloody' gauze head bandages; red-and-white Indonesian flag cloaks; glassless black-framed 'glasses' of the bespectacled '1945 Generation'; and shirts printed with a black silhouette of Bung Karno or the word *Demokrasi*. Within the ranks of these young 'old fighters' were parts of 'modern' military outfits—a white leather gun-less holster here, a mismatched uniform there—scattered in a way that suggested 'military' without identifying a specific unit. There were also 'traditional' powerful characters costumed in 'magical' black turbans, clip-on beards and temporary tattoos, or shouldering thirteen-foot boa constrictors, or stubbornly dressed in the old-fashioned coolie outfit of 'peasants'. This grand procession of quotations was indeed, as one PPP spectator somewhat cynically quipped, 'a really good parade'. Nevertheless, the unfortunate sight of all this casual revolutionary camaraderie and traditional intimacy, character after character each just out of arm's reach from the next, trudging along in a more or less orderly manner, created the queer impression of a perfectly disconnected 'solidarity'.

The primary aim of the parade was simply to keep moving. For a brief moment a spirited *réyog* ('trance dance') troupe stopped in front of the reviewing stand and quickened the tempo of its enticing rhythms. Lured by the attraction of the masked dancers, two boys sprang from the crowd to join in. In a second, nervous reviewing-stand officials signalled the troupe to move on to make room for those that followed. Throughout the PDI's afternoon came more followers, marching along behind. The familiar accumulative logic of *ikut-ikutan* was bracketed: at no point did spectators rush to join in (save the two dancing boys), nor did they cheer on the procession which seemed to move along slowly but surely of its own accord. More remarkable was the total lack of enthusiasm to attract new followers. There were no invitations to the crowd to join the PDI's ranks and no signs displaying possible campaign issues—the cost of education, uneven distribution of wealth, prevalence of corruption etc.—which might persuade voters. Having followed the parade (as, in fact, few did) to its destination, the huge grassy square (*alun-alun*) which opens out in front of both the central mosque and the old Solo palace, one found no inspiring political speeches—in fact no speeches at all—just tired marchers about to head off home. In front of the reviewing stand on Slamet Riyadi the impression was that this procession had come from nowhere and was going nowhere, and was simply providing a temporary focus for those gazing from the street's edge, as if waiting for something to happen. But nothing actually happened—no accidents, no incidents—and the PDI officials were obviously proud.

Although the 11 April parade had gone smoothly, the next day the government ordered that the central section of Slamet Riyadi should be strictly off-limits for all PPP and PDI campaigning. The ban covered not only mass parades but even the individual display of anything that could be construed as a sign of *partai politik*. The rationale for the ban was a legal convenience, a clause in Election Regulations that prohibited campaigning near the headquarters of one's opposition. Since the Golkar office was on Slamet Riyadi, that was that. Implicit in the rationale was the logic that Golkar was not actually 'political' and thus no threat to order in the streets. Both PDI and PPP were furious and once again Slamet Riyadi became a source of news and related rumours. One story in particular—Solo's 'Silir Incident'—preoccupied *warungs* during the evenings of the third week in April. It had been in the air for several weeks and had been reported briefly in the nationally prestigious *Tempo* magazine on 3 April. Perhaps because the story's protagonist was a notoriously brutal Solo underworld figure, or perhaps because the story itself had already been printed, it had not been talked about much. However, the almost simultaneous suspension of *Tempo*'s publishing rights and implementation of the campaigning ban on Slamet Riyadi suggested, it was argued, that something was happening in Solo, that *Tempo* had begun to report it and that this was indeed the story behind it.

In the early hours of 26 March, so the story went, four truckloads of AMPI men (paramilitary 'youth' squads organised by Golkar) pulled up at a small *warung* filled with a dozen local PDI followers. The AMPI contingent was led by Usi, a regionally known hoodlum and manager of Solo's most extensive and government-supported prostitution district, Silir. He was also an all-round muscle man for Golkar. In less than a minute Usi singled out and stabbed one of the PDI men who, almost as fast, succeeded in fleeing. Usi pursued but the PDI man made it to familiar territory, the maze of alleys and tight neighbourhoods attached to the old palace's southern walls. But here someone screamed 'thief!' and the poor man was almost clubbed to death by his eager neighbours before he could identify himself. The next morning more than 3,000 PDI followers marched to a local police command post and demanded immediate official action against AMPI. Because an official decision was not offered, that night trucks carrying hundreds of PDI men descended on Usi's home in Silir, destroyed AMPI cars, and took over the house; but Usi had fled. At this point one middle-aged PDI organiser, a Solo man known both for his smooth talk and for his violent outbursts, slowly persuaded the crowd that Usi had been arrested and that it was best to go home.

Behind the Silir story was an explosive logic: Usi was 'Chinese'.[6] This single detail made automatic sense of the mass movement against

---

6 *Cina*, a pejorative term for Indonesians and resident aliens of Chinese descent.

him, both that morning at the command post—how else could 3,000 march on it and not only get away with it, but receive a silent go-ahead to boot—and then again that night in Silir. In *warung* conversations the incident recalled the much celebrated Solo Incident of November 1980 when a minor traffic accident involving a cyclist and a 'Chinese' pedestrian touched off a series of violent mass actions aimed at local 'Chinese'-owned shops, actions which within days spread throughout Central Java.[7] More than any other event in Solo's recent history, the 1980 Solo Incident was cited during campaign rumourings to vividly demonstrate not so much Solo's anti-'Chinese' attitude but the remarkable far-reaching forces that could be set off by an accident, even a small accident, when it occurred in Solo. This 'Chinese' connection gave the Silir Incident a peculiar potency, not because it raised issues concerning local 'Chinese' business practices—indeed, Silir was immensely popular—but simply because it linked the incident with the 1980 violence. The terms of the incident in Silir remained patently political: PDI versus Golkar. Usi happened to be the pivotal figure in a peculiar logic of accidents. It was as if the traffic accident which triggered the 1980 Solo Incident coincided with the accidents that, it was claimed, triggered the 1982 campaign incidents like the one in front of the Hotel Cakra. Most likely this coincidence, reinforced by the supplementary coincidence of the *Tempo* closure and Slamet Riyadi ban, created the compelling feeling that an inevitably uncontrollable moment was close at hand in the Solo campaigns. The *warung* buzzed with references to a *sa'at*, an approaching 'moment when...'. Whenever a campaign incident occurred without touching off a mass response like that of the 1980 Solo Incident, one often heard the phrase, *durung sa'até* ('it wasn't "time" yet, its "moment" had yet to come').

Sunday 18 April officially belonged to the PPP. Again truckloads of PPP followers flanked by motorcyclists roared the streets. However, since Slamet Riyadi was now off-limits there was no possibility that the PPP's campaign would dominate the city the way the PDI had the previous Sunday. Perhaps because of this, there emerged a point of convergence, a destination: Pasar Kliwon, an old market area at the centre of Solo's most populous 'Arab' quarter and home to one of the city's most powerful mosques. The traffic flow itself produced a parade radically different from the PDI's. Thousands of mobile PPP supporters and crowds of spectators following along poured into the bottleneck that becomes the main street through Pasar Kliwon. All of the energy that high-speed campaigning carries was suddenly transformed into a mass so dense that it barely moved. There were no costumes, police, performers or reviewing

---

7 When the 'Solo Incident' was told as a story, it usually began with the accident. Accounts of the 1980 Solo Incident can be found in Bambang Siswoyo (1981) and *Tempo*, 13 December 1980, pp. 12–14 and pp. 54–8.

stands; in their place, shouts of '*Hidup Ka'bah*' and '*Allahu Akbar*' echoed all around. The boundary between the street and its edges, between followers and spectators, collapsed jubilantly. Whole families leaned out of the shuttered windows of the old second-storey apartments that line the streets and poured bucketfuls of religious cooling water on those below. That morning there had been important speeches by PPP leaders from Jakarta.[8] By afternoon Pasar Kliwon itself seemed to embody the PPP when for the first and only time during the long 1982 campaigning in Solo an entire community was somehow on the move.

Sunday and Monday 25–6 April presented the PDI and PPP with their last official days of campaigning. With Slamet Riyadi still out of bounds and all major parading past, there was no alternative but to do what they had been doing all month—race along the streets in open trucks and tight clusters of motorcycles—only more furiously than ever. Occasionally the noise cut across Slamet Riyadi, taunting the army and police in position there. Often it was impossible to make out from the blur which party was represented, if any at all. Often too, a lone motorcyclist could be spotted wearing each of the three representative numbers, one after the other, or all together. The noise could even be heard late at night.[9] The trucks of followers and especially the motorcyclists seemed to be bypassing politics; but in fact this represented a state of affairs that was all the more politically radical. People began to remark that this was a Saturday-night affair (*malem Minggon*) which had exceeded itself because it was full of *emosi* ('dramatic anger', 'emotionality'). Why *emosi*? Because this was *politik*! The 100 cc tempest became a peculiarly political omen that questioned the reigning order by unquestionably disturbing the peace.

The response of the army and police to the illegal night campaign movement was the same as on late Saturday nights when, seasonally, Slamet Riyadi became an illicit motorcycle drag-strip: they completely ignored the motorcyclists. Instead they chased back the groups, often crowds, of onlookers accumulating first on one corner, then on another, in episodic *kucingan* ('cat and mouse'). Reasoning that the motorcyclists were motivated by a trance-like control induced by the cheers of spectators, the Solo police held the crowds, not the motorcyclists themselves, responsible. Nevertheless, given the sheer number of motorcyclists roaring through the streets of Solo in April 1982, the police did not really expect to separate the spectators from such an attraction. Thus throughout the campaigns crowds of onlookers represented a double threat to the police, the army and, ultimately, the New Order government. On the one

8   Among the speakers was Ridwan Saidi who advised the audience: 'In the Week of Quiet ahead, a lot of tricky "spooks" will roam about, making power plays and coercing the populace. When the spooks appear and go into action, just scream: Thief! Thief!' (*Pelita*, 24 April 1982).

9   This was in spite of a ban, in effect since 6 April, on night campaigns in Central Java.

hand crowds were thought to be the active motivation behind a political noise which drove the motorcyclists on. On the other crowds seemed always to be waiting for the sound of an incident that could be followed. During the last week of April a dozen or so army troops and police were stationed at every major intersection along Slamet Riyadi. They were conspicuously not watching campaign trucks and motorcycles sail past from all directions.

On the final campaign day, 27 April, Golkar was slated to hold its last grand city-wide parade, for which Slamet Riyadi was not off-bounds. Just before the parade Golkar officials circulated fliers with cautionary reminders for their followers: 'Watch out for certain groups fabricating issues meant to sabotage the election and discredit Golkar; look out for subversives disguised as Golkar; report all threats to Golkar immediately.' Large convoys of army troops joined the police already positioned on Slamet Riyadi. Solo's few ambulances and fire-engines, along with a sizeable collection of other official city vehicles (including several dump-trucks), stood ready at the intersections.

The motorcyclists and marchers who led the parade were noticeably different from those of the PDI and PPP movements. Golkar's T-shirt uniforms were brand spanking new, white and carried along by thousands of pairs of spotless sneakers padding down Slamet Riyadi in muffled triumph. There was little precision but extreme order in these ranks of civil servants-plus-families. They carried a banner which read 'Parade of Development' and announced the floats that followed. Large flow charts designed to demonstrate the Fertile Society's graphic success passed by, as did minibus-loads of women—Golkar Women: Pillars of the State. Golkar youth in new pickups displayed placards with the same formulaic commands that dominated daily headlines: 'We must (*Kita harus! Haruslah!*) preserve, conserve, implant, improve etc., the culture, the order, the spirit, the character etc.!' A car-length cardboard pencil pointed out that 'Education is Important'. A *papier-mâché* mosque appeared with women in pious costume and a sign: 'Golkar Respects All Religions, Especially Islam'. A traditional wedding with ceremony-in-progress followed: 'Golkar Respects Traditional Customs'. *Papier-mâché* schools, electric plants, ideal hospitals and waste-disposal systems passed by too, along with all the other departments dutifully representing Development as well as 'Father Development', Suharto himself. Except for a couple of clowns from Solo's failing *wayang wong* troupe, there was little in the procession that really excited spectators. In fact there was little action until torrential rain intervened and army troops, police and Golkar officials rushed to the aid of paper floats in distress. An entire sugar factory began to dissolve, then split lengthwise, and finally just slid off into the street behind the truck that had been carrying it. Within hours the 1982 campaigns in Solo came to an official end, rain or no rain.

That night, on the eve of the Week of Quiet, the rains cleared and campaigners were busy once again; but now they were tearing down the thousands of posters that over the six-week campaign schedule had accumulated everywhere, from neighbourhood WCs to Slamet Riyadi billboards. This political clean-up (*pembersihan*) was carried out with unusual enthusiasm. One energetic group of men followed another in removing all signs of the campaigns, all traces of *politik*. By morning posters had disappeared as miraculously fast as they had first appeared in mid-March. In their place the theme *tenang* ('quiet', 'calm') filled newspapers:

Today we enter into the Week of Quiet after enduring a 45-day campaign period and before Election Day on May 4th. The Week of Quiet is meant for calming ourselves and clearing the air so that we can calmly and with a cool head execute the national election. Perhaps during the Week of Quiet we can begin an effort to neutralise [*menetralisir*] and then eradicate all the results of the excessive acts [*ekses-ekses*] which occurred during the campaigning, so that no mutual hate or grudges arise.[10]

On the surface Solo was in fact calm; but at night new rumours of violence spread during what became a gossip-filled week of quiet. The prime story concerned the last week of the campaigns. On 22 April a PDI man wearing his party's emblem stopped for petrol at a station on off-limits Slamet Riyadi near the Golkar headquarters. He was confronted and shot dead, it was said, by an army man who claimed to be protecting the headquarters from arson. During the funeral for the victim the next day, PDI pall-bearers spotted an army man approaching the procession aggressively. Rumour has it that the crowd turned on him and chased him down an alley where he was hacked to death with sickles. This, it was reckoned, accounted for the heavy turnout of the army at the final Golkar parade on the 27 April. Scores of other rumoured incidents followed: stories of collisions, threats and confrontations. Then just before election day a final, brief rumour circulated, its very simplicity signalling an end to all stories: *sa'até wis liwat* ('the "moment" had passed').

Except for the occasional sound of army trucks, the streets of Solo on election day were absolutely still. As one newspaper reported, even the WTS (*wanita tanpa susila*), the 'women of damaged morals', were not to be found. It was often remarked that the vacated city recalled the annual Lebaran ritual holiday when all markets are closed and millions of Indonesians have returned to their village homes to beg forgiveness from elders and social superiors at the very end of the Muslim month of fasting. The scene within neighbourhoods, of small groups of people, mostly families, dressed up and strolling to and from local destinations, was also reminiscent of Lebaran. At the 869 polling stations

10 *Kompas*, 29 April 1982.

scattered throughout Solo a steady and controlled traffic of voters flowed in and out, past army troops positioned at each entrance. Inside men and women voters customarily sat on opposite sides of the room, chatting quietly, as if this were a traditional ritual reception. With regularity names were called and the summoned voter entered a cloaked booth to *nyoblos* ('pierce') one of the three party emblems on the paper ballot before slipping it into the locked ballot box. By 2 p.m. the voting was finished. Although it was officially encouraged, very few voters stayed on to watch the ballot-counting process; the day's orderliness itself seemed to indicate yet another clear victory for the government choice. In the end Golkar collected 64.3 per cent of the vote nationwide.[11] More remarkable than the size of Golkar's victory was its uncanny regularity. In the three national elections sponsored by the New Order over the eleven years from 1971 to 1982 Golkar's national tally has varied only 2 per cent. But most remarkable of all, particularly in light of the numerous *grubyug* movements, rumours of incidents and real expectations which grew at a fantastic rate throughout April right up to election eve, was the silent fact that the events of the campaign were rarely, if ever, brought up again in *warung* conversations. After election day only a fool asked what had happened. Occasionally he received the reply, 'Oh, seemed lively enough' or 'basically, a *sukses*'. But the likely response was: 'Nothing happened, nothing at all.' The anticipated moment had simply passed by; any momentum which might have been read into the April events in Solo went unrealised. To the extent that the election itself recalled the campaign anticipations, even it too was soon forgotten. From the street-side point of view of the *warung*, by the end of May it was as if the whole business had just never happened.

THE AFTERMATH

Although *warung* conversations had turned to other topics, *Pemilu* 1982 still preoccupied government administrators as well as the press in the weeks after the election. Official ballot counts were calculated and recalculated with apparent precision and released with deliberate slowness. This was done, according to one Solo administrator, not because the technology for quick calculation was missing, but because the government wanted to protect the masses from the possible 'shock' of a sudden surprise. Such a shock, it was maintained, might start people talking

---

[11] The PPP received 27.8 and PDI 7.9 per cent nationwide, down from 29.3 and 8.6 per cent, respectively, in 1977. In the 1982 DPR the military government controlled 342 of 460 seats. The PPP retained 94 and the PDI 24 seats, down from 99 and 29 in 1977. In Solo Golkar claimed 55.5 per cent of the vote, the PPP 17.8 and the PDI 26.8 per cent. Golkar's gain from 51.2 per cent in 1977 was at the expense of the PDI which fell from 31.5 per cent in 1977 (Suryadinata, 1982: 76, 80).

again. While the exact figures of Golkar's success were being registered, local government officials focused their attention on the final ceremonies of the long election period. During the week or so that followed election day, *syukuran*—rites devoted to expressing thanks to God and all others involved in the successful completion of a task, usually a ritual task—were held by most administrative levels of government, from top to bottom. Thus, as the Indonesian newspaper *Sinar Harapan* reported, on 8 May at Solo's city hall:

There took place a *syukuran* and '*sungsuman*' ... because the *Pemilu* had taken place in an orderly and smooth fashion. Mayor Sukatmo explained that the *Pemilu* was over now and that the previously tense, heated atmosphere must be removed. *Syukuran* also took place in the outlying areas. The District office in Sukoharjo held one two days after Election Day, at the same time that the army troops assigned to that area were dismissed. In addition, the Sub-district head of Kartosuro, Dr Suharto Hartoto, held a *syukuran* which continued with an intimate evening shared by the political parties, Golkar, election officials and army company and platoon troops. The *syukuran* was entertained by dancing and singing. In neighbourhoods the *syukuran* were smaller, more local affairs.[12]

The quotation-marked '*sungsuman*' ('bone-marrow porridge') referred the newspaper's readers to a predominantly Javanese custom usually tied to a *syukuran* held at the conclusion of more complex domestic rituals, like weddings, which draw heavily on the labour of neighbours and kin. Ritually consumed, the marrow porridge is meant to restore strength and knit together social fractures which may have occurred during the concluded ritual's often extensive preparation. In a single word, *sungsuman* reread the entire election event as an enormous, successfully completed ritual task. In mid-May, after the *syukuran*, *sungsuman* and evenings of formal 'intimacy' were over, the army troops departed and 'normal life' (*kehidupan normal*) returned to the Solo area.

In Jakarta, exactly one week after election day, Kopkamtib Chief Laksamana Sudomo summoned the chairmen of Golkar, the PPP and the PDI to give ceremonial thanks to President Suharto for successfully organising the 'great task' (*karya besar*), *Pemilu* 1982. Then, in a Lebaran-like gesture, each of the three chairmen 'offered his deepest apologies to the entire Indonesian people for any possible excessive promotion of his respective party/group during the campaign period'.[13] In return Sudomo thanked the chairmen (whom he referred to as 'contestants') for their help in making the election *aman* ('secure'), *tertib* ('orderly') and *lancar* ('smooth-running'). Finally, in a peculiar show of gratitude, the

---

12 *Sinar Harapan*, 12 May 1982. *Syukuran* were by no means limited to Solo. For the Yogya area, see *Kedaulatan Rakyat*, 17 May 1982. In Jakarta, Gen. Eddie Nalapraya 'entertained' local Islamic officials with a *syukuran* (*Kompas*, 15 May 1982).

13 *Kompas*, 15 May 1982.

Kopkamtib Chief pinned 'medals' on each of the three contestants: the PPP's chairman was awarded a Golkar emblem, Golkar one of the PDI, and the PDI one of the PPP. With this formal symbolic exchange, *Pemilu* was ceremonially finished.

There was, however, another part of the general *Pemilu* process still left to be completed. At one point in the awards ceremony the PPP Chairman J. Naro commented that although the campaign 'storm' was over, there still remained a 'sprinkling' of ill feelings which, if neglected, might bring on a 'chronic ailment'. Naro appealed to the Kopkamtib Chief to act as the 'doctor' on the case. Sudomo responded by placing an imaginary stethoscope to his ears; in fact the operation was already in progress. Naro's request concerned the resolution of cases involving persons arrested during campaign disturbances. Because many of the arrested suspects were said to be PPP followers, the party chairman apparently wanted to clear his party of official responsibility and, at the same time, display some concern for those arrested. One week later Sudomo issued an official statement that all '*ekses-ekses*' which occurred during the 1982 *Pemilu* would be taken care of by the end of May.

Of the numerous 1982 campaign *ekses(es)*, like that in front of Solo's Hotel Cakra, it was the 18 March Lapangan Banteng Incident in Jakarta that received the broadest national attention and most extensive official response. Its detailed coverage suggested the complex stakes contained in the notion '*ekses*'. The incident had occurred during a massive Jakarta Golkar rally when shouts of '*Hidup Golkar*' were suddenly countered by hurling of rocks and shouts of '*Hidup Ka'bah*'. Before army reinforcements were able to disperse the crowds Golkar's performance stage was in flames and cars, buses and shops near the rally site were destroyed. At first the press appeared to attribute this incident of *ekses* to the heat of the day, the size of the crowd and the sway of rock star and Golkar entertainer Elvie Sukaesih's hips. *Tempo* concluded its initial report with: 'Perhaps because they were hungry, hot, disappointed, as well as frustrated that noonday, in the middle of a crowd crammed onto a field increasingly narrow: Amok.'[14] This was, after all, the 'campaign season' (*musim kampanye*), a stormy time of periodic *politik* when crowds of people are easily carried away. Of the 318 arrested, mostly schoolchildren, 274 were released because they were, in Sudomo's words, just *ikut-ikutan*—'following the others', 'tagging along'. While the *ikut-ikutan* rationale initially made sense of the incident, the fact that forty or so suspects were still under arrest raised new questions: were they somehow behind the

---

14 *Tempo*, 27 March 1982, p. 15. The report also commented: 'This '*anarki*' was rather different from the 15 January 1974 incident. In that incident eight years ago, the motives and targets were clear: anti-foreign investment, especially Japanese, and anti-luxury. But in the actions taken by the angry youths this time, it was not clear what they wanted other than to destroy cars and shops' (p. 14).

incident, or were they themselves manipulated by an invisible character
behind it all? In short, was there a *dhalang* ('puppeteer')? At follow-up
press conferences with the Kopkamtib Chief reporters pursued rumours
that the incident was the result of *pemainan politik*, a political game
directed by someone off stage. Was the PPP implicated? Sudomo answered that he had already contacted the PPP's chairman, Naro, and that
it was quite possible that the characters involved in the incident acted
on their own, independent of party policy. Was then the government's
own Minister of Information Ali Moertopo implicated? 'Take pity on my
good friend the Minister', responded Sudomo, holding Moertopo's hand
at the press conference.[15] Thus *Tempo*'s second report on the incident
began: 'The Lapangan Banteng Incident in fact still overshadowed the
campaign after two weeks. This was felt most in Jakarta: rumours spread
continuously.'[16]

The constant rumours of a *dhalang* countered the threatening sense
that the campaign crowds had moved on their own accord and were themselves the ultimate source of the Lapangan Banteng *ekses*. Most of the
arrested—but not all—were said to be *ikut-ikutan*, unwitting followers of
a script possibly directed by someone else. And yet this 'someone else'
was never identified; the question never grew into a full-blown incident
of its own. No sooner had Sudomo opened the possibility of a *dhalang*
than he seemed to close it by maintaining constant contact with the PPP's
Naro and the government's Moertopo. Even those eventually brought
to trial were not accused of directing the disturbances. What emerged
from the incident was a general sense of *ekses* which conflated the two
rationales for interpreting political disturbances—the campaign season's
turbulent *ikut-ikutan* forces on the one hand and *pemainan politik*'s invisible *dhalang*-like authority on the other. The two rationales were joined
together into a circular logic which ran more or less as follows: a stormy
political climate was created by certain politically motivated characters
taking advantage of a stormy political climate. With this, the charged political implications of the sense that crowds or rumours were moving on
their own were short-circuited. What was produced and what remained,
unsurprisingly, was *ekses*, as a natural precipitation in campaign seasons.
Hence Sudomo had already opened his Crisis Control Centre (*Pusat
Pengadalian Krisis* or *Pusdalsis*) 'hotline' two days before the Lapangan Banteng incident. Similarly two months later the Kopkamtib Chief
could expect that all *Pemilu ekses-ekses* business would be 'finished'
by the end of May. But it was the most invisible authority of the entire
election period, Suharto himself, who underscored the very regular place
that cases of *ekses* have in New Order politics. Without interrupting his

15 *Tempo*, 10 April 1982, p. 12.
16 *Tempo*, 3 April 1982, p. 12.

normal *Pemilu* silence, the off-stage president issued a brief statement through Vice-President Adam Malik: 'The Lapangan Banteng Incident is just an ordinary kind of case and already under control.'[17]

The term '*ekses*' had been around for some time before the 1982 election. As Ken Ward pointed out, it was one of a number of expressions developed in 1971 by Golkar's *Bapilu* (Body for Managing the General Election—an Ali Moertopo creation) to counter charges of Golkar steamrollering. These expressions 'gained immense popularity in 1971: *ekses*, *overacting* and less concretely *issue*. An *issue* is an accusation or insinuation which one's opponents may make but which friends and independent onlookers would do well to disbelieve. Any violence that occurred in the form of intimidation of party members was then either an issue raised by the parties to "discredit" Golkar, or could be attributed to mere excess of zeal on the part of local activists who were given a new organisation with orders to swell its membership rapidly. Such overzealousness thus produced *overacting* which, however regrettable, should not be allowed to obscure the ideals Golkar really stood for. Similarly, once any intimidation that took place was recognised to be no more than an *ekses*, Golkar's image need not be considered tarnished' (Ward, 1974: 50–1). In 1982 the terms 'issue' and 'overacting' operated in the same way as in 1971: the former turned all criticism of Golkar into sheer slander, while the latter excused intimidation by Golkar as mere enthusiasm. The meaning of *ekses*, though, had shifted. Its reach had extended to include not only Golkar over-enthusiasm but, in a sense, all *Pemilu* over-enthusiasm, especially that of the two political parties. Thus by extension *ekses* grew to cover *politik*: all campaign disturbances, whether seasonal *ikut-ikutan* movements or seasoned *pemainan politik*, came to have an almost natural feel in the increasingly familiar new order of things. As *ekses-ekses*, incidents were responded to as if they were not surprising—just ordinary cases already under control. Thoroughly expected of campaign seasons, *ekses* has a sort of built-in retrospect which 'takes care of things' before their time, as if they have already happened.

While *ekses* represents campaign incidents, it also reflects what it is not. Reporting on Golkar's final 25 April campaign parade in Jakarta, Sudomo noted that it was 'performed extraordinarily well—orderly, smooth-running and very regulated. All of the participants in the parade obeyed the rules.'[18] He then went on to report, 'regretfully', that all along the edge of the campaign route there occurred disturbances which, when totalled, left six dead, 97 wounded and 130 arrested.[19] More than any other, this last incident of the campaign period highlighted the contrast

17   *Tempo*, 27 March 1982, p. 13.
18   *Suara Karya*, 27 April 1982.
19   Two days later Sudomo gave orders to 'shoot on the spot' anyone caught obstructing *Pemilu* 1982, 'especially on 4 May', election day (*Sinar Harapan*, 28 April 1982).

between *ekses* and its mirror opposite: in the face of *ekses* emerges *su-kses*. Constructed contrastively, *sukses* embodies all that *ekses* is not and appears as an ideal model of order. Confronted with disturbances along its edges, the Golkar parade was an extraordinary *sukses* because its participants remained undisturbed, followed the rules, and obediently exemplified discipline and order (*tata tertib*). But equally significant to its construction, *sukses* is attained by actively removing the *ekses-ekses* that faces it. On 25 April this meant six dead, 97 wounded and 130 arrested. In the process *sukses* displays an ideal model for ordering. Thus *Pemilu* involves more than just a calculated risk on the part of the government. In the New Order it represents a somewhat sinister application of Clifford Geertz's classic formula for religious performance in which rituals are 'not only models of what they believe, but also models for the believing of it' (Geertz, 1973: 114). Already apparent, victory is secured, repeatedly.

After the election Solo's own Javanese newspaper *Dharma Kandha* completed its *Pemilu* 1982 reportage with the summary headline: 'Indonesian People Really Politically Conscious: GOLKAR VICTORY ABSOLUTE, POLITICAL PARTIES DYNAMIC.' The story's opening paragraph read:

> The People are amazed and exclaim: Wow, the election was just like Lebaran; everyone together, old and young, men and women, dressed up in their very best; almost no shops, *warungs*, or restaurants open; all freely and gladly joining in the celebration of *Pemilu*. It really was like a *Pesta Demokrasi*! If one followed the campaign events, one felt insecure; but when Election Day arrived, everything really was different and ran smoothly and *sukses*-fully. If that's the case, now the Indonesian People really are politically conscious.[20]

In its customary familial style, *Dharma Kandha* quoted an imaginary exclamation as if it had been heard 'in the streets'. If one followed the campaign events, 'one felt insecure [*rasané ati kaya kaya miris*]'. But on election day everything was different: 'It really was like [*temenan kaya*] a *Pesta Demokrasi*.' By 1982 *Pemilu* had emerged as a ritual model which, with *sukses*, could be lived up to. In performing *Pemilu*, the official roles were unmistakable: Golkar's victory is absolute while the two political parties are, in a word, 'dynamic'.

It is not surprising that Indonesian and foreign observers of *Pemilu* have noted—with varying degrees of official pride, dismissive cynicism and academic curiosity—*Pemilu*'s ritual-like appearance. Indeed *Pemilu* 1982 was promoted essentially as a ritual: a Lebaran-like *Pesta*

---

20 *Dharma Kandha*, Minggu Ke-III, May 1982. The headline reads: '*Rakyat Indonesia Sadhar Politik Temenan: GOLKAR MENANG MUTLAK, PARPOL DINAMIS.*' I am grateful for Nancy Florida's suggestions on the translation of this and other passages in this chapter.

Demokrasi perceived by local administrators as a colossal domestic ceremony, a national life-cycle rite. In addition recognisable 'traditional rituals' (*upacara tradisional*)—*syukuran* and *sungsuman*, for example—were present, as were their equally recognisable bureaucratic counterparts, opening/closing ceremonies (*upacara pembukaan/penutup*). By extension many of the events specific to *Pemilu*—parades, the Week of Quiet, voting days—attained a certain ceremonial feel in 1982 because of the increasing regularity of the *Pemilu* process itself. Even the campaign incidents, when identified as *ekses*, fit into the general formula of '*sukses*' by which *Pemilu* 1982 was processed and 'normal life' restored, ritually.[21] In Solo the fact that campaign incidents were rarely mentioned again in *warung* conversations after election eve invites such an interpretation. If the rumoured incidents had been politically motivated rather than just a regular part of the *Pemilu* process, where, then, did all the momentum go? The problem with this kind of ritual interpretation, however compelling it may be, is that such a reading tends to de-politicise its subject. What is lost by treating *Pemilu* as if it were a ritual is the sense that *Pemilu* is political, in part, precisely because it is treated by the New Order government as a ritual. A ritual interpretation of *Pemilu*—by New Order officials and foreign observers alike—carries with it, willy-nilly, certain political consequences. Deeply rooted in its own conventional assumptions of cultural order, anthropological interpretation of 'ritual' often tilts in favour of, well, *sukses*.

On the streets of Solo during the 1982 campaigns one had the dramatic sense that something else, something other than the ritual restoration of order, was also at stake. Although the presence of army troops along Slamet Riyadi might have been taken as a sign of order, these 'security' (*keamanan*) forces in fact signalled just the opposite, order's absence, no matter how calm (*aman*) everything occasionally appeared. This sense of another reality, behind or beyond calm appearances, was sharpened during the campaign, but was by no means particular to it. Tied to the New Order's concern with *keamanan* is its programme of *pembangunan* ('development', 'construction'); in a state of *keamanan, pembangunan*

---

[21] Responding to the 1977 election, anthropologist N.G. Schulte Nordholt (1980) asks: 'What is the use of these elections if by all means of manipulations the results are fixed anyway?' (p. 179). Through an analysis of symbols rooted 'in the 'cosmic order' of Old Java'—symbols drawn from traditional classificatory systems of pre-Hindu Javanese society, Javanese mystical beliefs about the relationship between subject and divine monarchy, and no less a monument to cosmic order than the Borobudur itself—Schulte Nordholt argues that 'the national elections might be seen as a rite with the purpose of restoring the wholeness of chaotic society and nature. The chaos which had become manifest in a terrifying way during the campaign had to be overcome' (p. 181). In 1982 terms: '*sukses*' reigns as '*ekses*' is overcome. Meanwhile, in the midst of the 1982 campaigns, the *Far Eastern Economic Review*'s cover story reasoned that 'religious and primordial symbols overshadow political debate' (1982: 24–9).

is supposed to grow. But here too exists the sense of another reality, represented nightly on national television evening *pembangunan* reports where the scenes of model neighbourhoods and villages on the screen never match up with local scenes, no matter how much *pembangunan* appears to have been implemented. Slogans of *keamanan* and *pembangunan* are so much a part of everyday life in Solo that the difference between what they are signs of and what they are not is almost transparent. A sense of difference remains; it is just terribly familiar. During *Pemilu* it becomes acute. Like the army *keamanan* troops, Golkar-Solo's 27 April *pembangunan* parade stood for what it was not. Not until the rains fell did the crowds of spectators begin to show some excitement.

Probably because of their very familiarity, these differences were not what was discussed in *warung* during the campaign period. Instead rumours of the numerous campaign incidents preoccupied conversations. Unlike in Jakarta, there was little newspaper coverage of local incidents. The government was normally sensitive about news reports of 'regional' incidents. However, it was unusually cautious concerning Solo, not permitting branch offices or local editions of major newspapers in the city. This essentially left the weekly ritual pronouncements of *Dharma Kandha* (and its Indonesian counterpart *Dharma Nyata*) on the one hand, and the *warung* stories on the other, which combined to produce an extraordinarily split-image view of *Pemilu* events. Without newspapers to cover the local incidents as *ekses*—be it campaign amok or political *dhalangry*—rumours of incidents in Solo moved on, gathering a momentum of their own. (It was not until *Tempo* was banned that both its atypical coverage of the 'Silir Incident' and the magazine itself became *warung* topics.) Like the campaign motorcycles, once in gear the rumours too seemed to be heading somewhere, to another point beyond the political traffic on Slamet Riyadi, towards a 'moment' (*sa'at*).

The mid-April emergence of the notion of *sa'at* brought with it an almost contradictory half-vision of what might lie ahead. Torn loose from the relatively domesticated identification of the Indonesian *ikut-ikutan*, the Javanese *gumrubyug* movements echoed the accelerating sense of direction rumoured as *sa'at*. Embodying the sound of crowds on the move, *gumrubyug* directly opposed the logic of *keamanan* troops whose power rests in their ability to represent what is not present—the authority of the government on the one hand and 'secured calm' on the other. At a stand-off with *gumrubyug* there seemed to be little for the troops stationed on the street corners to do during the last week of April other than not watch campaigners roar by. The real threat of crowds on the move is that they will suddenly turn on you. No less a *keamanan* trooper than Sudomo himself commented: 'The climate of that "crowd" is what made my hair turn white .... Whether it's called *Malari, Lapangan Banteng* or whatever, the "crowd" always makes me nervous.'[22] But the Javanese *gumrubyug* did not understand the significance of the English loan-trope 'crowd' as it headed towards its *sa'at* in Solo. The other side of the vision accompanying rumours of a *sa'at* was total lack of movement—*macet* ('stalled', 'stuck', 'conked out'). For the government, *macet* represents a general fear that the bureaucracy's chain of command will break down; but more specifically it signals the moment when economic wheels stop turning. Just after the Lapangan Banteng incident it was reported: 'Jakarta Economic Activity "*Macet* Total". 240 Persons Arrested.'[23] Together this unlikely combination of threats—*gumrubyug* and *macet*—struck at the heart of New Order logic by simultaneously overriding *keamanan* and stalling *pembangunan*.

During the campaigns it was the duty of army troops and police along the borders of parade routes to hold back the crowds of spectators lest they *gumrubyug*. The job of parade officials, though, was to keep things moving. Just after the ban on Slamet Riyadi 'political party' parading, the unusual official-less 18 April PPP parade slowly transformed itself into the dense mass that merged with Pasar Kliwon. However, most campaign marchers—even the 11 April PDI *réyog* troupe—normally followed orders to move on and avoid *macet*.[24] These regulated flows of campaign followers mirrored the government's ideal image of the overall *Pemilu* process: *lancar* (not speeding, not idle, but smooth-running). On the streets of Solo the ideal counter-image was the sight of a motorcycle whizzing past, its young rider reclining, perfectly relaxed and posed as a still-life portrait of taking it easy, *santai*, at 100 kph.

As the 'moment' seemed closer at hand, there emerged from *warung* rumours the peculiar sense that the smooth-running process of *Pemilu* would *macet*. This sense carried all the fascination of an enormous political traffic accident.[25] An explicitly 'political' victory—that the PPP

---

[22] *Tempo*, 27 March 1982, p. 18. Sudomo himself used the English word 'crowd'.

[23] *Jurnal Ekuin*, 20 March 1982.

[24] That *reyog* troupes—once the signal of non-'order' as well as active recruiters for PKI and PNI in 1955—should now follow orders represents the height of domestication. In fact for some groups orders were not even necessary, as *Tempo*'s report on an East Jakarta PDI rally indicates: 'The Ponorogo *reyog* group, which at first had entertained the crowds, quickly stopped its deafening noise, without orders, when PDI Secretary General Sabam Sirait appeared at the podium. But the mood was still enthusiastic...' (*Tempo*, 27 March 1982, p. 12).

[25] Long after *Pemilu* 1982 was over, a crowd of spectators formed along the wide street in front of Solo's main post office. The spectators were waiting for accidents which came one after another in quick succession, when motorcyclists lost control and hit the pavement, swerved into other traffic, or just skidded off the road. There was an oil spill. No one attempted to warn the approaching motorcyclists or stop them; that seemed to be taken care of by the oil. Even the policeman, who had just dropped onto the oil with his white Honda, joined the rest of the spectators. I left for fear of blood; but now I doubt whether that was at stake in the scene, in spite of its inevitability. Instead the image of all these

or PDI would actually win—was never discussed, nor was the language of 'victory' ever used. Instead the rumours' momentum suggested that the election process itself would suddenly break down and the election day would have to be cancelled. On election eve, when word spread in the *warung* that the 'moment' had passed, it anticipated a silence in the weeks to come. Although the post-*Pemilu* press overflowed with reports on the election period—its results, highlights, incidents and measures of political consciousness—*warung* conversations shifted to other stories. *Sukses* was not mentioned; but this was not new. Absent too were the campaign stories. Unlike the official press, the *warung* now had no real interest in these incidents. Not to talk of rumoured incidents past was not to see them, in retrospect, as *ekses*, and in a sense not to see them at all. This unconcerned, utterly casual silence was at perfect odds with the post-*Pemilu* 'political' soul-searching and consciousness-raising of the government and press. It seemed to confirm suspicions that while *Pemilu* was a *sukses*, voters were somehow not really politically conscious. 'Did the masses consciously give their support to a particular *Pemilu* contestant?' asked *Topik* magazine.[26] *Warung* conversations did not worry much over this question. When *Pemilu* was raised in *warung* in the last weeks of May 1982, it was with reference to *Pemilu* 1987. A last whisper of rumours wondered whether the two 'political parties' would be active in 1987, who might lead them, and what would happen if the parties were abandoned, or if they weren't. The rumours did not last long, but they signalled the possibility of another *sa'at*.

One of the striking facts about *Pemilu(s)* is that the most active campaigners are youths in their teens and early twenties. They now belong to a New Order generation born after 1965 and trained in New Order schools. And yet they are the ones most frequently criticised as thoroughly undisciplined and politically unconscious. Considered alongside the relatively recent rise of *Pemilu* to its ritual status, this unruly fact suggests a rather strange coincidence of histories in 1987: that of a *Pesta Demokrasi* 1987 on the one hand and (for lack of a better term) a '1987 Generation' on the other. If the logic of *sa'at* repeats itself, *Pemilu* 1987 may secure its 'ritual' position as a *Pesta Demokrasi*. Then again, *Pemilu* 1987 could very well follow through the compelling logic of *sa'at* and ritually exceed itself. In any event, looking back now on the 1982 General Election in Solo, Ken Ward's initial thought holds true: 'Historical events often seem more important to their witnesses than they do to the

---

shooting-gallery ducks going down without a single shot fired was probably a sweetly amusing alternative to *aman-tertib-lancar*: a moment when the machine slips on its own oil. In this light it is significant that the 130 spectators arrested during the 25 April Golkar parade in Jakarta were accused (among other charges) of smearing the streets with oil (see *Kompas*, 27 April 1982).

26 *Topik*, 10 May 1982, p. 5.

historians who judge them later'. The same could be said of rituals and their ethnographers.

POSTSCRIPT, 2002

The events recalled in the preceding essay occurred some twenty years ago at a time that we now know to have coincided almost exactly with the midpoint of New Order rule in Indonesia. One might say these events occurred at the height (or depth) of the Suharto regime's prolonged trajectory of repression. The highly politicised years of the early 1960s, which then gave way to the massacres of 1965–6, already seemed long past by 1982, as did even the protests and riots of the early 1970s. By the 1980s comments such as those—common in 1974—of the political analyst Ken Ward quoted at the outset of this essay ('As I write in the wake of the January 1974 demonstrations that rocked Djakarta, the solidity of the New Order appears to have been a very ephemeral thing indeed .... Few Indonesians would wager that another twenty years will be given to the New Order to carry out its programme of accelerated modernisation') seemed doubly misplaced: initially for their expression of extreme shock (had there not been signs beforehand?), and subsequently for their apparent sense of false alarm. In 1982, as the General Election approached, the New Order machine seemed to move with remarkable effortlessness on its twin rails of security and self-assurance. And we know now, of course, the Suharto regime would manage to extend its peculiar hold even further, much further, and by the end, in 1998, to have logged thirty years plus. I say 'peculiar' because the New Order was always, in a sense, 'the ephemeral thing' that Ward had acutely observed in 1974, a thing perpetually poised on the threshold of derailment; for it was as if even 'normal' times (like those of the 1980s) were always cast against a curtain of uncertainty. A strangely exhilarating sensation of fragility and precariousness emerged whenever security forces were deployed, even for the most mundane of assignments. It was as if the very security of the thing always seemed to call to mind a state of affairs at direct odds with appearances of control. Such sensations were most palpable—almost routinely so—during the mobile campaigns anticipating Indonesian general elections every five years.

The preceding essay was published in *Indonesia* (a Cornell University Modern Indonesia Project journal that closely tracked New Order politics) in 1986 (Pemberton, 1986). Thus the essay was published precisely in anticipation of Indonesia's 1987 General Election. It was not written to predict that election's outcome (as the pronounced ambivalence of its conclusion discloses), much less to reassure foreign investors (upon whom the Suharto regime very much depended) that Indonesia was 'secure' terrain. Rather the essay meant to recall events that might evoke a sensation, perhaps, of the real ephemerality of the thing. It meant to recall a certain uncertainty. The focus of the essay differed significantly from previous accounts of Indonesian elections in two fundamental respects. First, the essay's true focus was not the refined calculus of percentage politics—when 'successful', such elections always produced almost exactly the same results, a given from the start—but instead the campaigning's particular feeling of political movement, in the most physical sense of the term. Second, the essay was sited primarily in the streets of Solo, a Central Javanese city far from preoccupations with the capital politics of Jakarta, though hauntingly close to the epicentre of the New Order élite's ruling cultural fantasies. Suharto personally identified with Solo's purportedly exemplary articulation of Javanese culture. If the election process derailed in Solo, repercussions would 'spread' (according to many Solo people and ruling Jakartans alike) throughout the land 'like fire'. Such was the spectre of uncertainty that accompanied general elections in Solo, an uncertainty as routine as the elections themselves.

While the essay thus meant to shift attention away from Jakarta politics and the conventional calculations that so dominated mass media and much academic analysis, it ran the risk, in turn, of appearing to give credence to a form of 'local cultural' accounting that is, in my opinion, equally pernicious. Given Solo's considerable cultural capital, such a risk was especially evident. Previous coverage of the elections that followed more patently cultural lines had concluded, for example, that 'the national elections might be seen as a rite with the purpose of restoring the wholeness of chaotic society and nature. The chaos which had become manifest in a terrifying way during the campaign had to be overcome' (Schulte Nordholt, 1980: 181). Such a conclusion was particularly troubling during New Order times in light of the Suharto regime's own obsessive invocation of 'culture' (*kebudayaan*) as a reference, with the general election itself presented explicitly as a 'national ritual' (*upacara nasional*). It was as if New Order rhetoric and anthropological interpretation were uncannily synchronised and colluded to produce, in a word, *sukses*. The essay thus attempted, quite self-consciously, to counter such conclusions. (One needed only to recall Sukarno-era elections to reveal just how un-'Javanese' Javanese could be.) Be that as it may, not long after the essay was published I received a comment from an Australian scholar noting his 'appreciation' for the manner in which I had (he maintained) revealed New Order elections as representations, essentially, of Javanese ritual behaviour. Nothing, of course, could have been further from my intent. I was struck by the professional skill with which cultural analysts (devoted to identifying cultural actors), like political analysts (devoted to locating political actors), managed not to acknowledge far-reaching effects of this thing calling itself the New Order, with all its forces of *sukses* and *ekses*. And I was struck as well by the almost systematic absence of reflection on whatever it might be—another sort of force, perhaps—that would remind this thing of its own ephemerality.

On the streets of Solo during the campaigns of 1982 no word better projected the spectre of this other force than the English loanword 'crowd'; for this 'crowd' signalled a force that was utterly undeniable when it emerged, appearing to move entirely on its own, and yet whose source was not clearly identifiable, its exact point of origin was unlocatable. The 'crowd's' sudden appearance seemed to define a moment as potentially *the* moment (*sa'at*) and thus served as a reminder that there could be an end. Then, like a ghost, it would vanish as quickly as it had first appeared. One was tempted to say that this ghost was that of the *Rakyat* ('The People'), but such an utterance was inherently scandalous. (Could one really say that 'The People' had just rioted?) And vanish it did that year, precisely on election day, 4 May 1982.

This spectre of the 'crowd' would reappear periodically in Indonesia over the next decade and a half, most tangibly during the national election campaigns of 1987, 1992 and 1997, with election days nevertheless always registering essentially the same results. May 1998, as is well known, then ushered in events in the form of protests, which transformed, in turn, into horrific riots, looting and widespread destruction in urban centres. Within days Suharto resigned. By this time a new term had replaced 'crowd' to describe the force driving such destruction: *massa* ('the masses') perhaps, though for many this term, like 'crowd', carried with it a quasi-alien feel. While 'crowd' had been the phantom projection of the New Order state security apparatus, *massa* was now much more a spectre projected by Indonesia's newly emergent middle class, increasingly unsettled by underclass movements, increasingly fearful.[27] The May protests had been initiated with middle-class support calling for financial reform and acting as if representing *Rakyat* ('The People'). However, great masses of people soon began to move into unnerving trajectories of destruction at direct odds with such middle-class assumptions of representation. Born amidst times promising a social revolution yet to be achieved, yet to be completed, and then domesticated during thirty-two years of New Order rule as a residue of The Revolution deemed already past, *Rakyat* was now pursued by the spectre of forestalled revolutionary change, by the spectre of its own incompleteness.[28] It remained for

---

[27] I am indebted to James Siegel's startling account of the events in Jakarta during May 1998, particularly his insights concerning the term '*massa*' (Siegel, 1998). I am indebted as well to Benedict Anderson's reflections on popular violence in Indonesia (Anderson, 2001: introduction).

[28] In the early 1960s, before such New Order effects of enframement and domestication, *rakyat* and its spectre were still effectively conjoined in the phrase '*massa rakjat*', a progressive revolutionary force summoned up in leftist discourse. This phrase is beginning to resurface now among some Indonesian activists. I am most grateful to Nancy Florida for

newly 'reformed' Indonesian elections to perform the unwieldy task of reconciling the differences between 'The People' and its ghosts.

In the meantime much of Solo had been destroyed. Rioting and arson had taken a material toll of greater proportions here than in any other city on the island of Java. The magnitude of the destruction was astonishing. Eventually even Solo's City Hall—presumably the official centre for the staging of future elections—was engulfed by flames.[29] It was as if decades of prognostications concerning events that 'spread like fire' had transformed into an uncanny reality and returned, as it were, home. At the time I recalled, for a moment, Elias Canetti's recollection of 15 July 1927, a day of events in Vienna that compelled Canetti to pursue the figure of the crowd for the rest of his scholarly career:

The fire is what held the situation together. You felt the fire, its presence was overwhelming: even if you did not see it, you nevertheless had it in your mind, its attraction and the attraction exerted by the crowd were one and the same. The salvoes of gunfire by the police aroused boos, the boos new salvoes. But no matter where you happened to be under the impact of gunfire, no matter where you seemingly fled, your connection with others (an open or secret connection, depending on place) remained in effect. And you were drawn back into the province of the fire—circuitously, since there was no other possible way. (Canetti, 1982: 249–50)

Circuitously, concluding the 1986 essay, I made reference to the possibility of a '1987 Generation' in an attempt to convey, at that time, a sense of tangible uncertainty. In Solo nowadays one may speak, with a strange sense of certainty, of the '1998 Generation'. But then what?

Anderson, Benedict, 2001, *Violence and the State in Suharto's Indonesia*, Ithaca, NY: Cornell University Southeast Asia Program.

Bambang Siswoyo, P., 1981, *Huru Hara Solo Semarang*, Indonesia: Bakti Pertiwi.

Canetti, Elias, 1982, *The Torch in My Ear*, New York: Farrar, Giroux [trans. Herman Neugroschel].

Geertz, Clifford, 1973, *The Interpretation of Cultures*, New York: Basic Books, 1973.

Lembaga Pemilihan Umum [Electoral Institute], 1983, *Buku Pelengkap II Pemilihan Umum 1982*, Jakarta.

Nishihara, Masashi, 1972, *Golkar and the Indonesian Elections of 1971*, Ithaca, NY: Cornell Modern Indonesia Project.

bringing this significant conjunction to my attention.
29 Solo's City Hall was set on fire in October 1999 as riots and arson continued in the city, periodically, well after May 1998.

Pemberton, John, 1986, 'Notes on the 1982 General Election in Solo', *Indonesia*, no. 41, pp. 1–22.

Schulte Nordholt, N.G., 1980, 'The Indonesian Elections: A National Ritual' in R. Schefold, J.W. Schoorl and J. Tennekes (eds), *Man, Meaning and History*, The Hague: Nijhoff, Verhandelingen van het Koninklijk Instituut voor Taal, pp. 179–203.

Siegel, James T., 1998, 'Early Thoughts on the Violence of May 13 and 14, 1998, in Jakarta', *Indonesia*, no. 66, pp. 75–108.

Suryadinata, Leo, 1982, *Political Parties and the 1982 General Election in Indonesia*, Singapore: Institute of Southeast Asian Studies.

Ward, Ken, 1974, *The 1971 Election in Indonesia: An East Java Case Study*, Clayton, Victoria: Centre of Southeast Asian Studies, Monash University.

ELECTIONS IN IRAN

RELIGION, NATION AND THE PUBLIC SPHERE

Mahmoud Alinejad

'We had an Islamic revolution, which produced a concrete outcome: an Islamic political order. Thus we are no longer engaged in the struggle to establish an Islamic State. The main task now is to preserve reform and strengthen this (already established) political order...'[1]

'The main question of our nation (today) is the question of religious democracy, which has been both the goal and outcome of our great Islamic revolution...'[2]

'The establishment of the rule of the people through religious democracy is a unique experience, which would become a reality only with the help and participation of the people themselves .... Our people are conscious and responsible citizens entitled to (citizenship) rights...'[3]

'I do not agree that the taste or view of one particular group or tendency is tantamount to Islam. People vote for the views or programmes of individuals or groups, which might naturally be deficient. If we reduce Islam to the taste or view of one particular group, then any deficiency of that view or group could be conceived as the deficiency of Islam. I believe this is not in the interest of Islam. People must know that they are voting for man-made programmes and human tendencies, which are by no means sacred...'[4]

'The (coercive) imposition of narrow and outmoded views (on the nation), and the use of violence and (other) unjustified methods in the name of religion are the biggest treachery against religion ... and an important cause of laicism...'[5]

It was with such rhetoric that in May 1997 Mohammad Khatami, then a little-known, middle-ranking, Shi'i cleric, won Iran's seventh post-revo-

---

1 Excerpt from Khatami's interview with the Iranian Daily *Jomhuri Eslami* (The Islamic Republic) in February 1997 (Khatami, 1997).
2 Khatami's speech in his swearing in ceremonies on 8 August 2001 (*Daily Norooz*, 9 August 2001).
3 President Mohammad Khatami's campaign booklet entitled *Religious Democracy and Sustained Development*, May 2001. The booklet was published in the run-up to the June 2001 Presidential Elections in Iran.
4 Khatami's speech in *Husseiniyyeh Jamaran* (17 March 1997) during his election campaign in 1997.
5 Khatami's speech in his swearing in ceremonies on 8 August 2001, after he won a second term in office.

lutionary presidential elections by securing a landslide victory, and that he repeated his victory four years later, in June 2001. Since the May 1997 Presidential Elections electoral politics has evidently found a new meaning and hence a new place in Iran's Islamic politics. It has certainly ceased to be a mere instrumentality at the service of the political establishment for regular expression of allegiance to the ruling system. Henceforth the public has laid claim on elections, in the name of 'reform', turning them into a channel for open reflection of the demands of the nation on the state.

What inspired the idea of 'reform' in the elections of 1997 was the project of sustaining a religious state in a changed local and global context. It followed a continuous pattern, since the victory of the Islamic Revolution of 1979, of defining religion as a political culture and making cultural policy serve the purposes of the political aspirations and developmental needs of the 'Islamic State', which claimed to be representing Iran as an 'Islamic nation'. Yet if in the 1980s and early 1990s the nation was presumed to be monolithically religious, since 1997 a significant turn in society and polity has forced recognition of diversity and even conflict in the Islamic nation. The centrality of the continued challenge of nation-building to Khatami's project of reform cannot be overemphasised. After all, the political legitimacy of the Islamic State in Iran (not unlike other modern states) could not be maintained over the long haul without a sense of 'Islamic nation' that it would represent (Alinejad, 2002).

This chapter deals with the new place of elections in Iran's Islamic politics as a means of articulation of nationhood, representing long-term aspirations for 'freedom' and 'independence'. Focus is on the domestic efforts at the public level for entrenching the electoral process as the medium for assertion of national will and citizenship rights. In reformist literature the electoral process is promoted as a means of restoring the vote of the people to its constitutional role in the legitimacy of power. To this may be added: developing an indigenous discourse of democracy and expanding the public sphere. Whether, or to what extent, these aspirations have materialised is another matter. In pointing to the role of the public sphere in giving elections their new place, the chapter will note the new forms of public engagement in politics and their increasing importance as the source of legitimacy of the state. It will be noted that while the 1997 elections produced a mediated (predominantly religious) public sphere, this public sphere has, in turn, made elections an indispensable element of the legitimacy of power and the assertion of a religious nationhood. Of particular importance is the function of elections as a medium for capturing the imagination of millions of young male and female professionals, intellectuals, students and even blue-collar workers, shopkeepers and farmers as discerning voters. These new publics are rapidly appropriating the modern culture of elections in a bid to assert their constitutionally recognised citizenship rights in the context of the dominant 'religious polity' and 'religious public sphere'.

ISLAM, POLITICS AND DEMOCRACY

Until not so long ago the predominantly Western literature on democratisation was dominated by theories that proved (beyond a shadow of a doubt) that Islam was antithetical to democracy. It was somehow taken for granted that Muslim societies (unlike Western ones) lacked the historical experience and hence the political and cultural capacities that have made democratic development a reality in the West. A 'cluster of absences', in the words of Leonard Binder, prevented the development of democracy (as it is known in the West) in the Muslim world (Binder, 1988). 'In this view, the absence of a concept of citizenship and of a legal-political culture of compromise and flexibility marks a critical deficiency' (Piscatori, 2000). Not surprisingly the currents of Western thought, which insisted on the unique experience of democracy in the West, have had their counterpart in the Muslim world, which emphasised, in turn, the uniqueness of the Islamic experience. Traditionalist religious leaders (from Sheikh Fazlollah Nuri in the early twentieth century to his present day followers) have emphasised that the idea of democracy carries in it an inherently 'alien' and 'secular' value system. Accordingly this value system seeks to replace the *Shari'at* (God's law) by man-made law, the belief in the sovereignty of God with the idea of popular sovereignty, and the ideal of the rule of God's chosen representatives with the idea of majority rule. Hence, a mutual and malignant commitment to the incompatibility of Islam and democracy developed, which often pitted the two against each other.

Essentialist arguments about the uniqueness of the Western or Islamic experience have often made conflict inevitable, as both sides go on taking superior ground for their own uniqueness. While the former boasts of the privileged political culture of citizenship and the rule of (man-made) law, the latter prides itself in saving humanity from the structured system of domination and manipulation of man by man, promising a spiritual and just world ruled by divine law. Both sides have often exaggerated the weight of the 'place of origin' factor to justify the incompatibility of Islam and democracy; nonetheless, the intellectual and doctrinal justifications for these exaggerations have persisted against the background of post-colonial politics. Hence, a 'fully democratic' electoral process could not be entrenched in the Muslim world owing to the absence of functional (legal-structural) predicates and appropriate normative roots on the one hand, and the 'alien' nature, and particularly the secular intellectual source, of the Western idea of liberal democracy on the other.

Doubts about the incompatibility of Islam and democracy had always existed, but had to take a back seat, as more than a century of experience with modernity had ostensibly failed to instil democratic values in the Muslim world. Electoral politics, for example, had come into currency in the Ottoman Empire during the nineteenth century, and in Iran stirring for a parliamentary government began in the early twentieth century. But despite the intellectual, legal and institutional means developed in various Muslim societies in order to sustain and regulate electoral politics, democracy as practised in the West seemed to be significantly lacking there. Certainly the requirements of post-colonial politics dictated the extension of democracy to the Muslim world (Turkey, Iran, Pakistan, Egypt, Jordan, Algeria etc.) as government instrumentalities; but obviously this could not instigate a democratic spirit. The indigenous political discourses and normative social practices which had consistently promoted human dignity and social justice against political and social repression and coercion (often perpetrated by regimes supported by the former imperial powers) were still linked to religious spirit and hence considered essentially 'non-democratic'.

That the post-colonial politics in the Muslim world often produced modern states seekingto maintain themselves through repressive policies provided sufficient ground for the arguments that saw no chance for anything more than rudimentary and instrumental use of elections in Muslim politics. This phenomenon is attributed by the prevalent Western theories to the patrimonial and authoritarian political practices, social structures and religious traditions in which Muslim societies are rooted. But the modernist defenders of Islamic traditions view this as a product of the post-colonial design for the domination of the Muslim world, whereby native dictatorial regimes were implanted and propped up to protect Western interests. The inconspicuous place of genuine, free and open elections in the Muslim world provided both sides with evidence to support their often conflicting accounts of why democracy was substantially lacking there. Yet despite (and even alongside) such snobbish intellectual attitudes, the utilitarian necessities of post-colonial politics gradually instigated an acknowledgement in both Western and Islamic political discourses (in the form of alternative theories) that it was not only possible, but also desirable for Muslim politics to be democratic. Democracy proved in practice to be more than a Western privilege, as national and international campaigners for democracy (of various persuasions) expounded its universality. Even the Islamists (long accused of being anti-democratic) began to profess the universality of democratic values (and particularly the electoral process), making democracy an imperative, rather than a choice, in Muslim politics.

It was in such circumstances that unanimity developed in post-revolutionary Iran on the value of electoral politics, as a measure of compliance

with the requirements of democracy (*mardom-salari*). The recognition
of elections as a democratic means to power came about despite (and
even alongside) the hostile views of some Islamists with respect to Western modernity as the original site of democracy. The association of democracy with Western imperialism did not deter Muslim Iranians from
increasingly acknowledging that elections should be understood, more
appropriately, as a native means of instituting the rule of the many as
against the rule of the few. Meanwhile a greater interest has been shown
in Western academic circles (if not in power circles) in understanding
the nature and functions of political Islam in the modern world in terms
other than 'backwardness' and 'irrationality', albeit often in terms of
'incomplete modernisation'. The recent academic shift in the study of
Muslim politics away from familiar pessimistic premises, whereby this
politics was viewed as inherently anti-democratic, is an example of this
discursive change.[6] In light of this discursive shift in political theory
credit is due to the diversity and ingenuity of the indigenous intellectual,
social and cultural currents that shape Muslim politics. Attention to developments in Iran brings to light several indigenous intellectual trends
that have long promoted Islamic variants of participatory politics. What
is more, despite their historical and cultural peculiarities, these trends do
not seem to differ in principle from the Western experience.

The Iranian advocates of 'religious democracy' (*mardom-salari dee-
ni*) have tackled the discourse of democracy in close connection with the
moral value of freedom as the basic requirement of virtuous faith in God.
Since the early-twentieth-century constitutional movement (1905–11)
several religious leaders and activists have conceptually associated the
moral value of freedom with the sanctity of human dignity. The historical
roots of this sanctimonious view of freedom are often sought in the early
Islamic commands to the faithful on liberation from slavish subjugation
to non-God (*taqut*) through resistance against injustice and oppression
(*zolm*).[7] The struggle to establish democracy as a religious value has
been supplemented in recent times by religious arguments for democracy (as a value in itself) in the work of a new generation of religious
intellectuals.[8] They have certainly benefited from their acquired knowl-

6 The work of Dale Eickleman and James Piscatori is only one example of this change
(Eickleman and Piscatori, 1996).
7 This was indicated in the early twentieth century by the constitutionalist Ayatollah
Mohammad-Hassan Na'ini's treatise on the merits of constitutionalism in Islam (*Tanbi-
holumma va Tanziholmella*), and taken up by his present day followers like Mohammad
Khatami.
8 Dr Ali Shari'ati, Ayatollah Mahmoud Taleqani and Mehdi Bazargan emphasised the
appreciation of Islam of the rule of the people in their work in the 1960s and 1970s. The
new generation of religious intellectuals including clerics and lay persons, like Mohammad Mojtahid-Shabestari, Mohammad Khatami, Mohsen Kadivar, Abdolkarim Soroush
and Saeed Hajjarian, have carried on the legacy of the earlier generation of religious intel-

edge of the Western experience (in an intense process of translation of the works of Western social theorists). But the originality of their efforts in incorporating the concept of democratic government into moral and legal arguments, which would fit within the Iranian-Islamic philosophical, mystical and juridical tradition, should not be overlooked.

Nonetheless, the persistence of advocates of the uniqueness of the Western experience continues to feed the rhetoric of the uniqueness of the Islamic experience, which is bent on warning against threats of Western values to Islamic purity. The strategy of refraining from engagement in modern secular politics, motivated by concerns about the doctrinal purity of Islam, had already acted as a serious impediment to the effective participation of Muslim Iranians in public life, although this impediment was substantially overcome with the revolutionary seizure of political power by Islamists in 1979. Yet it was not until May 1997 that genuine participation emerged as a main element of religious politics in Iran.[9] Ever since, intensifying competition for the positions of power has made the electoral process subject to unprecedented levels of agitation and scrutiny to ensure its authenticity.[10] And the electoral wins of the democratically-inclined Islamists through the electoral process promise to create, slowly but surely, real possibilities for the social approximation of such ostensibly contradictory concepts as 'religious democracy' and 'religious civil society'.

ELECTIONS AND THE EMERGENCE OF THE PUBLIC SPHERE

In order to understand the nature of electoral politics in Iran over the period under discussion, one should pay special attention to the role of a new intellectual movement that has been contributing (since mid-1990s) to the expansion of a mediated public sphere outside the strict control of the state. The development of a language of critique is the main feature of this process. The intellectuals virtually took over the mediated public sphere with their critical discourse, in which electoral politics was turned into a serious element of political legitimacy. But in time this mediated public sphere has become a site for the emergence of a differentiated and articulated public with a life of its own, with potential to transgress the red lines that mark the safe boundaries of a non-subversive language of critique.

---

lectuals to the 1990s and beyond.

9 In the 1997 elections the voter turnout increased by more than 70 per cent compared to the previous rounds of elections in 1985, 1989 and 1993. Khatami won these elections with 70 per cent of the popular votes (Badi'i, 2001 [1380]).

10 In the Parliamentary Elections of February 2000 close scrutiny of the electoral process by both sides of the political spectrum was unprecedented. According to some recounts in Tehran, instigated by a dispute between the conservatives and reformists, electoral error was less that 2 per cent.

The increasing public participation in the competition for power through the electoral process (as high as 80 per cent since 1997) seems increasingly to be beyond containment even by its initial beneficiaries. This profound politicisation of the public sphere should not be too surprising though, given that the new publics are, in essence, a product of the economic, demographic, educational and communicational developments that swept the country after the revolution, rather than an intellectual design. Nonetheless, the role of the creative imagination of the intellectuals in shaping public opinion cannot be ignored. Significant political, economic, social and cultural changes during and after the war with Iraq (1980–8), and the political and ideological responses that were provoked by these changes, were both responsible for bringing more and more marginal social groups into national public and, inevitably, political life. Besides, there was an increased role of the state in social life as both the representative of the nation and the servant of the public.[11]

The new developments in public culture under Ali-Akbar Hashemi Rafsanjani's two-term presidency (1989–97) involved the burgeoning of a new press, which not only reported but also inspired a variety of political, cultural, social and artistic activities. This gave rise to a new pluralistic political environment, which contradicted the repressive political atmosphere of the war period. The post-war political developments were in fact the open expression of the real diversities and differences in political and cultural ideas and tastes of various political factions and social forces that had been kept silent during the war, often because of security concerns. A major part of these differences pertained to a significant generation gap. The insistence of the elderly and traditionalist clergy on using the official media to inculcate monolithic and monologic messages to this heterogeneous and educated nation not only alienated the younger generation but also increasingly politicised and radicalised this alienation.

The politicisation of religion in Iran since the revolution—based on political interpretations of sacred symbols (narratives, texts, rituals etc.)—although limiting in many ways, nevertheless helped create new social spaces for interaction and negotiation. These new spaces for social interaction helped, in turn, forge a diversified public sphere both as the site of public debates on national interests and as a mechanism for the intervention of the public in political decision-making. For example, there was a surge in informal intellectual circles, often convening in private homes, which discussed common social, economic and political problems associated with the involvement of religion in

---

11 The state responsibility for service provision is enshrined in the constitution of the Islamic republic.

politics.[12] Part of a mediated public sphere was already in the making as a result of the seepage of intellectual debates on traditional religious beliefs and political loyalties into the public domain. Alternative readings of religion, for example, were raised in speeches, lectures and debates in the universities and seminaries. The main media for the spread of these new ideas beyond the confines of academia were printed publications. In time new reference groups emerged within this public domain. For example, with the importance of higher education among Iranian families, in both traditional urban neighbourhoods and even the rural communities, the political opinions of university students became increasingly important for their families and communities. Also the reformist activists-turned-journalists, who used printed publications to advance more progressive interpretations of religious and cultural traditions, gained in significance as new reference groups for the public in general and the educated youth in particular (Abdi and Rezaie, 1998 [1377]: 35).

The elections of 1997 thus provided an outlet for a new critical discourse that was already attracting increasing support among the general public and particularly the younger generation, who were faced with increasing evidence of political and moral double standards in the ruling circles. This new discourse made a substantive appeal to reason and rationality. For example, the rational language of critique displaced (albeit partially) the rumours which were bandied around about the cases of abuse of power and financial corruption by officials. This involved questioning of strict attachment to and merciless enforcement of restrictive and militant readings of religion and politics while evidence was mounting of economic mismanagement, moral decay and political and social discrimination. The vote in the 1997 elections was thus the reflection of a movement from below, fuelled by such factors as high literacy among the youth, the mobilisation of the youth for revolutionary purposes and the war effort, and the increased presence of women in the economic, social and political arenas. While these factors had increased the sense of independence and power of these sectors of the population, the lack of effective associations, political parties and other civil institutions formed an impediment to public expression of the demands of these groups for political participation. This could explain the explosive rush of these groups to polling booths on 23 May 1997 (and again on 8 June 2001), which provided an outlet for expression of the independence and power of these new publics.

Demands for a share in political power were advanced primarily by a new generation of reform-minded junior clerics and lay religious in-

---

[12] During 1995 and 1996 Mohammad Khatami attended one of these informal intellectual gatherings, which held regular weekly sessions in Tehran. It was in such a setting that the then little known Khatami was approached by other members of the circle (who are well-known officials, professionals and activists today) to run for president.

tellectuals through the electoral process. Furthermore, since the 1997 elections the republican virtues of the constitution of the Islamic republic have been increasingly invoked in order 'to restore the vote of the people to its constitutional authority' as the main agency of political legitimacy. This created the possibility of a far greater scale of political participation than had hitherto been seen. The question was no longer whether the public should participate in politics, but rather how the power of the people should be organised in the interest of democratic political competition.

The extension of the struggle for power to the public domain initially led to the formation of informal coalitions in what gradually came to be known as the 'right' and 'left' wings of the political spectrum. In the early 1990s this trend led to the dominance of the so-called right-wing coalition consisting of 'conservative' clergy and their non-clerical allies in the government and the ouster of most of the 'leftist' religious revolutionaries from positions of power. The dominance of conservative politics and the exclusion of alternative political views and tastes marginalised these views but did not eliminate them altogether. The marginalisation, particularly of those political forces whose religious and revolutionary commitment could not be easily denied, created possibilities for the formation of new coalitions that challenged, in the language of reform, the solid political dominance of the 'conservatives'.[13]

According to reformist literature, the attempt on the part of the conservative clergy to monopolise political power, and even control the personal behaviour of the people through repressive cultural and social regulation, pitted not only part of the government élite but also many other social groups against the conservative power. For example, the modern middle class, a product of modernisation under the deposed Pahlavi monarchy (1925–78), which was virtually disenfranchised by the aggressive push of the Islamic state to revive the strict codes of religious morality, began to reassert itself from the mid-1990s. According to a local analyst, the ruling clerical élite caused a political crisis, which was a result of their inability to create a general consensus around their cultural, social and economic policies, and hence their resort to coercion and repression to impose their views on society. The conservatives failed to recognise the need for the creation of civil institutions that were required to disseminate their political ideology and turn their ideas and tastes into common values (Abdi and Rezaie, 1998 [1377]: 11–12). Thus in the political atmosphere that preceded the 1997 elections the right-wing coalition, despite its control of all the major apparatuses of power, failed to create

---

13 I use the labels of 'reformist' and 'conservative' because of their significance in the current political language in Iran, and in the sense that they are used here; but one should always be aware of their multiple and shifting meanings.

broad social consent around its policies; and hence it created the opportunity for its political and ideological competitors to challenge its power. According to this analysis, Khatami's electoral victory and the rise of a popular reform movement in its wake should be examined in light of this ideological vacuum in the conservative coalition.

After the 1997 elections Iran's religious politics indeed became more open to competitive political participation and public criticism, giving rise to a campaign for more political freedom and civil liberties by a new political opposition manned predominantly by a new generation of intellectuals of religious and revolutionary background. The question of how to limit the powers of the conservative jurists and their non-clerical allies may be the most important concern of this campaign at both political and religious levels. The politico-religious dispute, which had begun immediately after the victory of the Islamic revolution in the drafting of the constitution of the Islamic republic, is now pursued in the struggle to find a resolution to the question of compatibility, or otherwise, between democracy and Islam. This quest has gathered increasing momentum in electoral politics and is driven mainly by the new 'religious intellectuals' and their printed publications.

The electoral process in Iran has had a twofold implication. On the surface mass participation in elections has been presented as a confirmation of the commitment of the Muslim public to Islamic political values, a means of representation of a collective identity based on religious revivalism and a radical critique of Western modernity. However, the appeal to mass mobilisation and its apparent anti-modern rhetoric often conceal the very modern nature of electoral politics, which tends to reveal the real diversity and differentiation of the Muslim publics. On the one hand the electoral process represents the collective aspiration of a religious-turned-political community for national identity based on religious culture. Yet on the other it has also to represent the struggle of smaller identity groups and sub-cultures, which demand expression within the constraints of the dominant Islamic (Shi'i) culture. The latter enterprise has given voice to the discourses of the mainly peripheral groups (youth, women, intellectuals, artists, ethnic and religious minorities etc.) which tend to appropriate Islam in order to expand the public sphere within the constraints of the dominant Shi'i culture. In other words, in the electoral process what is understood as 'Islamic identity' is being increasingly articulated in terms of a discursive field of political and social critique, expressed in an environment of competition, whereby newly erected identity structures demand recognition.

The shift of the contest for power into the public domain through the appeal of electoral politics has given the nascent generation of 'religious intellectuals' the opportunity to represent the thus far marginal but increasingly vocal, and even critical, social and political groups. Hence, the intellectual effort to expand the public sphere as a domain of national enfranchisement, political competition, free speech and civil society has come to face stiff opposition from an élite group of Shi'i *foqaha* (jurists) that is trying to maintain control over the boundaries of the public sphere. Thus the electoral process has emerged as a field of contest for capturing public support, and hence as a means of political legitimacy, by a generation of new democratically-minded Islamists who seek to turn Shi'ism into a 'civil religion'. In their arguments, the tradition of the Prophet and the Shi'i Imams had already rendered the Shi'i faith a civil religion that would allow for interpretations and practices other than those offered by the jurists, and hence provided a basis for religious pluralism and political tolerance. In this sense elections have given rise to a movement representing the upwardly mobile social and political forces that, while expressing allegiance to the Shi'i religious and revolutionary traditions, have mounted a challenge to the claims of the scholastic Shi'i jurists to exclusive authority over religion. Given the entrenched power and vested interests of certain individuals and groups of religious authority, it should be obvious why the protagonists of reform have had to deal with accusations of heresy, apostasy and even treason in their calls for alternative interpretations of religion.

No doubt the landslide victories of Khatami in the 1997 and 2001 elections have been instrumental in these developments, giving rise to a virtual opposition within the power establishment on the one hand and a challenge to the religious establishment on the other. Yet this situation should be understood not so much in terms of the conscious plans and interests of Khatami and his supporters but more in terms of a subliminal undercurrent of public resistance against absolutist political tendencies (which was the original motivation of revolution against monarchical autocracy). The newly emerging collective intellectual effort to develop an indigenous language of democracy serves as only one form (albeit a significant one) of articulation of this resistance. This native discourse and its substantive appeal to democratic rhetoric are thus a product of accumulated social discontent and political dissent, providing the public resistance to authoritarianism with a differentiated and purposeful articulation, while continuing to pledge allegiance to Islam. This situation has amounted to a serious challenge to Islamic political power in Iran, as the legacy of the 1979 revolution. What is more, it has also challenged the whole political and cultural enterprise of creating a religious society and polity as the proper environment for raising new generations of committed religious believers and loyal revolutionary souls.

REVOLUTION, SOCIAL CHANGE AND ELECTORAL ENTHUSIASM

Elections (despite their relatively long legal and institutional history in Iran) were definitely not experienced in a meaningful sense by the nation until 1997. This was certainly due to a number of deficiencies. The religious intellectuals have enumerated, for example, the lack of democratic experience under long-term despotic rule, the lack of a religious reformation of a Protestant type, the lack of effective civil institutions and civil liberties, the lack of an efficient and free market economy and industrial development like that of Western Europe. All these explanations certainly have merit, but do not explain the surge of public enthusiasm at the national level for participation in the Presidential Elections of 1997 and 2001, simply because this heightened enthusiasm came despite the lacks mentioned. What was not lacking, though, was a national political will to use the available public resources (e.g. elections and the printed press) as media for asserting the presence of the nation as a force to reckon with, without risking much violence and recrimination. These elections were in effect a medium of peaceful protest by a generation that was born out of a revolution, a revolution that had promised freedom, independence and a government of justice: an Islamic republic that would be at once emancipatory and egalitarian.

A joint study by two Iranian scholars (Khaniki and Kashi, 2001) shows that at least two generations and two generational experiences should be differentiated in post-revolutionary Iran. One is a generation that found self-consciousness in the revolution and flourished during the war, and the other a generation that began to develop self-understanding after the war. With respect to these two generations, one may speak of two value systems with distinct and at times conflicting structures. According to this study, owing to the weakness, or even absence, of appropriate mechanisms for the transmission of experience from the older generation to the younger, the generation gap in Iran manifested itself increasingly in the form of political demands on the state. What is more, it threatened to degenerate into a generational breakdown. In fact the incipient signs of such a breakdown began to appear in the years immediately after the end of the war, as a crack developed in the value system promoted in the war period, based on austerity, purity and sticking to principles.

The encouragement of individual material well-being motivated by tendencies that approved, and even encouraged, 'get-rich-quick' attitudes after the war offered a basically materialistic value system, which began to encroach on the austere values of the war period, Khaniki and Kashi argue. The revolutionary discourse, therefore, found itself under the threat of a so-called 'rational' (mainly economic) discourse that was winning advocates among increasing numbers of the revolutionary generation in ways that would further distance the younger generation from the revolutionary values. This led to a 'compulsive accentuation of ultra-revolutionary zeal' among the conservative elements of the revolutionary generation, which allowed for almost no tolerance for what they saw as 'new trends of deviance'. Not surprisingly, the emotional attachment to strict interpretations of revolutionary values and the culture of war had as its counterpart the development of a purely instrumental economic rationalism on the opposite side. The main carriers of the new discourse were the intellectuals (e.g. university graduates and students) who developed a shift away from the collective tendencies of the revolutionary discourse (based on asceticism and otherworldly aspirations) to a discourse that emphasised individual worldly interests. It was in this context that new political trends developed in support of 'economic development' (*tose'eh eghtesadi*) and attention to worldly needs and desires, as against the tendencies that sought true salvation in revolutionary suffering in this world, manifested in militancy and soldierly life. In the new discourse, scientific and technological expertise, economic growth, social progress, welfare and entertainment were given priority over the ethical, emotional and solemn messages of the revolutionary discourse.

In 1979 the revolutionary generation protested in a mass movement against the Pahlavi monarchy, which was seen as an irredeemable source of national indignity and moral decay. It undertook to oust the monarchical state in the name of freedom, independence and the Islamic republic. The post-revolutionary generation either inherited, or was born into, the Islamic republic but had yet to experience the freedom and independence that had been promised by the revolution. Moreover it had a whole host of new needs and desires associated with the new domestic, not to mention global, developments over the two decades after the revolution. The new generation was more independent, more urbanised, more educated and more informed than the generation of the revolution. Not least because it grew up during a period of significant demographic change, important shifts in the pattern of employment in an expanding job market, rapid expansion of mass education (particularly higher education) and an unprecedented growth in modern communication technology. Mass education, demographic shifts, new patterns of employment and entry onto the scene of the modern media brought the whole population into contact with political and social developments of the nation, and increasingly helped shape new identities that demanded recognition.

According to 1976 statistics Iran was almost half-illiterate and half-urbanised (47.5 per cent of the population were considered literate and 47 per cent lived in the urban centres). According to the census of 1996 though, almost 80 per cent of the population were literate[14] and almost

---

14 In the period 1976–96 literacy among women rose from 36 to around 70 per cent.

70 per cent were urbanised. The overall population grew in this period from around 36 million to around 65 million (with about 70 per cent of the population estimated to be under the age of thirty). The population engaged in formal education rose from around 7 million in the academic year 1978–9 to more than 19 million in 1996, indicating an increase of more than 250 per cent. In 1996 more than one million students were enrolled in higher education nationwide, with another 1.5 million holding university degrees. For every nineteen families (approximately) there were on average two people with university degrees or engaged in higher education. In the employment sector too there was an important change. While the state remained the main employer, the private sector recorded an unprecedented growth. Interestingly the rise in employment in the private sector was due overwhelmingly to the sharp increase in ownership of small businesses. A comparison of the official censuses of 1976 and 1996 indicates that whereas the number of wage earners in the private sector rose by only 6.5 per cent, the number of self-employed jobs rose in the same period by 189 per cent. Obviously these jobs, by their nature, provided more independence and hence more opportunity for being selective in choosing a lifestyle, developing management skills, participating in the national economy and making political decisions.

In the government sector there was an increase of more than 250 per cent in employment[15] and a large portion of these jobs went to the lower classes, a new pattern espoused by the revolutionary egalitarian aspirations. Also significant, in the employment sector women were making more inroads into high-status jobs than ever before. But the rate of electoral participation of women still remained low with respect to the rise in higher education among this social group (around 60 per cent). Meanwhile the mobilisation for war and the programme of economic rationing forced the state to expand communication networks into the remotest areas, thus further politicising the population, while deepening the sense of belonging to one nation.[16] Moreover the surge in employment and education and the spread of modern means of communication were not limited to the urban population. In the provincial and rural areas too the population had become more educated,[17] more demanding, more discerning in forming political opinion and more selective in making political choices. In addition, during the eight-year war with Iraq (1980–8) there was a huge displacement of population through internal migration

---

[15] Government employment grew from around 1.5 million in 1976 to more than 4 million in 1996.

[16] The 1996 census showed that out of 12.2 million families in the country only a little more than one million did not have a radio or television (Abdi and Rezaie, 1998 [1377]: 117–18).

[17] The literacy rate was 86 per cent in the urban areas and 70 per cent in the rural ones. For women in the urban centres it was about 82 per cent, and in rural areas about 62 per cent.

that transformed the old patterns of life in many areas. Big cities, in particular, had to host huge populations of refugees from the war-stricken geographical and cultural regions.

These developments were surely shaped by post-revolutionary politics, which despite its conservative nature had to maintain the revolutionary slogans while keeping up with the developmental needs of the state. Yet inevitably the huge changes in social life in the urban and rural areas meant that the relationship of the new generations of urban and rural people with the traditional sources of authority could not remain the same. One may argue that as a result of these chnages the power of the more traditional sources of authority diminished (e.g. school authorities versus students, parents versus children, men versus women, religious authorities versus the community of believers, and the official media versus alternative media). The alternative media, which helped the public find an independent voice, certainly weighed in, creating an environment in which new identities and new loyalties were forged. The new generations needed a voice, and the 1997 elections produced a mediated public sphere which gave it just that.[18] After all, the huge electoral support for Khatami's reformist agenda came largely from the votes of the youth (both male and female, between fifteen and thirty years of age), who were either children or not yet born at the time of the revolution.[19] The explosive turn of the public to elections almost two decades after the revolution was interpreted both as an indication of public dismay with the status quo and as showing the continued public trust in the possibility of correcting the ruling Islamic system from within. In both cases reformism appeared almost instantly as a movement against the overwhelming 'conservative' power, which represented the status quo. And the voices of dissent found some expression in the burgeoning but fledgling market of a reformist press, as the voices of 'civil society'.

RELIGION, REVOLUTION AND ASPIRATIONS FOR A RELIGIOUS NATION

Iran had since the early twentieth century a constitution in which the role of elections had been recognised. The move of some groups of intellectuals, clerics, merchants and enlightened aristocrats in 1905 to bring to the attention of the Qajar King the grievances of his subjects grew into what came to be called the constitutional revolution (1905–11). It involved the drafting of a constitution and the convening of the first Iranian parliament (*Majlis Showra Melli*). But the constitutional movement was a movement of a political, social and economic élite who wished to limit the power of the king for the good of monarchy, and for the benefits

18 For a discussion of the Muslim public sphere, see Eickleman and Anderson (1999).
19 The legal age for voting was set at fifteen.

that a limited expansion of the political sphere would offer the marginal élite (Kasravi, 1967 [1346]; Abrahamian, 1982). Yet the divisions and conflicts that emanated from the constitutional movement led to the meteoric political rise of Reza Shah (the first Pahlavi king) as a strong man. Dictatorial yet modernising, he ruled Iran in a crucial historical period from the early 1920s to the early 1940s and produced the structural and territorial components of a modern state. The Pahlavi monarchy produced a sophisticated bureaucracy, a modern army, a modern system of mass education (including institutions of tertiary education),[20] a modern legal system,[21] modern means of transport and mass communication[22] and all other structural elements of a modern state. Also in this period the territorial boundaries of Iran found cartographic precision, as a network of roads and railways made possible the drawing of the first modern maps and the setting up of border checkpoints. But this modern state failed to produce a nation that it would represent.[23] Prime Minister Mohammad Mossadeq and his oil nationalisation movement created a brief sense of nationhood in the early 1950s, but again the conflicts and troubles distanced the state from the religious leaders who could deliver the people required for the membership of the nation. According to most accounts, this was the main cause of the defeat of Mossadeq's nationalist movement and the rise of a second round of dictatorship under the second Pahlavi monarch, Mohammad-Reza (1941–78).[24]

The Islamic revolution of 1979, though, provided the main motivating elements of a new sense of religious nationalism, namely the religious notions of historical victimisation, a divine mission to restore justice and the culture of sacrifice (martyrdom).[25] These elements were the pillars

[20] The University of Tehran was founded in 1934.

[21] The civil code was introduced in 1936.

[22] This included the construction of roads and railways, the proliferation of printing and the introduction of telegraphic technology.

[23] Reza Shah, for example, created Iran's first standing army in modern times by crushing the armed nomadic tribes, which had historically acted as military contingents for tribal dynasties that controlled the monarchical states. For centuries these traditional warrior-tribesmen had successfully defended the unmarked territorial boundaries of Iranian monarchies. But in 1941, when the geographically delimited borders of modern Iran were invaded by the Allied forces, the tribal contingents had already been dispersed by Reza Shah to make room for his modern army, which was to be the new defender of his modern state. Yet this army proved to be lacking in a fundamental element: a nationalist spirit that would make the territory sacred and its defence a life-and-death duty. The army's rapid disintegration at the sight of the invading forces was proof that Reza Shah's ideological chauvinism had failed to inspire such a spirit. This lack of nationalist enthusiasm was not limited to the armed forces; all other elements of the state suffered from it.

[24] The destiny of Mohammad-Reza's advanced and expensive armed forces (rapid disintegration, this time in the face of revolutionary masses) was further proof that the Pahlavis' references to Aryan racial origins had long ceased to inspire a nationalist spirit in Iran.

[25] For a discussion of the concept of 'religious nationalism', see Van der Veer and Lehmann (1999).

of the cultural-revolutionary reading of the Shi'i faith, a reading that claimed to provide the Iranian-Islamic nation with a common cultural self-understanding. Shi'ism was thus presented as both a revolutionary faith and a collective culture, a powerful faith that would inspire a militant spirit and a hope for the '*monji* (saviour) of the human world'.[26] The revolution, though religious in form and content, did not cast away the constitutional legacy. A new constitution was drafted that contained many elements of the early twentieth-century constitution, but also added a great many new ones. This constitution of the Islamic republic (the main, most concise and most comprehensive political document inherited from the Islamic revolution) was significantly articulate in its elevation of the role of the people, not surprisingly because it was a product of a mass revolution. According to Article 6:

In the Islamic republic of Iran the management of the affairs of the state must rest on the vote of the people, either through elections (the presidential elections, the parliamentary elections, the council elections and the like), or through referenda...

And according to Article 56:

Absolute sovereignty over the world and mankind belongs to God. And it is He who has made man sovereign in his social destiny. No one can take away this God-given right, or put it at the service of specific individuals or groups. And the nation applies her right in ways and means that are stipulated in other articles (of this law).

Ayatollah Khomeini himself (as the charismatic leader of the revolution and the architect of the Islamic republic) frequently acknowledged the debt of the Shi'i clergy to the 'people' (*mardom*). 'The people are our masters', he repeatedly asserted. In the last leg of his exile in Paris (just before he returned to Iran in triumph), Ayatollah Khomeini retorted to a German journalist who asked what sort of political regime would replace the monarchy:

'The nation will decide the form of our government. We will put the proposal for an Islamic republic to the nation in a referendum .... This government should salvage the national life, provide the people with freedom, give back the country its independence, and replace an exploitative regime with (a regime of) economic justice.'[27]

26 The age-old mass rituals of *Ashura*—a grassroots religious ceremony that commemorates the sufferings and ordeals of the third Shi'i Imam on the national scale (preparing the believers for martyrdom)—combined with the nationwide hope for the *Mahdi* (the Concealed Imam), who would return from his Great Concealment (*Gheibat-e Kobra*) to restore a government of absolute justice, provided a proper religious-cultural basis for an imagined yet meaningful national identity.

27 Cited from an interview with Ayatollah Khomeini in Paris on 7 November 1978, conducted by the German magazine *Der Spiegel* (Khomeini, 1994: 148).

As to how Islam and republicanism could be combined, he replied to a French journalist: the republican side (of the Islamic republic) follows the same sense of republic that is prevalent everywhere else; 'yet this republic is based on a constitution rooted in Islamic law.'[28]

The facts of religious demography made the Shi'i faith and culture a factor much more inclusive than the Aryan race (or even the Persian language) in inspiring a collective identity, so essential for the sense of loyalty to the Iranian Shi'i territory.[29] The Islamic revolution provided precisely for this sense of religious nationality, based on historical victimisation, a readiness for sacrifice and a hope for future salvation. But it was not until May 1997 that it produced the conditions for transition from being a populist movement to becoming a political environment for national enfranchisement. From the *imaginaire* of a monolithic revolutionary mass (in the early 1980s), which covered up all differences under Ayatollah Khomeini's call for *vahdat-e kalameh* (unity of the word), emerged a public domain (in the late 1990s) which increasingly revealed the real diversities (and even conflicts) of the nation. These divisions and diversities had somewhat successfully been concealed in the 1980s by religious solidarity built around the ascetic-revolutionary views of Ayatollah Khomeini. The charismatic Ayatollah, as the head of the 'first truly Islamic state' in modern times, had little difficulty in creating a solid social constituency, i.e. millions of revolutionary youth with enough loyalty to engage in a 'heroic' war against the external enemy (Iraq) (Alinejad, 2002). The state's efforts at using legislation, education, communication, mass mobilisation and even coercion were combined with the charismatic influence of Ayatollah Khomeini to build religious faith and culture into a moral-legal element in the legitimacy of the Islamic State. What is more, in this process religion was made, in time, the cornerstone of a national *imaginaire*.[30]

SHI'I JURISPRUDENCE AND THE ISLAMIC NATION-STATE

An Iranian religious intellectual and political strategist, Saeed Hajjarian,[31] refers to Ayatollah Khomeini as 'the jurist of transition'. Khomeini, according to Hajjarian, was a jurist who presided over both Iran and the Shi'i *fiqh* (jurisprudence) in a crucial period of transition from tradition to modernity. This radical Shi'i *faqih* (jurist) certainly made a transi-

---

28   Cited from an interview with Ayatollah Khomeini in Paris on 13 November 1978, conducted by the French newspaper *Le Monde* (Khomeini, 1994: 145).

29   Shi'ism is a faith to which more that 90 per cent of Iranians are born.

30   For a discussion of the concept of 'national imaginary', see Anderson (1983).

31   Saeed Hajjarian is a leading Iranian Muslim intellectual. Before the attempt on his life in March 2000, which has confined him to a wheelchair, he was also a successful journalist and an astute political strategist. He was considered to be the key figure in the victory of the reformist candidates in the Parliamentary Elections of February 2000.

tion from tradition to modernity in his received juridical knowledge. He moved Shi'i *fiqh* from its traditional oppositional position within the confines of the clerical institutions (seminaries, mosques, endowments etc.) to a position of political power in modern times at both national and transnational levels (Hajjarian, 2001 [1380]: 92). According to Hajjarian, by combining religion and politics Ayatollah Khomeini (and other Shi'i jurists who followed him) turned *fiqh* into an element of 'national sovereignty'. By taking over political power the religious institution virtually obliged itself to protect national interests, or, to put it in religious language, 'the common good' (*masaleh-e ammeh*). The introduction of the concept of *maslehat* (expediency) into the Shi'i political discourse by Ayatollah Khomeini led eventually to the creation of a distinct institution. The Expediency Council (*Majma'e Maslehat*), enshrined in the constitution in 1989 in a referendum which endorsed a series of constitutional amendments, was given authority to intervene (on the basis of *maslehat*) to settle disputes and conflicts over concerns relating to violation of the *Shari'at*. This was a clear example of the attention of the Islamic state to the priority of national interests over any other concern. In this sense, Hajjarian suggests, not only did Ayatollah Khomeini make a political revolution against the Pahlavi monarchy, he also created a doctrinal revolution in Shi'i *fiqh*.

Whereas Sunni *fiqh* had already incorporated the element of *maslehat* because of its cooptation by the state, Shi'i *fiqh* had remained loyal to the letter of the *Shari'at*, largely because of its opposition to the state up until the victory of the Islamic revolution. As a result of the revolution and the foundation of an Islamic state, the Shi'i *ulama* left their closed scholastic circles to get involved in national and global politics. Based on the juridical, theological and mystical traditions of Islam, Ayatollah Khomeini's thesis of *velayat-e faqih* (the supreme politico-religious authority of the jurist) was destined to enhance the capacity of political Islam in the face of the new challenges of modernity. What he did was, in effect, lay the ground for concurrent nationalisation and globalisation of Islam—a project that would lead to calls for 'Islamic democracy' and 'civil society' in the late 1990s.

Given that the nation-state had become an inescapable structural form for political sovereignty, the thesis of *velayat-e faqih* served not only as the doctrinal basis for the revolutionary rise of the jurists to power, but also as the initial impetus for a modern religious nationalism. Religiously speaking, with the takeover of the state by the jurists, the *velayat* of the *faqih* could not remain a *velayat* of a kind found in traditional juridical treatises. Traditional *fiqh*, as a system of personal religious obligations of members of the religious community, entitled the *valy* (the person in authority) to take charge of the affairs of the people under his authority (often the minors and the insane) even without their consent. The requirements of the modern nation-state, though, implied that citizens were mature members of the nation and hence entitled to certain individual rights. In the new setting, therefore, *velayat* had to be understood in a way that would make possible recognition of the mutual rights and obligations of the state and society. Hajjarian (2001 [1380]: 93) locates such a *velayat* in early Islam (as in Imam Ali's *Nahjulbalagha*) whereby mutual rights and obligations linked the ruler and the subjects.

In practical terms the limitations of obligatory interpretations of the thesis of *velayat-e faqih* became increasingly evident in the early to mid-1990s. As the religious symbol of national sovereignty, and as an authoritative leadership with both popular and spiritual appeal, the position of *velayat-e faqih* (personified in Ayatollah Khomeini) had certainly provided for a sense of a religious nation during the period of war with Iraq in the 1980s. Yet the problem of this religious sense of nation was that the domain of its enfranchisement had become too limiting in peacetime, when economic development was the first priority, and the charisma-based leadership was losing its grip. The insistence of some religious and political tendencies on the privileged constitutional position of the Shi'i jurists in a way that limited the domain of political participation (and even the right of citizenship) to dedicated followers of the juridical authority began to show its flaws in the early 1990s. It came to serve as a source of dormant political, religious and legal divisions and conflicts. From the mid-1990s tension surged not only at the legal and social levels but also in the political and cultural spheres. For by that time Iran had grown too populous, young, diverse, technically advanced and socially complex to remain loyal to political authority based solely on a juridical understanding of religion (Alinejad, 2002).

As the death of Ayatollah Khomeini had left the essence of the charisma-based legitimacy in crisis, the state had to design policies that would address this legitimacy problem. However, the conservative domination of the political and cultural scene entailed attempts at enforcing restrictive political and cultural policies, aimed at creating a pseudo-theocratic state promoting strict public piety with little, if any, attention to political openness and economic development. This move, though, suffered from a fundamental lack: the lack of a political legitimacy resting on national consent and consensus, something that in the absence of the charismatic leadership of Ayatollah Khomeini and the emergencies of the wartime, and in the light of huge social and demographic changes in the country, was almost impossible to recreate without a fundamental shift in the political culture. In the run-up to the elections of 1997, therefore, increasing signs appeared of the real political, social and cultural diversities of the nation.

It was in such a context that the reformists began to speak of legal legitimacy based on the constitutional role of 'the vote of the people', and the 'accountability' and 'transparency' of the power structure. The conservatives, on the other hand, insisted on the superior authority of the jurists, also enshrined in the constitution. In the 1997 Presidential Elections the reformists and conservatives came face to face, for the first time, in the public domain, with the reformists using the small media of the press versus the big medium of television, which was under the control of the conservatives. Ever since, the nature of elections has changed, becoming, for the first time, truly competitive. The statements made by Khatami during his election campaign in 1997 anticipated a major shift in the way power was distributed and exercised in the previous years. This shift was helped in the following years by the emergence on the scene of a vocal media-based public sphere, which became a major source of electoral support for Khatami and his followers in the elections that were yet to come. Thus Khatami's rhetoric and the campaign of a group of so-called 'reformist religious intellectuals' on his behalf set a new precedent in Iran's political culture. They moved the people to feel compelled to take an active part in election after election in support of the idea of reform. And in the life of the ordinary public, Khatami's idea of reform meant more than anything else a change in the status quo. The secret of the success of the Khatami campaign lay in its appeal to the voters who had no previous inclination to vote: those who had stopped voting because of dismay with the closed political process, and even many of those who had never voted. Interestingly, much of the electorate did more than just go to the polling centres casting their ballots. They also participated in and contributed to the reformist campaign, both through personal agitation among family and friends and in the workplace, and by using the media (mainly the printed press, but also pamphleteering) to support Khatami and the cause of 'reform'.

ELECTIONS AND THE VIRTUES OF A REPUBLIC

The May 1997 elections have been characterised as a synthesis of legal constitutionalism and revolutionary republicanism, all within the environment of a deeply rooted religious culture (Hajjarian, 1998 [1377]). According to this account, these elections were a means to reverse the process of containment of the revolutionary aspirations for freedom and justice, which had gone on for almost two decades owing to various extraordinary circumstances (external war, civil strife, economic sanctions, cultural invasion etc.). In the reformist literature the popular appeal of the election culture from May 1997 onwards is often attributed to the constitution of the Islamic republic. Yet there is an inherent ambiguity in the constitution. The coining of the concept of an Islamic republic itself, which combined a religious faith and tradition with the virtues of a republic, had anticipated this inherent ambiguity. If we envisage an ideal type republic, it may be conceived, at least in legal terms, as a system of government where general suffrage (which gives the people the right to free, direct and secret voting) is recognised as the basis of taking political office. The constitution of the Islamic republic provided, in theory, for all these elements. But in practice these elements were constrained by the constitutional role of the *foqaha* as guardians of the nation and as a supreme politico-religious authority with almost unlimited powers. In political-institutional terms, conservative interpretations of the constitution and customary political practice have effectively limited the role of the people's vote.[32]

With the 1997 elections the power was not displaced completely from its more traditional seats. But the view of power, and particularly the way it was exercised, certainly changed. Moreover a site for putting up serious challenges to the traditional religious authorities was opened up in the public domain. It was in this context that the idea of civil society was promoted as a buffer zone between the state and society. Henceforth civil society was understood as a site of civil institutions (such as the press, elected councils, professional and student associations etc.), institutions that would articulate the needs, demands and criticisms of the respective sections of the public *vis-à-vis* the state. As a result of the connection between religion, elections and democracy a whole host of new social actors were attracted to the public sphere. Clerical and lay intellectuals of traditional and modern schools of thought emerged as essayists, journalists, academics, authors, artists etc. to serve as the voices of political and religious reform. Yet they had to work in a situation where Shi'i *fiqh* dominated in the realm of politics and Shi'i culture was established as the core of national identity.

The new forms of publicness that emerged during Khatami's first term in office had a great impact on the exercise and legitimacy of power by producing crucial electoral support for his idea of reform. Khatami's programme of reform and his efforts to entrench Islamic democracy received a boost in his second electoral victory in June 2001. As in 1997 these elections attracted a large number of the voters to the polling stations to exercise their citizenship rights, confident that these rights were religiously and legally sanctioned. The old sources of legitimacy, such as the charisma of the leader and the traditional authority of the clergy, did not seem able to continue to displace the legal legitimacy of a repub-

---

[32] As a result of political negotiation, debate and even confrontation in the years following the revolution, the direct vote of the people in the election of the president and the members of the Parliament came to be closely supervised by an appointed body, the Guardian Council (*Showra-ye Negahban*). The Guardian Council is a body stipulated in the constitution with extensive authority, including the authority to reject the legislation of the Parliament if it is found in violation of the *Shari'at* or the constitution. The Council is also charged by the constitution with the authority to interpret constitutional ambiguities.

lican reading of the constitution, but they certainly invested republicanism with religious sanctity. The national electoral support for Khatami, and for the reformist politicians and activists for that matter, seem to continue as a sign of respect for policies of cultural and political openness. Nonetheless, the project of Islamic democracy and civil society still suffers from a multitude of theoretical and practical ambiguities and limitations, which deprive it of effective institutional power. Well into Khatami's second term of presidency serious questions remain as to the extent to which the people's vote can be translated into real power in Iran's venture of reform.

Abdi, A. and A. Rezaie (eds), 1998 (1377), *Entekhab-e Nou* [New Choice], Tehran: Tarh-e Nou.

Abrahamian, E., 1982, *Iran between Two Revolutions*, Princeton University Press.

Alinejad, M., 2002, 'Coming to Terms with Modernity: Iranian Intellectuals and the Emerging Public Sphere', *Islam and Christian-Muslim Relations*, vol. 13, no. 1, pp. 25–47.

Anderson, B., 1983, *Imagined Communities*, London: Verso.

Badi'i, M., 2001 (1380), 'A Comparative Review of the Presidential Elections since the Revolution', *Norooz*, *Tir*, no. 4, 25 June.

Binder, L., 1988, *Islamic Liberalism: A Critique of Development Ideologies*, University of Chicago Press.

Eickleman, D.F. and J.W. Anderson (eds), 1999, *New Media in the Muslim World: The Emerging Public Sphere*, Bloomington, IN: Indiana University Press.

Eickleman, D.F. and J. Piscatori, 1996, *Muslim Politics*, Princeton University Press.

Hajjarian, S., 1998 (1377), 'Talaqi-ye Jomhuriyyat va Mashrutiyyat' [The Crossroads of Republicanism and Constitutionalism] in A. Abdi and A. Rezaie (eds), *Entekhab-e Nou* [New Choice], Tehran: Tarh-e Nou.

——, 2001 (1380), *Az Shahed-e Qodsi to Shahed-e Bazari* [From the Sacred Beauty to the Market Beauty], Tehran: Tarh-e Nou.

Kasravi, A., 1967 (1346), *Tarikh-e Mashruteh Iran* [A History of the Iranian Constitution], Tehran: Tarh-e Nou.

Khaniki, Hadi and Muhammad Kashi, 2001, 'The Generation Gap in Iran', unpublished paper.

Khatami, M., 1997, *A Collection of the Transcripts of the Interviews and Speeches of Seyyed Muhammad Khatami*, Tehran: March.

Khomeini, R., 1994, *Sahifeh Noor*, vols 3 and 4.

Piscatori, J., 2000, *Islam, Islamists and the Electoral Principle in the Middle East*, Leiden: ISIM.

Rezaie, A., 2000, 'Expanding the Public Sphere in a Fragile Civil Society: The Cases of Iranian Newspapers, May 1997–March 2000', unpublished.

Van der Veer, P. and H. Lehmann (eds), 1999, *Nation and Religion: Perspectives on Europe and Asia*, Princeton University Press.

INDEX

Abomey, 184
Aceh, 131
Adams, John, 49
Alavez, Máximo Flores, 174–5
Ali, Imam, 245
Altos, 173
Andhra Pradesh, 94, 96–7
Aquino, Aristarco, 168
Asia-Europe Foundation (ASEF), 121–2
Asian Network for Free Elections (AN-FREL), 119
Assam, 94
Asshiddique, Jimly, 129n34, 130
Australia, 1, 25, 120
Australian Ballot, 1–2, 52, 53, 55, 56, 57, 59, 60
Australian Council for Overseas Aid (AC-FOA), 119
Ayutla, 168

Bahujan Samaj Party, 93
Baker, James, 71
Bali, 119
Ballot Act (1872): 16, 19, 29–32; consequences of, 31–41; prelude to, 21–30
Ballot Society, 24–5
Banser, 137–8
Banté, 185
Bastia, 143, 144
Bazargan, Mehdi, 230n8
Benin: 2, 10, 12; Constitution of, 184; National Assembly, 186; National Conference (1990), 186; see also clientelism, democracy, electoral culture
Bentham, Jeremy, 22
Berkeley, Henry, 24–5, 26
Bharatiya Janata Party, 85, 91
Bharatiya Lok Dal, 85
Bidwell, John, 52
Bihar, 93, 94–6
Bopa, 184, 185, 191
Bophal, 85
Breyer, Justice Stephen, 71, 75
Bright, John, 24, 27, 29
Britain: 2, 4, 5, 44, 54, 107; Ballot Act (1872), see Ballot Act (1872); Corrupt Practices Act (1883), 34–5, 40–1;

General Election (1842), 23; General Election (1868), 27, 29, 31, 34, 35–6; General Election (1874), 33, 34, 35–6, 38; General Election (1880), 35, 40; General Election (1885), 40–1; House of Commons, 23–5, 27–9, 35; House of Lords, 23–5, 28–9, 32; Poor Law Amendment Act (1834), 21; pre-(1872) voting in, 19–21; Reform Act (1832), 16, 17–18, 20, 23–6, 30, 33; Reform Act (1867), 16, 17, 26–7, 30, 33; Reform Act (1884–5), 16, 41; Representation of the People Act (1918), 32, 49; see also democracy, electoral culture
British Council, 122
Buchori, Mochtar, 122
Buddhism and Buddhists, 85
Bush, George W., 9, 69, 76

Calcutta, 88
California, 61, 63
Cameroon, 190, 191
Carollo, Joe, 70
Carter Centre, 120–1, 124
Carter Institute, 119
Carter, Jimmy, 119, 121
Cartwright, Major, 22n9
caste: 89–93, 97, 98; Chamars, 93; Dhobis, 95; Jats, 91; Scheduled Castes (Untouchables/Dalits), 80–1, 87–8, 92–3, 95, 97, 98; Scheduled Tribes, 80–1; Vaishyas, 93; Yadavs, 93
Catholicism and Catholics, 171
Cave, Stephen, 32n31
chads, 60, 74–6
Chamars, see caste
Chartists, 22, 24
Chayuco, 174, 175
Chhattisgarh, 96
Chiapas, 166, 173
Christianity and Christians, 198, 201, see also Catholicism and Catholics
clientelism: in Benin, 3–4, 10, 181, 182, 186–9, 190–1, 192, 193; in Corsica, 10, 142–54; in India, 90, 92; in Indonesia, 119; in Sub-Saharan Africa, 180
Cobden, Richard, 24

251